LONGMAN

Anna Uhl Chamot

Jim Cummins

Sharroky Hollie

Longman Cornerstone A

Pearson Education, 10 Bank Street, White Plains, NY 10606

Staff credits: The people who made up the *Longman Cornerstone* team, representing editorial, production, design, manufacturing, and marketing, are John Ade, Rhea Banker, Liz Barker, Don Bensey, Kenna Bourke, Jeffrey Buckner, Brandon Carda, Daniel Comstock, Gina DiLillo, Johnnie Farmer, Patrice Fraccio, Zach Halper, Sarah Hughes, Ed Lamprich, Niki Lee, Christopher Leonowicz, Katrinka Moore, Linda Moser, Liza Pleva, Edie Pullman, Tara Rose, Tania Saiz-Sousa, Loretta Steeves, Andrew Vaccaro

Text design and composition: The Quarasan Group, Inc.
Illustration and photo credits: See page 361.

Library of Congress Cataloging-in-Publication Data
Chamot, Anna Uhl.
Longman Cornerstone / Anna Uhl Chamot, Jim Cummins, Sharroky Hollie.
p. cm.
Includes index.
Contents: 1. Level 1. —2. Level 2. — A. Level 3. — B. Level 4. — C. Level 5.
1. English language—Textbooks for foreign speakers. (1. English language—Textbooks for foreign speakers. 2. Readers.) I. Cummins, Jim. II. Hollie, Sharroky. III. Title.

ISBN-13: 978-0-13-514805-1
ISBN-10: 0-13-514805-7

Printed in the United States of America

1 2 3 4 5 6 7 8 9 10–CRK–12 11 10 09 08

About the Authors

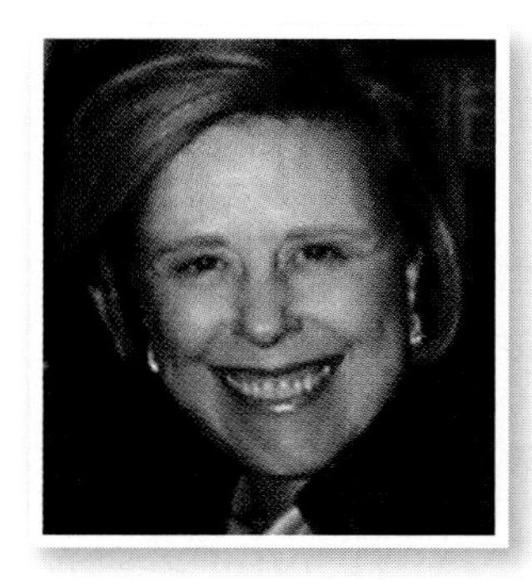

Anna Uhl Chamot is a professor of secondary education and a faculty advisor for ESL in George Washington University's Department of Teacher Preparation. She has been a researcher and teacher trainer in content-based, second-language learning, and language-learning strategies. She co-designed and has written extensively about the Cognitive Academic Language Learning Approach (CALLA) and spent seven years implementing the CALLA model in the Arlington Public Schools in Virginia.

Jim Cummins is the Canada Research Chair in the Department of Curriculum, Teaching, and Learning of the Ontario Institute for Studies in Education at the University of Toronto. His research focuses on literacy development in multilingual school contexts, as well as on the potential roles of technology in promoting language and literacy development. His recent publications include: *The International Handbook of English Language Teaching* (co-edited with Chris Davison) and *Literacy, Technology, and Diversity: Teaching for Success in Changing Times* (with Kristin Brown and Dennis Sayers).

Sharroky Hollie is an assistant professor in teacher education at California State University, Dominguez Hills. His expertise is in the field of professional development, African-American education, and second-language methodology. He is an urban literacy visiting professor at Webster University, St. Louis. Sharroky is the Executive Director of the Center for Culturally Responsive Teaching and Learning (CCRTL) and the co-founding director of the nationally-acclaimed Culture and Language Academy of Success (CLAS).

Consultants and Reviewers

Rebecca Anselmo
Sunrise Acres Elementary School
Las Vegas, NV

Ana Applegate
Redlands School District
Redlands, CA

Terri Armstrong
Houston ISD
Houston, TX

Jacqueline Avritt
Riverside County Office of Ed.
Hemet, CA

Mitchell Bobrick
Palm Beach County School
West Palm Beach, FL

Victoria Brioso-Saldala
Broward County Schools
Fort Lauderdale, FL

Brenda Cabarga Schubert
Creekside Elementary School
Salinas, CA

Joshua Ezekiel
Bardin Elementary School
Salinas, CA

Veneshia Gonzalez
Seminole Elementary School
Okeechobee, FL

Carolyn Grigsby
San Francisco Unified School District
San Francisco, CA

Julie Grubbe
Plainfield Consolidated Schools
Chicago, IL

Yasmin Hernandez-Manno
Newark Public Schools
Newark, NJ

Janina Kusielewicz
Clifton Public Schools/Bilingual Ed.
& Basic Skills Instruction Dept.
Clifton, NJ

Mary Helen Lechuga
El Paso ISD
El Paso, TX

Gayle P. Malloy
Randolph School District
Randolph, MA

Randy Payne
Patterson/Taft Elementaries
Mesa, AZ

Marcie L. Schnegelberger
Alisal Union SD
Salinas, CA

Lorraine Smith
Collier County Schools
Naples, FL

Shawna Stoltenborg
Glendale Elementary School
Glen Burnie, MD

Denise Tiffany
West High School
Iowa City, IO

Dear Student,

Welcome to *Longman Cornerstone*!

We wrote *Longman Cornerstone* to help you succeed in all your school studies. This program will help you learn the English language you need to study language arts, social studies, math, and science. You will learn how to speak to family members, classmates, and teachers in English.

Cornerstone includes a mix of many subjects. Each unit has four different readings that include some fiction (made-up) and nonfiction (true) articles, stories, songs, and poems. The readings will give you some of the tools you need to do well in all your subjects in school.

As you use this program, you will build on what you already know and learn new words, new information and facts, and take part in creative activities. The activities will help you improve your English skills.

Learning a language takes time, but just like learning to skateboard or learning to swim, it is fun!

We hope you enjoy *Longman Cornerstone* as much as we enjoyed writing it for you!

Good luck!

Anna Uhl Chamot
Jim Cummins
Sharroky Hollie

Your *Cornerstone* Unit!

Cornerstones are important for a building and important for learning, too.

Meet the program that will give you the cornerstones you need to improve in English and do better in all your subjects in school.

Kick Off Each Unit

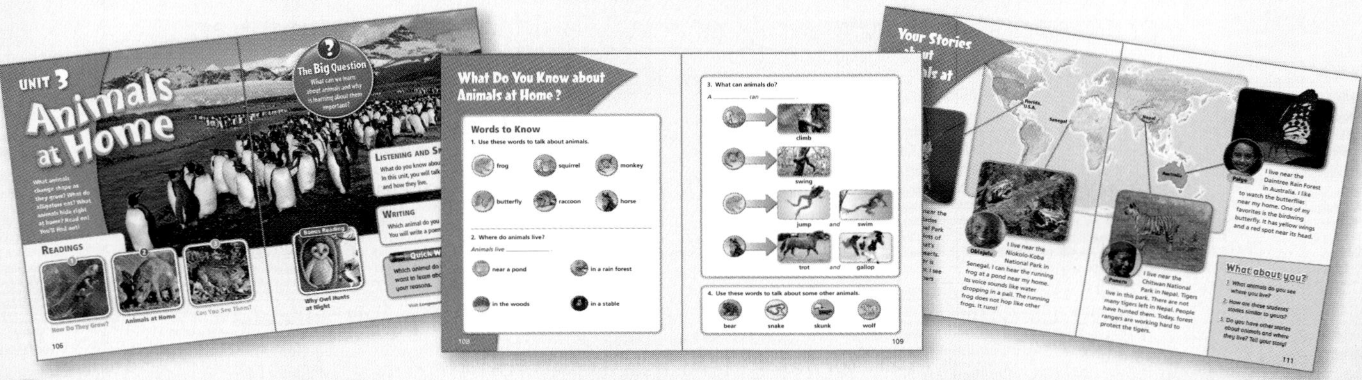

Big Question
The Big Question pulls all the readings together and helps you focus on big ideas.

Words to Know
Learn new vocabulary for the unit theme.

Mini-Autobiographies
Meet other students and hear what they say about the unit theme.

For Each Reading

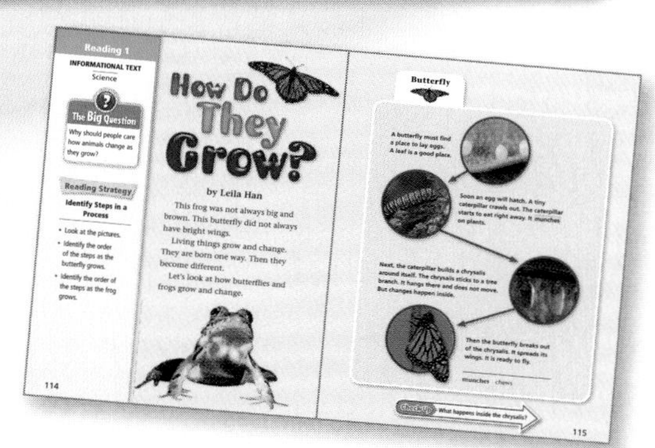

Vocabulary
Get to know the words *before* you read.

Readings 1, 2, and 3
Read with success! Get help from glossed words and Check-Up questions.

After Each Reading

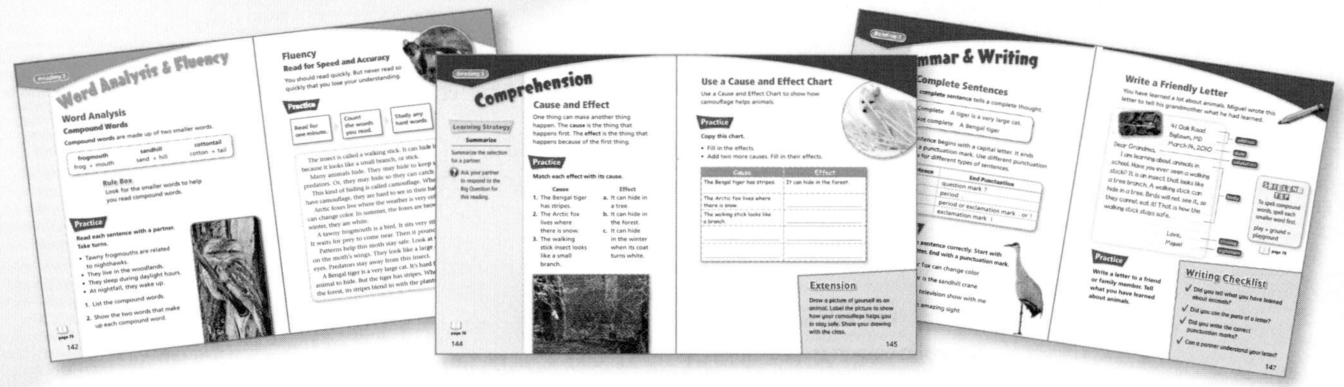

Word Analysis & Fluency
Become a better reader by learning about phonics and how words are formed. Then practice reading with ease on fluency pages.

Comprehension
Focus on a comprehension skill and practice it using a graphic organizer.

Grammar & Writing
Learn rules of grammar to help you communicate. Then improve your writing skills.

Wrap Up Each Unit

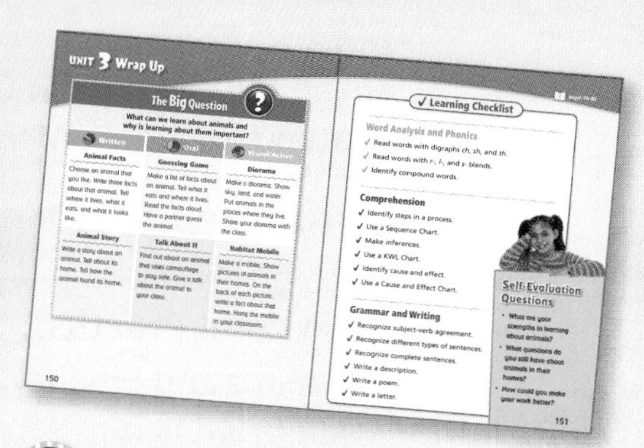

Bonus Reading
Take a break and read for fun.

Wrap up
Discuss the Big Question with your class. Choose an Assessment Project to show all you have learned.

UNIT 1 Contents

Communities

The Big Question

UNIT 2 Contents

Meeting Challenges

The Big Question

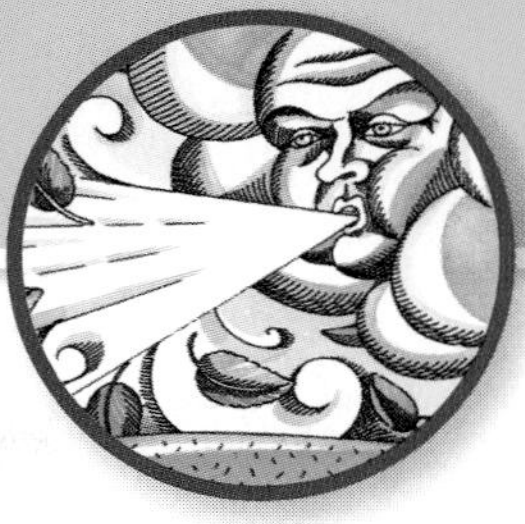

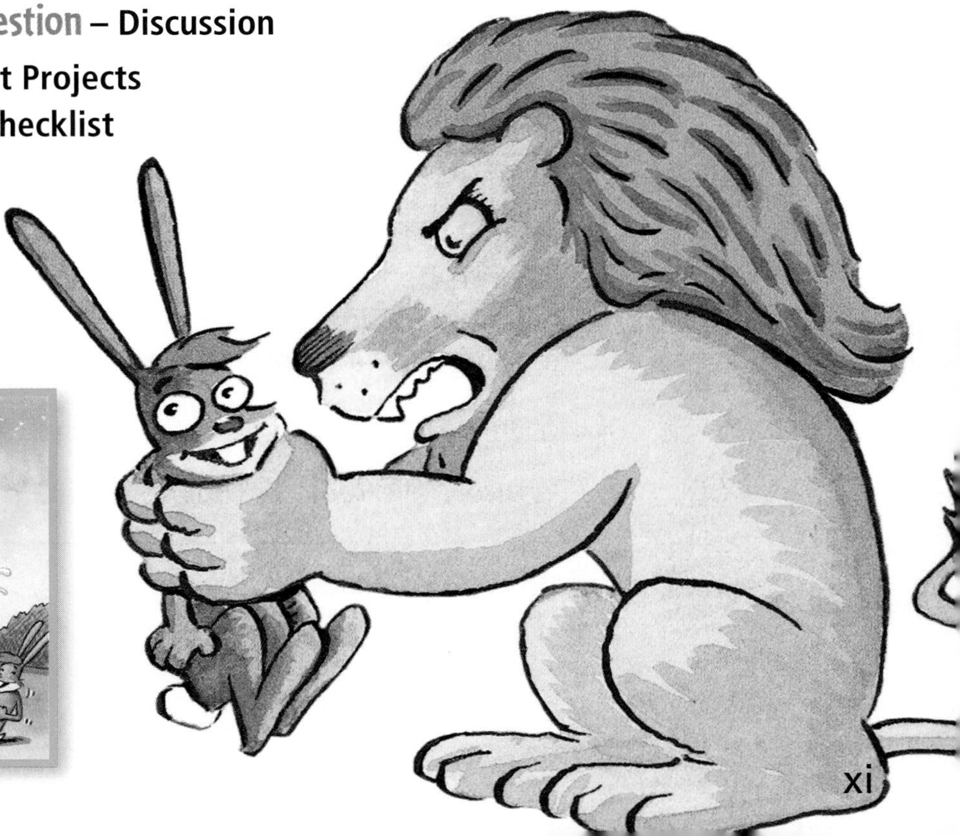

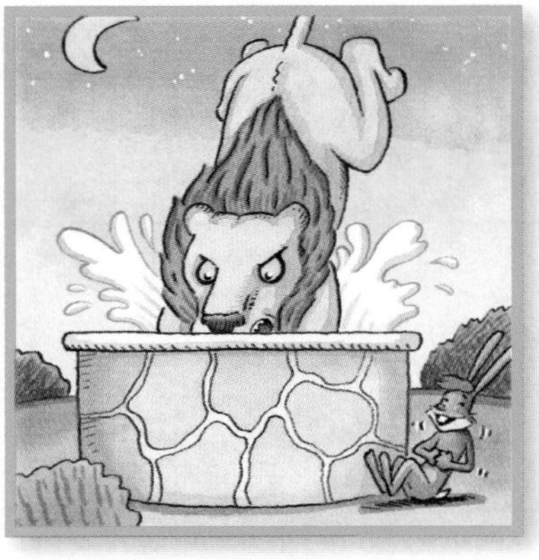

Animals at Home

The Big Question

UNIT 4 Contents

Great Ideas

The Big Question

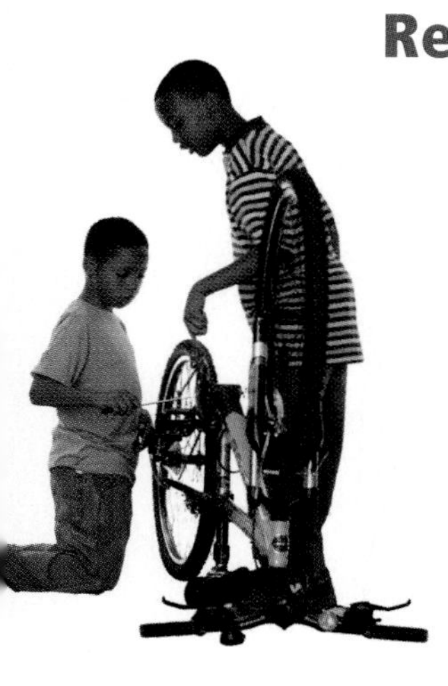

UNIT 5 Contents

Neighbors in Space

The Big Question

Reading 3: Literature/Myths

Bonus Reading: Informational Text/Science

UNIT 6 Contents

Arts Festivals

The Big Question

Reading 3: Functional Writing/Newspaper Article

Bonus Reading: Functional Writing/Journal

– **Discussion**

- ✓ Assessment Projects
- ✓ Learning Checklist

UNIT 1 Communities

Your community is where you live with your family. It is where you play with your friends and go to school.

Readings

1 Cool Hector

2 Making Friends

3 My Family

The Big Question

What are some ways that communities are alike and different?

Listening and Speaking

You will talk about what children do in different communities.

Writing

What do you like to do with your family? You will write about a special day.

Bonus Reading

Schools around the World

Quick Write

Look at the pictures that go with the readings. Pick one. Write what you think that reading will be about.

What Do You Know about Communities?

Words to Know

1. Use these words to talk about communities.

city

town

neighborhood

village

2. Who works in your community?

A _______________ works in my community.

bus driver

police officer

mail carrier

teacher

3. What do people do in your community?

In my ____________, people ____________.

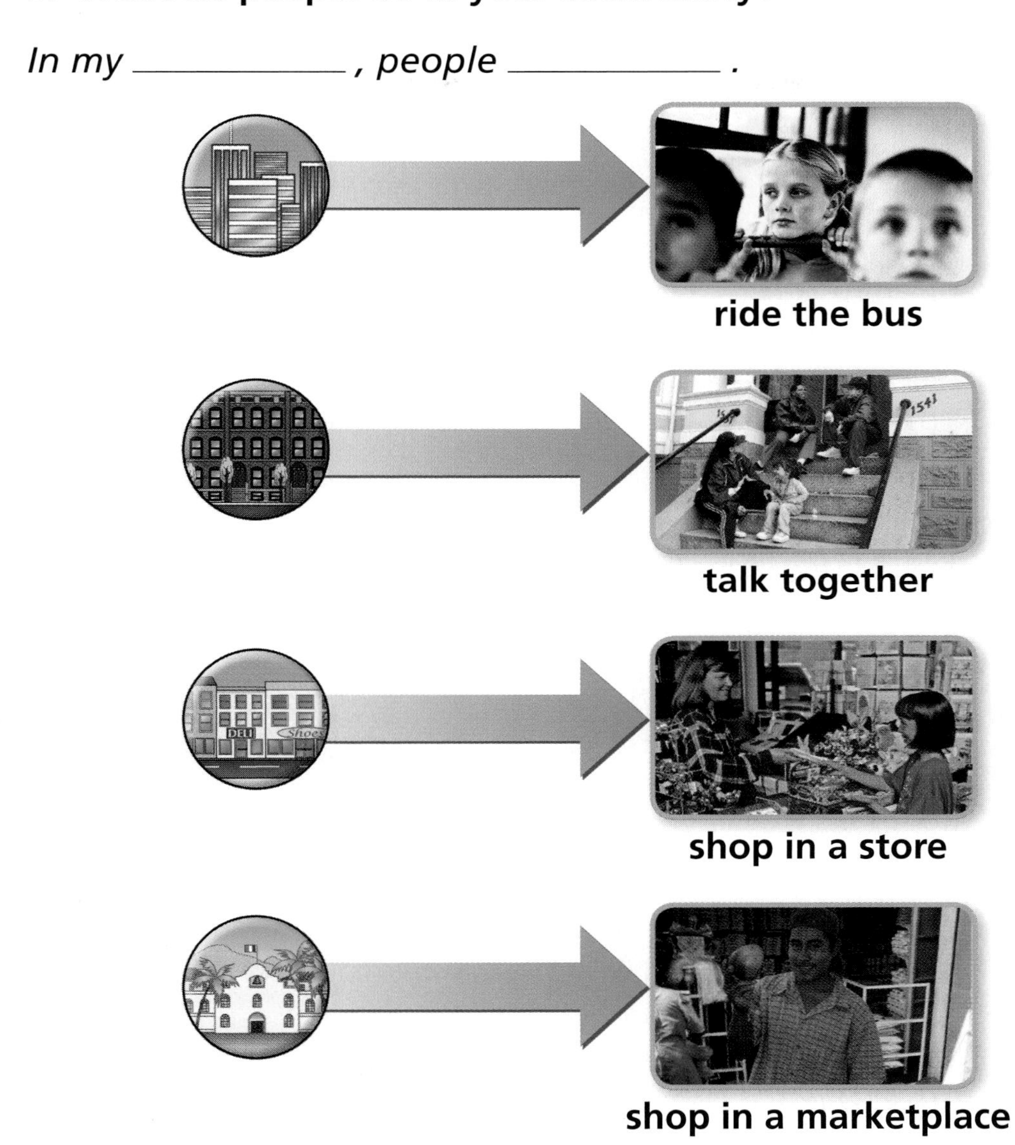

ride the bus

talk together

shop in a store

shop in a marketplace

4. Use these words to talk about where children play.

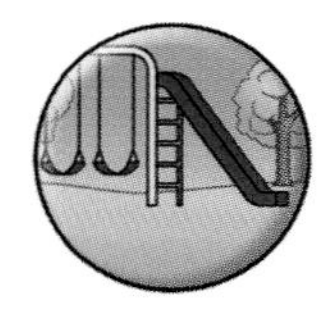

playground

soccer field

beach

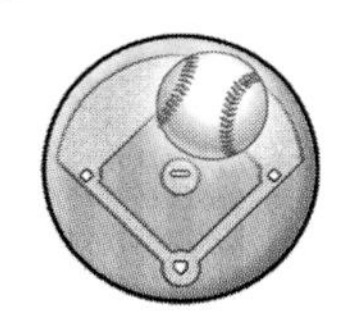

baseball field

Your Stories about Communities

Chris

My family and I live in a suburb. The suburb is near a big city in Illinois. A suburb has many houses. My friends and I take the yellow bus to go to school. In the afternoon, we do our homework. Then all the children play outside.

Lucia

My family and I live in a small town in the Andes. The Andes are mountains in Chile. There is no school in my town. I go to a school in another town. It is thirty miles away! The ride to school is long, but I love living in the mountains.

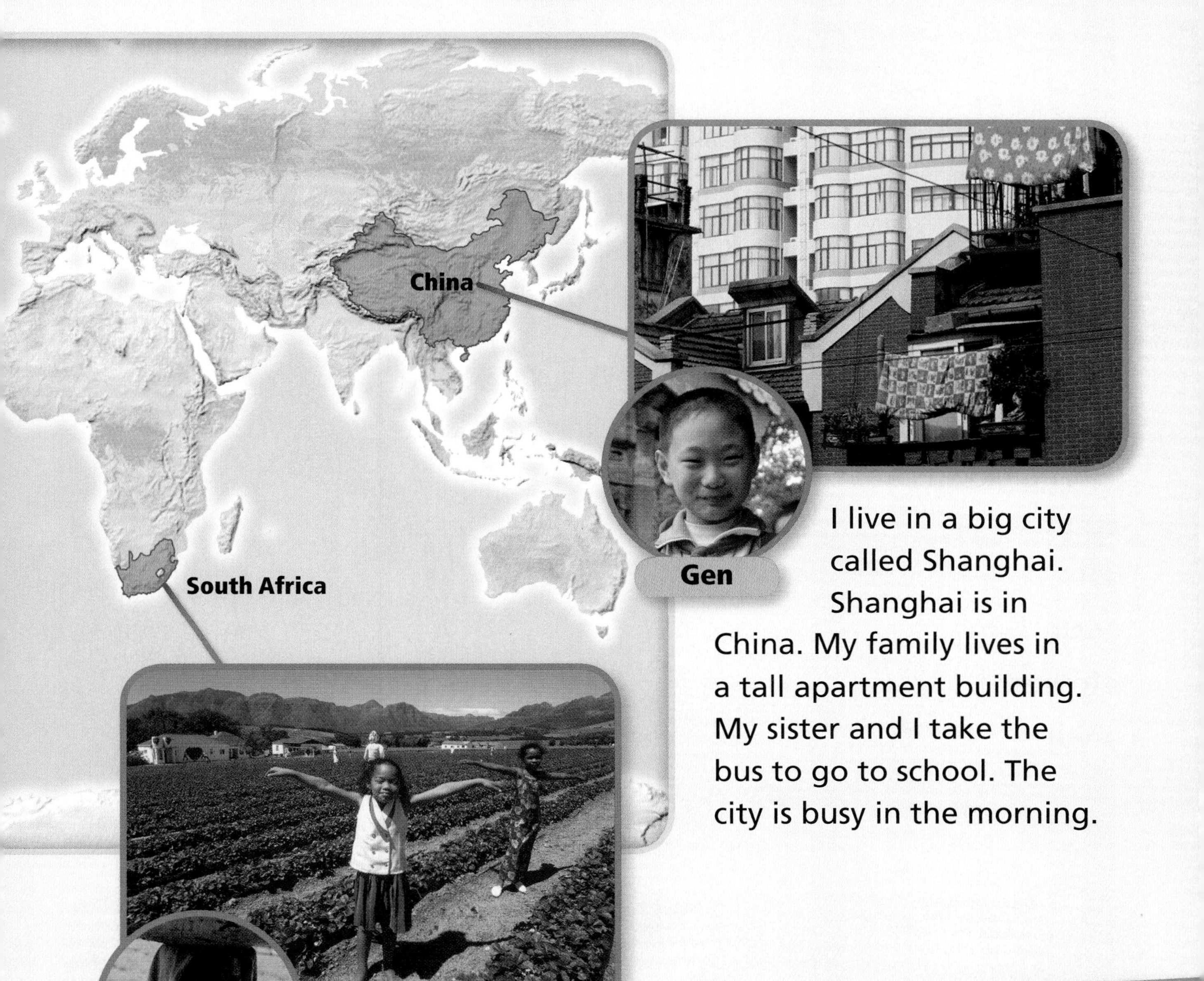

I live in a big city called Shanghai. Shanghai is in China. My family lives in a tall apartment building. My sister and I take the bus to go to school. The city is busy in the morning.

I am from South Africa. I live on my family's farm. We grow strawberries. There are other farms near us. All the children get together in the morning to go to school. We help around the farm, too.

What about you?

1. What kind of community do you live in?
2. How are these students' stories similar to yours?
3. How do you get to school? Tell your story!

Vocabulary

Cool Hector

Key Words

- **neat**
- **city**
- **luck**
- **flower**
- **mail**

Cool Hector **is a poem about a boy going around his neighborhood.**

Words in Context

1. This bike is so **neat**!

2. There are a lot of people in the **city**.

3 What **luck**! I caught the ball!

4 I give my grandmother a **flower**.

5 The mail carrier delivers the **mail** every afternoon.

Practice

Use each key word in a sentence.

Make Connections

Hector likes to talk to people in his community. What do you like to do in your community? Why?

Academic Words

community
place where people live

role
part that someone or something plays

pages 3–4

Reading 1

LITERATURE

Poetry

Why is each person an important part of the community?

Reading Strategy

Understand Character

- Hector is the main character. What does he do?
- Find clues in the poem that tell you what Hector is like.
- What kind of person is Hector?

Cool Hector

by Vivian Binnamin
illustrated by Ellen Joy Sasaki

Hector skips along the street.
He thinks, "This city is SO neat!"
To lots of people on his way,
he says, "¡Hola! How's your day?"

When Hector walks right by the park,
a big, black dog begins to bark.
Hector sees a disk fly by.
He catches it on his first try.

Hector goes into the store,
picks out an orange and then one more.
He sees a pretty flower to buy.
Hector's really quite a guy!

---

guy boy or man

Check Up How does Hector feel about the city? How do you know?

Hector sees the mail truck.
"Oh!" he says aloud. "What luck!"
Ms. Rodriguez drops some mail.
Hector's there. He does not fail.

Hector likes to ride the bus,
so he hops the Number Ten with Gus.
Gus lets Hector close the door.
(Hector did it once before.)

Hector buys something to eat,
choosing something cool and sweet.
Then he gives his mom the ice.
Hector's really very nice.

ice frozen food made from fruit

pages 5–6

Reading Strategy

Understand Character

Looking for clues can help you learn about a character.

- What clues help you learn what Hector is like?
- How did looking for clues help you learn about Hector?

Think It Over

1. Where is Hector?
2. What does Hector do by the park?
3. How does Hector help people?
4. How do you know that Hector is nice?

Phonics

Short Vowels

The **vowels** are *a, e, i, o,* and *u*. The other letters are called **consonants**. The words in the chart have short vowels.

can	bed	sit	top	bus

Rule Box

A word may have a short vowel when:

- the word has just one vowel.
- the word has a consonant before and after the vowel.

c a t	p u p
C V C	C V C

Practice

Work with a partner. Take turns.

- Read the sentences.
- Find the words with the CVC pattern.

1. The cat ran up the tree.

2. The girls sit on the bed.

3. Do not pick up the pup.

4. Gus drives the bus.

page 7

Fluency

Read for Speed and Accuracy

You should read quickly. But never read so quickly that you lose your understanding.

Practice

Read for one minute. → Count the words you read. → Study any hard words. → Read and count again.

Hector skips along the street.	5
He thinks, "This city is SO neat!"	12
To lots of people on his way,	19
he says, "¡Hola! How's your day?"	25
When Hector walks right by the park,	32
a big, black dog begins to bark.	39
Hector sees a disk fly by.	45
He catches it on his first try.	52
Hector goes into the store,	57
picks out an orange and then one more.	66
He sees a pretty flower to buy.	72
Hector's really quite a guy!	77
Hector sees the mail truck.	82
"Oh!" he says aloud. "What luck!"	88
Ms. Rodriguez drops some mail.	93
Hector's there. He does not fail.	99

Reading 1

Comprehension

Character

A **character** is a person in a story or poem. You can learn about characters by what they say or do.

Practice

Read each sentence. Then choose the word that tells what Hector is like.

a. helpful	**b.** busy
c. nice	**d.** friendly

1. ____ Hector says "¡Hola!" to people.
2. ____ Hector walks by a park, goes to a store, and rides the bus.
3. ____ Hector picks up the mail.
4. ____ Hector gives his mom the ice.

Learning Strategy

Retell

Retell the poem to a partner.

Ask your partner to respond to the Big Question for this reading.

page 8

Use a Character Web

You can use a Character Web to tell what a person is like.

Practice

Copy this Character Web. Tell what Hector does. Tell what Hector is like. The first one is done for you.

Hector says "¡Hola!" to people he meets. Hector is friendly.

Hector

Hector ______.
Hector is ______.

Hector ______.
Hector is ______.

Hector ______.
Hector is ______.

1. Which action tells you that Hector is helpful?
   - a. He picks up mail for Ms. Rodriguez.
   - b. He rides the bus with Gus.
   - c. He buys two oranges at the store.
   - d. He catches a disk by the park.
2. How do you know that Hector likes to be busy?
3. How do you know that Hector is happy?

Extension

What do you like to do in your community? Create a picture that shows what you like to do. Share your drawing.

Grammar & Writing

Nouns

Words that name people, places, and things are **nouns**.

In the sentences below, the words in red type are nouns.

People	Places	Things
Hector	store	orange
guy		flower

Hector goes into the store,
picks out an orange and then one more.
He sees a pretty flower to buy.
Hector's really quite a guy!

Practice

- **Read the sentences with a partner. Take turns.**
- **Write each noun.**

1. A boy rides a bike.
2. Our friends smile and wave.
3. A neighbor walks his dog.
4. The school is near my house.
5. My sister goes to the store.

page 9

Write a Description

A **description** tells what someone or something is like. Paz wrote this description of a park in his neighborhood.

The park in my neighborhood is very busy. My friends and I play ball. The little children play in the sandbox. The parents sit on benches and talk. Everyone is doing something.

Practice

Choose one place in your community. Write a description of it. Tell what the place is like.

- Start with a sentence that names the place.
- Write sentences that tell about the place.

SPELLING TIP

Notice that the word ***sit*** has a CVC pattern. Remember to use the CVC pattern when you write.

page 10

Writing Checklist

- ✓ Did you name the place?
- ✓ Did you tell what the place is like?
- ✓ Share your description with a partner. Can a partner picture the place?

Reading 2

Vocabulary

Making Friends

Making Friends is a story about two new children in a school.

Key Words

- **dessert**
- **friend**
- **fold**
- **mix**

Words in Context

1. Which **dessert** would you like to eat?

2. Meg likes to run with her **friend**, Tom. What do you like to do with a friend?

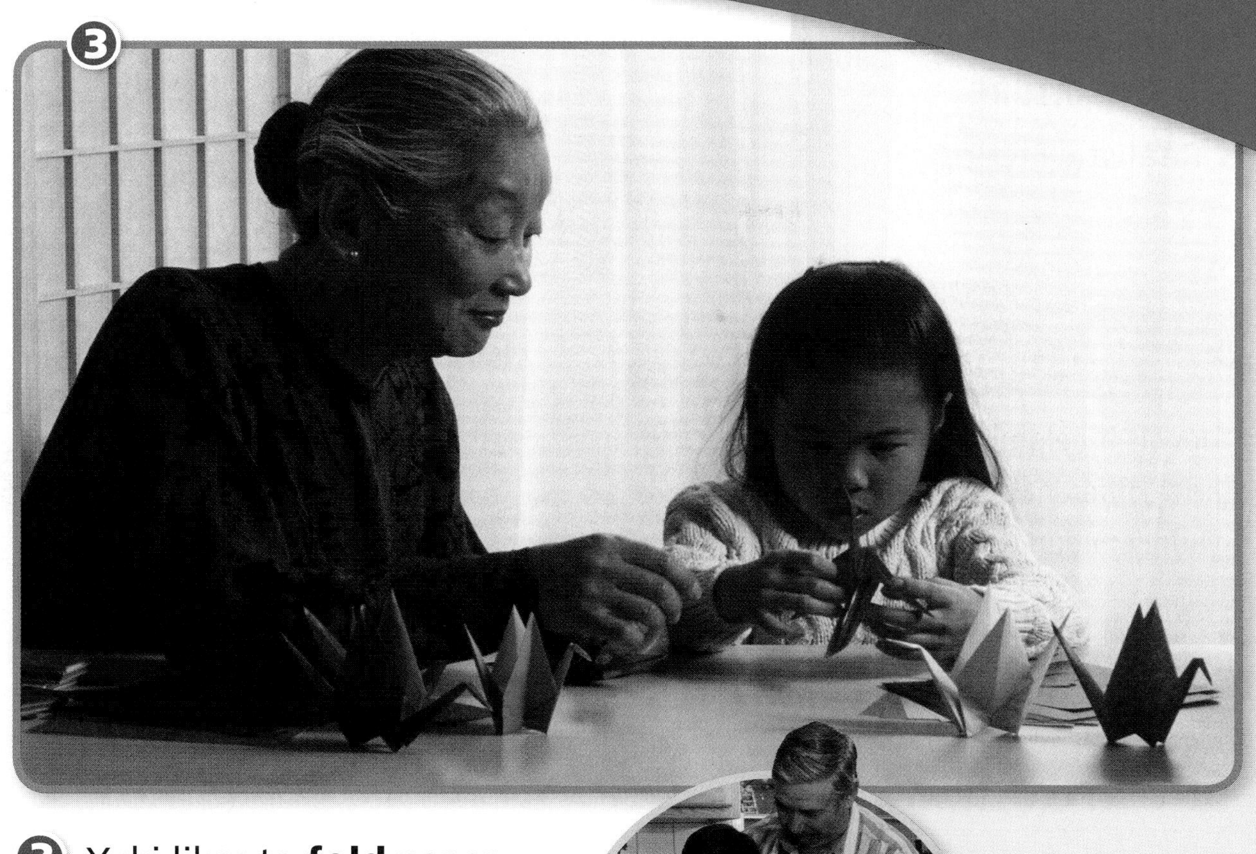

③ Yuki likes to **fold** paper.
She makes paper birds.

④ Juan can **mix** things.
He helps his grandfather cook.

Practice

Use each key word in a sentence.

Make Connections

Families may visit a new place. Do you remember a time when you were in a new place? How did you feel?

Academic Words

culture
the way a group of people does things

create
make something

pages 11–12

Reading 2

LITERATURE

Realistic Fiction

How is it helpful to have different people in your community?

Making Friends

by Dan Ahearn
illustrated by Laurie Keller

Reading Strategy

Make Predictions

- Read the title.
- Look at the illustrations.
- Predict what this story will be about.
- As you read, think about what may happen next.

The girls and boys in Miss Jones's class are from many different lands. But every family does fun things. Girls and boys can teach these fun things to friends.

Kate teaches a song to Juan. Juan tells a story to Kate. Maria shows Ben how to play a game. Most of the girls and boys are smiling. They are having fun.

But Hana and Carlos are sad.

---

different not like something or someone else

Check Up What did the girls and boys teach?

Hana just came to this school. She is from Japan. Hana does not have a friend yet.

Carlos just came here. He is from Mexico. Carlos does not have a friend yet.

Miss Jones tells Carlos to sit by Hana. She asks Hana to teach a fun thing to Carlos. Hana says she can make paper animals. Her mother showed her how. Carlos thinks that is a fun thing to do.

Japan country in Asia

Hana takes out some paper. She makes a paper crane. A crane is a bird. Carlos asks Hana to show him how to make a paper crane. Hana shows him how to fold the paper. Carlos makes a paper crane, too.

Now what can Carlos do? Carlos can make a dessert. But he needs his mother to help. He will teach Hana how to make a dessert.

Check Up What will Carlos teach Hana?

Hana goes to Carlos's house. His mother gives Carlos the things he needs. He can mix them. Carlos shows Hana how to make the dessert. Hana can mix the things, too.

His mother cooks the dessert. Carlos and Hana watch. It is fun making dessert! Soon, the dessert is ready. Hana tastes the dessert. It is so good!

At school, they will show other girls and boys what they learned.

Hana shows the dessert they made. Carlos showed her how to make the dessert.

Carlos shows a paper crane he made. Hana showed him how to make the paper crane.

The other girls and boys taste the dessert. They make paper cranes. Carlos and Hana show them how.

Hana and Carlos can do new things. All of the girls and boys can do new things, too. Hana and Carlos now have many friends.

pages 13–14

Reading Strategy

Make Predictions

- What did you predict?
- Were your predictions correct?
- How did making predictions help you understand the story?

Think It Over

1. Why are Hana and Carlos sad at the start of the story?
2. What does Hana teach Carlos?
3. What does Carlos teach Hana?
4. Why are Hana and Carlos happy at the end of the story?

Phonics & Fluency

Phonics

Long Vowels with Silent *e*

Each vowel can stand for more than one sound.

a		i		o		u	
hat can	hate cane	hid lick	hide like	hop not	hope note	hug cub	huge cube

- The words in the gray boxes have short vowels.
- The words in the white boxes have long vowels. The long vowel says its own name.

Rule Box

The vowel is long when it is followed by a consonant and the letter *e*. The letter *e* is silent.

Short Vowel	Long Vowel
m a d	m a d e
C V C	C V C e

Practice

Work with a partner. Take turns.

1. Write two new CVCe words for each vowel: *a, i, o,* and *u.*
2. Read the words to a partner.

page 15

Fluency

Read with Expression

When you read aloud, use your voice to show feelings.

Practice

Read silently. → Read aloud. → Get comments. → Read aloud again.

Hana takes out some paper. She makes a paper crane. A crane is a bird. Carlos asks Hana to show him how to make a paper crane. Hana shows him how to fold the paper. Carlos makes a paper crane, too.

Now what can Carlos do? Carlos can make a dessert. But he needs his mother to help. He will teach Hana how to make a dessert.

Hana goes to Carlos's house. His mother gives Carlos the things he needs. He can mix them. Carlos shows Hana how to make the dessert. Hana can mix the things, too.

His mother cooks the dessert. Carlos and Hana watch. It is fun making dessert! Soon, the dessert is ready. Hana tastes the dessert. It is so good!

Extension

Hana's way of folding paper is called **origami**. Look on the Internet or go to the library. Find out how to do origami. Make a paper animal. Show it to the class.

Comprehension

Learning Strategy

Retell

Retell the story to a partner.

 Ask your partner to respond to the Big Question for this reading.

Sequence of Events

Events are things that happen in a story. Events happen in a certain order. This order is called the **sequence**.

Practice

Read these events from *Making Friends*. Write the events in the order that they happen in the story.

- Carlos and Hana are sad.
- Carlos shows Hana how to make a dessert.
- Carlos and Hana share what they learned with the other girls and boys.
- Carlos and Hana watch Carlos's mother cook the dessert.
- Hana shows Carlos how to make a paper bird.
- Hana goes to Carlos's house.

page 16

Use a Sequence Chart

A Sequence Chart can help you think about events in the order that they happen.

Practice

Copy the chart. Answer the questions.

1.	2.	3.	4.
Hana and Carlos don't have friends.	Hana shows Carlos how to make a paper bird.		Hana and Carlos share what they learned with the other girls and boys.

1. Which event should be in box 3?
- **a.** Hana and Carlos are sad.
- **b.** Hana shows Carlos how to make a dessert.
- **c.** Hana and Carlos have fun with their new friends.
- **d.** Carlos shows Hana how to make a dessert.

2. Add a new box at the end. Choose an event to add.
- **a.** Hana and Carlos are sad.
- **b.** Hana and Carlos become friends with the other girls and boys.
- **c.** Carlos's mother cooks the dessert.
- **d.** Carlos needs his mother's help.

Extension

Think of something you know how to make. Teach a partner how to make it.

Grammar & Writing

Proper Nouns

A **common noun** names a person, place, or thing. A **proper noun** names a specific person, place, or thing. Proper nouns always begin with a capital letter.

Common Nouns	Proper Nouns
teacher	Miss Jones
girl	Kate, Maria
friend	Hana, Carlos
country	Japan, Mexico, United States
school	Rockland Elementary School
bridge	Golden Gate Bridge

Practice

- **Work with a partner. Read each common noun below.**
- **Write two proper nouns for each common noun.**

1. friend

2. teacher

3. boy

4. school

5. city

6. state

page 17

Write a Story

Think about a time when you made a friend. Dora wrote about making a new friend.

I am new in Vallejo. My family moved here from Laredo. I miss my best friend, Maria.

Today, I went to Hill Elementary School. I sat next to Akiko. She smiled at me. She asked me to sit with her at lunch. We both like baseball and books. Now I have a new friend.

Practice

Write about making a new friend.

- Tell how you became friends.
- Tell what you like about your friend.
- Share your story with a partner.

SPELLING TIP

Remember that proper nouns begin with a capital letter.

page 18

Writing Checklist

✓ Did you tell about making a new friend?

✓ Did you tell what you like about your friend?

✓ Can a partner understand your story?

Reading 3

My Family

Vocabulary

In *My Family,* a girl describes her family. She tells what her family does together.

Key Words

- **celebrate**
- **crowd**
- **company**
- **weekend**
- **gathers**

Words in Context

1. I like to **celebrate** my birthday. It makes me feel special.

2. **Here are many children in one place. These children make a crowd.**

3. We like to have **company** for dinner.

④ The **weekend** is Saturday and Sunday. We do not have school. We work in the community garden.

⑤ All the family **gathers** around to hear Grandmother sing.

Practice

Use each key word in a sentence.

Make Connections

In the story *My Family*, a girl tells what she likes to do with her family. What do you like to do with your family?

Academic Words

similar
almost the same

area
part of a place

pages 19–20

Reading 3

LITERATURE

First Person Narrative

How is your family a community?

Reading Strategy

Make Connections

As you read, think about your family.

- What does your family celebrate?
- Who comes when you celebrate?
- What special things do you do?

My Family

by Hanna Jamal
illustrated by Kathryn Mitter

My family likes to celebrate. We like to be together.

Monday through Friday, everyone is busy. We go to school. We go to work. We do homework. We do chores.

But on the weekend, we get together. Then we have good times.

---

chores jobs that you have to do often

I like it when we celebrate at home. The whole family is part of the celebration.

Everyone is doing something. My grandmother tells stories to the children. My cousins play games. My aunts and uncles talk and laugh. My grandfather does not talk much. But he always smiles.

There is plenty of food to eat. There is plenty of noise! You can tell that everyone is excited to be here. It makes me happy to see the whole family together.

---

celebration party

cousins children of aunts and uncles

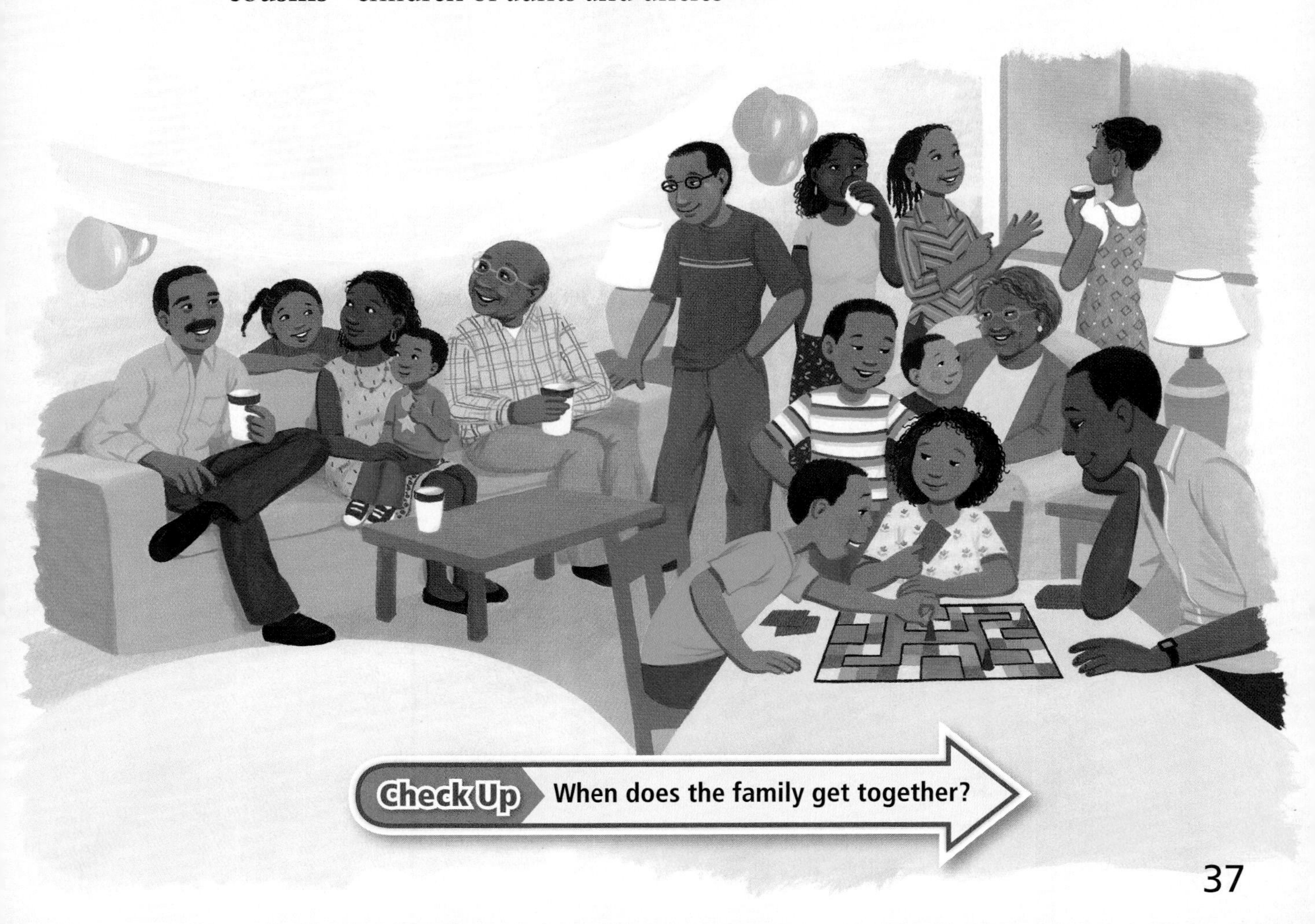

Sometimes, we celebrate a special day. Today we celebrate my grandmother's birthday. We all work together to plan her party.

My mother bakes a cake. My cousins and I put up streamers. We each have a gift to give to my grandmother.

We sing the birthday song. My grandfather smiles. He sings, too.

---

streamers long, thin colored paper

There are lots of candles on my grandmother's cake! We watch her blow out the candles. We ask her what she wished for. But she will not say.

My grandmother has fun at her birthday party. She is happy to have the family together.

I think I know what she wished for. Her wish is to have many more family celebrations.

---

candles sticks of wax that burn and give light

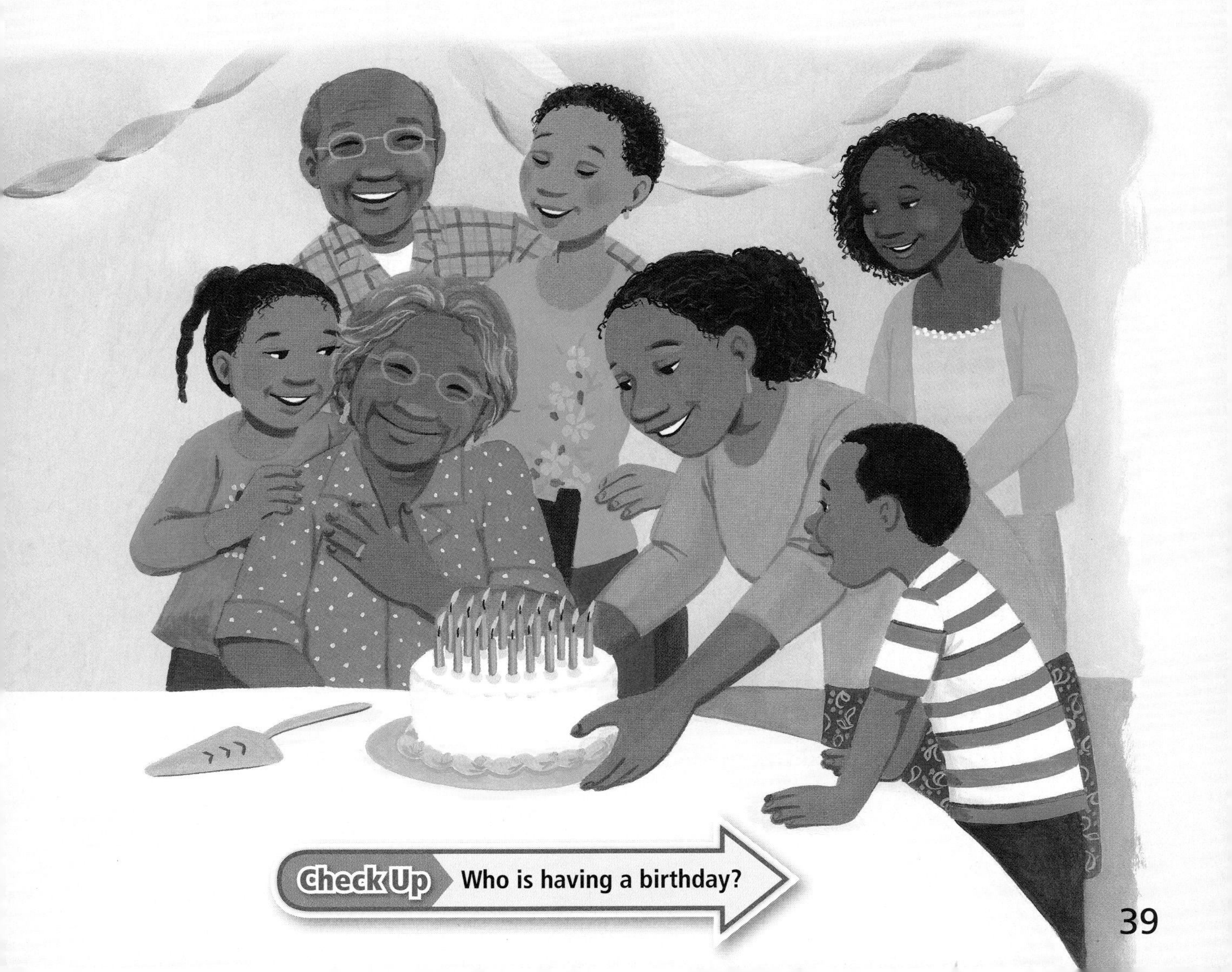

Check Up Who is having a birthday?

Sometimes, friends join our family celebrations. Company gathers in our yard. Neighbors, friends, and family come over. There is a big crowd.

Everyone brings something to the party. There is plenty of food. Dad cooks. Mom makes salad. We drink lemonade. We eat dessert.

We laugh and talk. We play games and have fun. You can tell that we are having a good time. I like to see everyone together.

---

salad a dish of raw leafy vegetables

lemonade a sweet drink made from lemon juice

At last, the party is over. The neighbors go home. Our friends go home, too. The aunts, uncles, and cousins say goodbye. My grandmother and grandfather say good night.

Now it is quiet. But next weekend, we will have another celebration. We will see the whole family together again.

pages 21–22

Reading Strategy

Make Connections

- How is your family similar to the one in the story?
- How is your family different from the one in the story?
- How did making connections help you understand the story?

Think It Over

1. When does the girl's family get together?
2. What does the family do for the grandmother?
3. Why is it quiet at the end of the story?

A Closer Look at...

A Family Tree

Grandmother
She is my mother's mother.

Grandfather
He is my mother's father.

Aunt
She is my uncle's wife.

Uncle
He is my mother's brother.

Mother
This is my mother.

Cousin
He is my aunt and uncle's son.

Amelia
Hi! I'm Amelia. This is my family tree.

Grandmother
She is my father's mother.

Grandfather
He is my father's father.

Father
This is my father.

Brother
This is my brother.

Sister
This is my sister.

Activity to Do!

These two pages use words and pictures to tell you about family trees.

- Think about your family.
- Make a family tree using pictures and words.
- Post your family tree in your classroom.

Word Analysis & Fluency

Word Analysis

The Letter *Y*

The letter *y* can be a vowel. It can be a consonant, too.

Vowel: long *e*	Vowel: long *i*	Consonant
city party	my try	you yes

Rule Box

The letter *y* may have a long e sound at the end of the word.

The letter *y* may have a long *i* sound at the end of the word.

The letter *y* may be a consonant when it is at the start of a word or syllable.

Practice

Work with a partner. Take turns.

1. Read the words in the chart. Listen for the sounds of the letter *y*.

2. Add six words to each list.

page 23

Fluency

Look Ahead

Sometimes readers look for hard words before they read. They then try to figure them out.

Practice

Pick one passage. → Find any hard words. → Practice saying those words. → Read the passage aloud.

1 Monday through Friday, the family works. On the weekend, the family has fun. The family celebrates. They get together and have good times.

2 Sometimes, we celebrate a special day. Today we celebrate my grandmother's birthday. We all work together to plan her party.

My mother bakes a cake. My cousins and I put up streamers. We each have a gift to give to my grandmother.

3 Sometimes, friends join our family celebrations. Company gathers in our yard. Neighbors, friends, and family come over. There is a big crowd.

Everyone brings something to the party. There is plenty of food. Dad cooks. Mom makes salad. We drink lemonade. We eat dessert.

Reading 3

Comprehension

Make Connections

Your family may be like another family. It may be different. You can ask yourself questions to learn about families.

- How are my family celebrations similar to the celebrations in the story?
- How are my family celebrations different from the celebrations in the story?

Learning Strategy

Summarize

Summarize the story for a partner.

Ask your partner to respond to the Big Question for this reading.

Practice

Look back at the story.

1. What do the aunts and uncles do at family celebrations?

2. How does the family celebrate the grandmother's birthday?

3. What does the family do when company comes over?

page 24

Use a T-Chart

You can use a T-Chart to show how things are alike and different.

Practice

Copy this chart. Answer the questions below. Tell about the family in the story. Tell about your own family.

Story Family	Your Family
1. They get together on the weekend.	1. ________
2. The aunts, uncles, cousins, grandmother, and grandfather come.	2. ________
3. ________	3. ________
4. ________	4. ________

1. When do you get together?
2. Who comes to the celebrations?
3. What do different family members do?
4. What do you do with family and friends?

Extension

Think of a special thing you do with your family. Describe this to a partner. Tell who is there. Tell what you do.

Grammar & Writing

Plural Nouns

Remember that nouns name people, places, and things.

- A **singular noun** names one person, place, or thing.
- A **plural noun** names two or more people, places, or things.

To form the plural of	Examples
most nouns, add *-s*.	aunt → aunts game → games
nouns ending in *s, ss, ch, sh,* or *x*, add *-es*.	dish → dishes box → boxes
nouns ending in a consonant and *y*, change *y* to *i* and add *-es*.	story → stories party → parties

Practice

Copy each singular noun below. Write the plural form of each noun.

1. cousin
2. hobby
3. bus
4. lunch
5. penny
6. cake

page 25

Write a Paragraph

Juan wrote about a special day for his family. As you read, look for the plural nouns.

Last week, we had a birthday party for my grandmother. She loves parties. The whole family worked together. My cousins put flowers around the house. My aunts made two cakes. My sisters put candles on the cakes. My brothers put up balloons in the living room. Then we hid. When my grandmother opened the door, we all yelled, "Surprise!"

SPELLING TIP

Remember the ways to make different nouns plural. Check your plural nouns when you write.

page 26

Practice

Write about something you like to do with your family.

- Describe what you like to do.
- Tell why you like to do this.
- Share what you write with a partner.

Writing Checklist

✓ Did you describe something you like to do?

✓ Did you tell why you like to do this?

✓ Can a partner understand your paragraph?

Bonus Reading

INFORMATIONAL TEXT

Magazine Article

Schools around the World

by Mia Dionetti

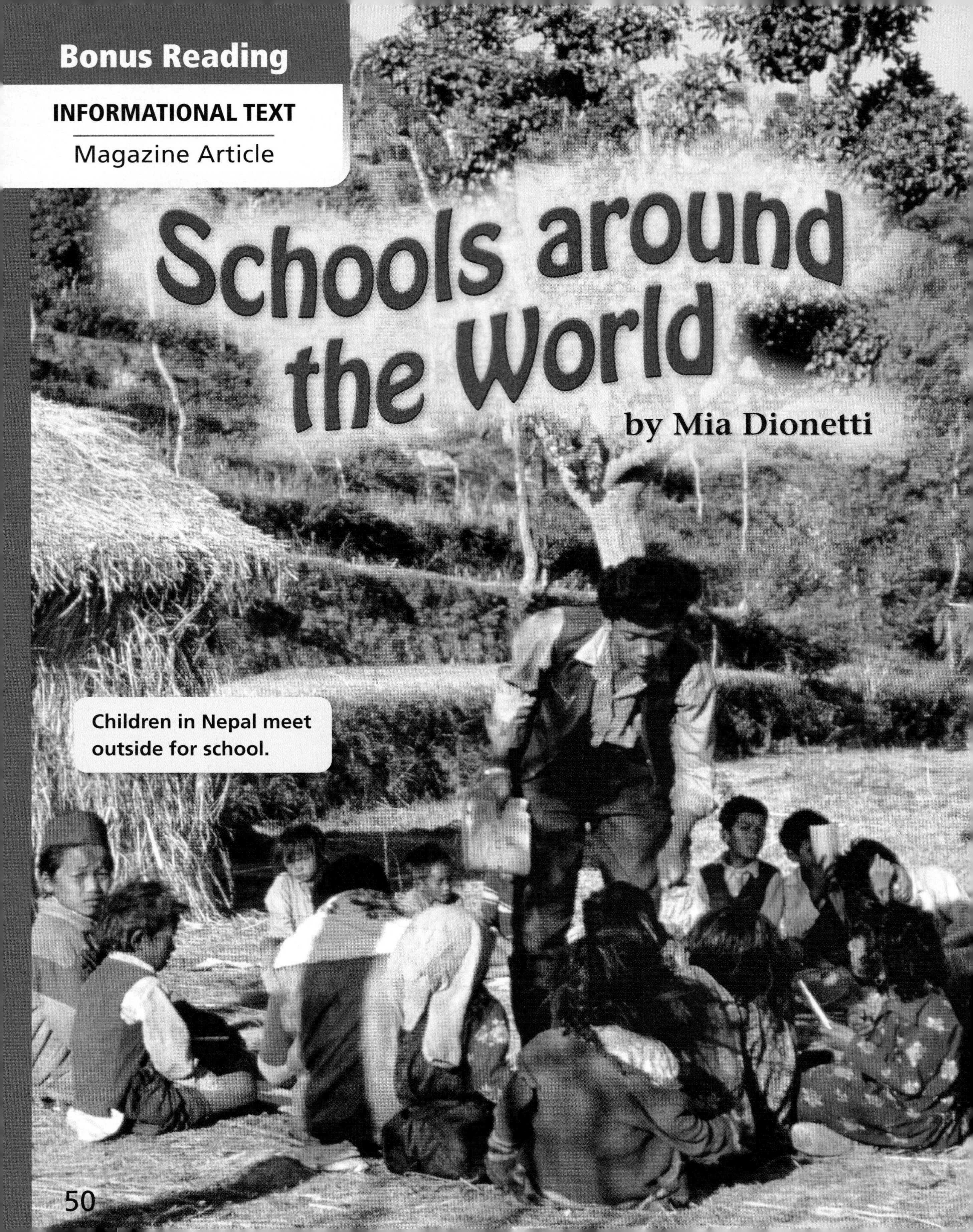

Children in Nepal meet outside for school.

Children in Sudan go to school in a tent.

This is a classroom in China.

Children all over the world go to school. The schools are similar in some ways. The schools are different in other ways.

In Nepal, all children can go to school. But some children do not go to school. Some live far away from a school. Others work to help their families instead of going to school.

How old were you when you started going to school? In China, children start school when they are four years old. Everyone walks to school. There are no school buses.

Boys and girls go to school together in Sudan. But more boys than girls go to school. Each class has many children. Their teacher helps them. The children raise their hands when they want to talk.

What is your school like? How is your school different from these schools? How is your school similar?

UNIT 1 Wrap Up

The Big Question

What are some ways that communities are alike and different?

 Written	 Oral	 Visual/Active
Lists	**Conversation**	**Postcards**
List three things you like about your community and three things that you wish you could change. Do the same for a community from one of the stories.	Talk with someone who has moved to your community from another place. Find out how the two communities are alike and different. Share what you learn.	Make a postcard that shows the community in *Cool Hector*. Make a postcard that shows your community.
Letters	**Town Song**	**Comic Strip**
Write a letter to a character in one of the stories. Tell three things about your community. Then write a letter from that character, telling you about his or her community.	Write new words to *The Wheels on the Bus* to create the song *The People in Our Town*. Teach others to sing your song.	Choose a community in another country. Find out about it. Create a comic strip that shows how children go to school or have fun in that community.

✓ Learning Checklist

Word Analysis and Phonics

✓ Read words with short vowels.

✓ Read words with long vowels with silent *e*.

✓ Identify the letter *y* as a vowel or a consonant.

Comprehension

✓ Understand character.

✓ Use a Character Web.

✓ Identify sequence of events.

✓ Use a Sequence Chart.

✓ Make connections.

✓ Use a T-Chart to compare.

Grammar and Writing

✓ Identify nouns.

✓ Recognize and use proper nouns.

✓ Recognize and use plural nouns.

✓ Write a description.

✓ Write a story.

✓ Write a paragraph.

Self-Evaluation Questions

- How does learning about other communities help you understand your own community?
- What are some other things you would like to learn about different communities?
- What would you do differently next time?

UNIT 2 Meeting Challenges

Solving problems and trying new things can be a challenge. People work hard to meet challenges.

READINGS

1

Birds in the Garden

2

The Rabbit and the Lion

3

The Contest

The Big Question

All of us have challenges at times. How can people meet challenges?

Listening and Speaking

It can be a challenge to learn a new thing. What challenge do you have? How can you meet this challenge?

Writing

What problem have you had? How did you solve your problem? You will write about how you solved a problem.

Bonus Reading

A Year Later

Quick Write

Look at the Bonus Reading picture. What challenge is this character meeting? Write what you think.

What Do You Know about Meeting Challenges?

Words to Know

1. Use these words to talk about meeting challenges.

 **practice**

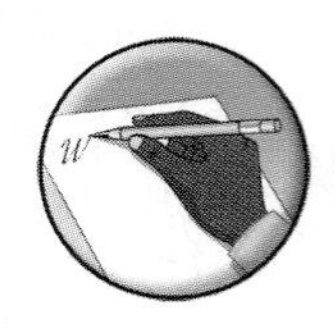 **study**

 **learn a skill**

 **train**

 **rehearse**

2. How do you meet challenges?

I can ______________ .

 **practice**

 **learn a skill**

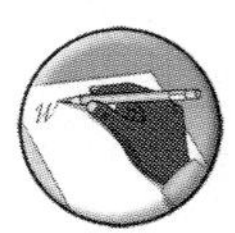 **study**

 **train**

 **rehearse**

3. What happens when you work to meet your challenges?

If I _____________, I can _____________.

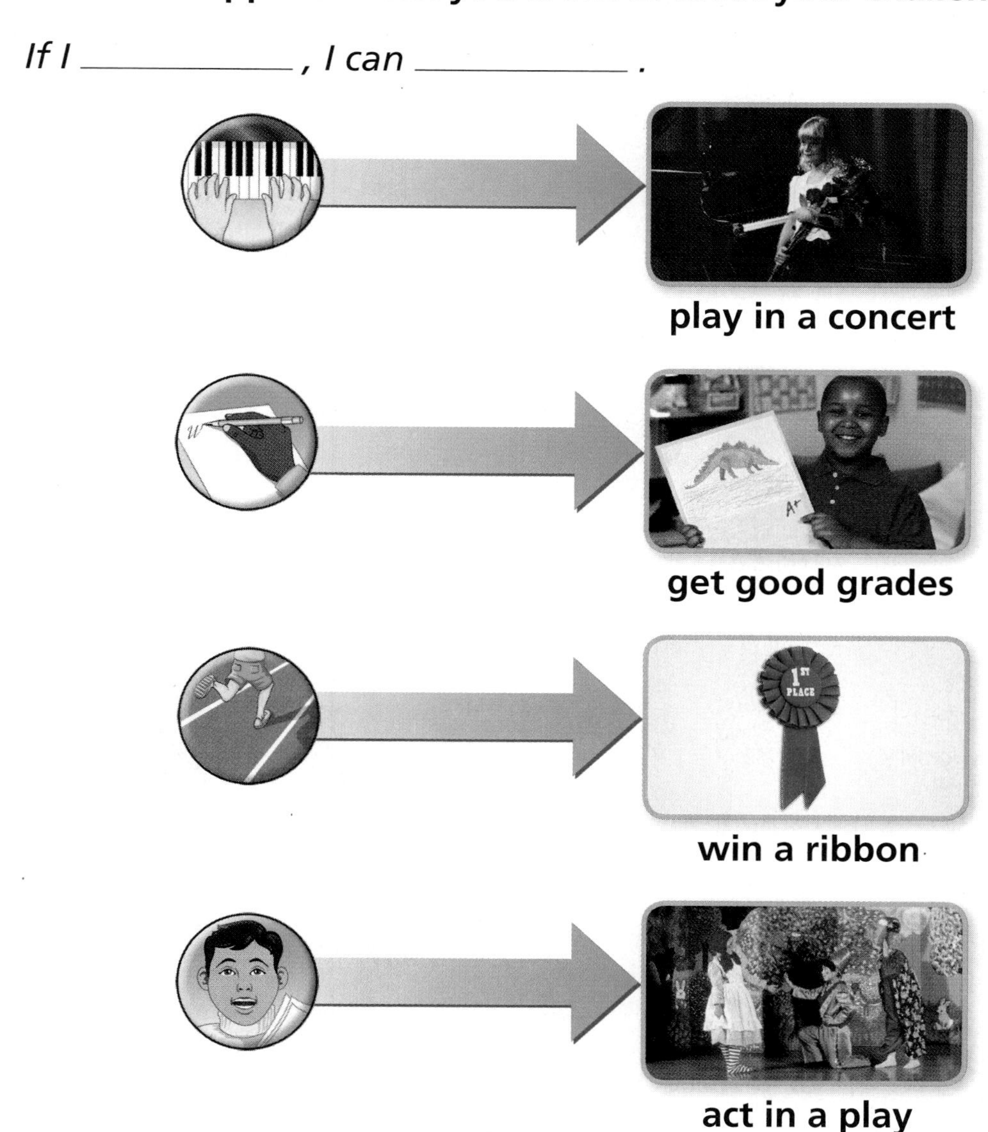

play in a concert

get good grades

win a ribbon

act in a play

4. Talk about people who help you meet challenges.

coach

parents

principal

Your Stories about Meeting Challenges

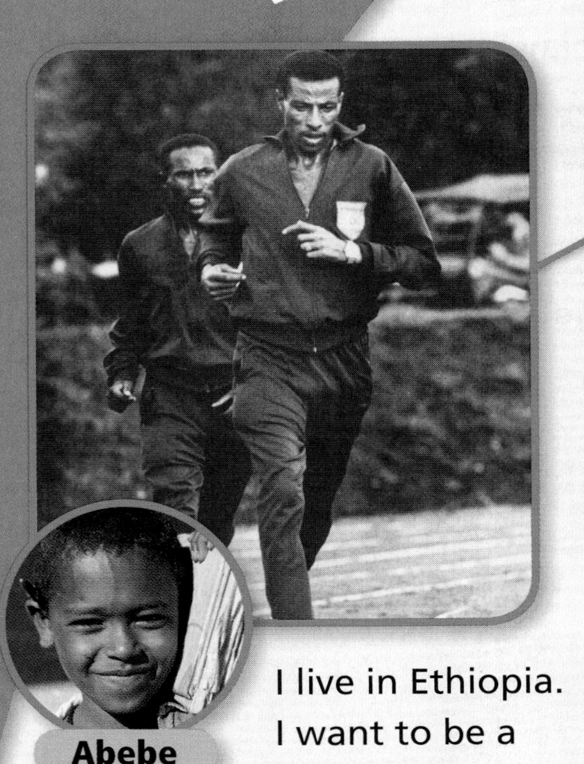

I live in Ethiopia. I want to be a good runner. Each morning, I train before I go to school. Each afternoon, I train after school. Then I go home and do my homework. If I train hard, I can be a great runner.

I live in India. Every day after school, I do my homework. Then I go to see my chess coach. I play chess with her for two hours. If I work hard, I can enter a chess contest.

Pedro

In Costa Rica, we have many rain forests. Our rain forests are in danger. Some people want to cut down the trees. Then the animals will not have homes. My parents and I try to help. We teach people about the animals in the rain forest.

I practice *tae kwon do* three times a week. *Tae kwon do* is a martial art from Korea. It is hard, but I like it. We learn to kick. We learn to move fast. If I practice, I can become strong.

What about you?

1. When have you faced a challenge?
2. How are these students' stories similar to yours?
3. How did you meet a big challenge? Tell your story!

Birds in the Garden

Vocabulary

In *Birds in the Garden*, a family stops birds from eating things in their garden.

Words in Context

Key Words

neighborhood

garden

seeds

plants

In our **neighborhood**, we have a community **garden**. People grow flowers there. They grow vegetables, too.

First we put **seeds** in the ground. Then the seeds grow into **plants**. We water the plants. They grow and grow.

Plants Grow

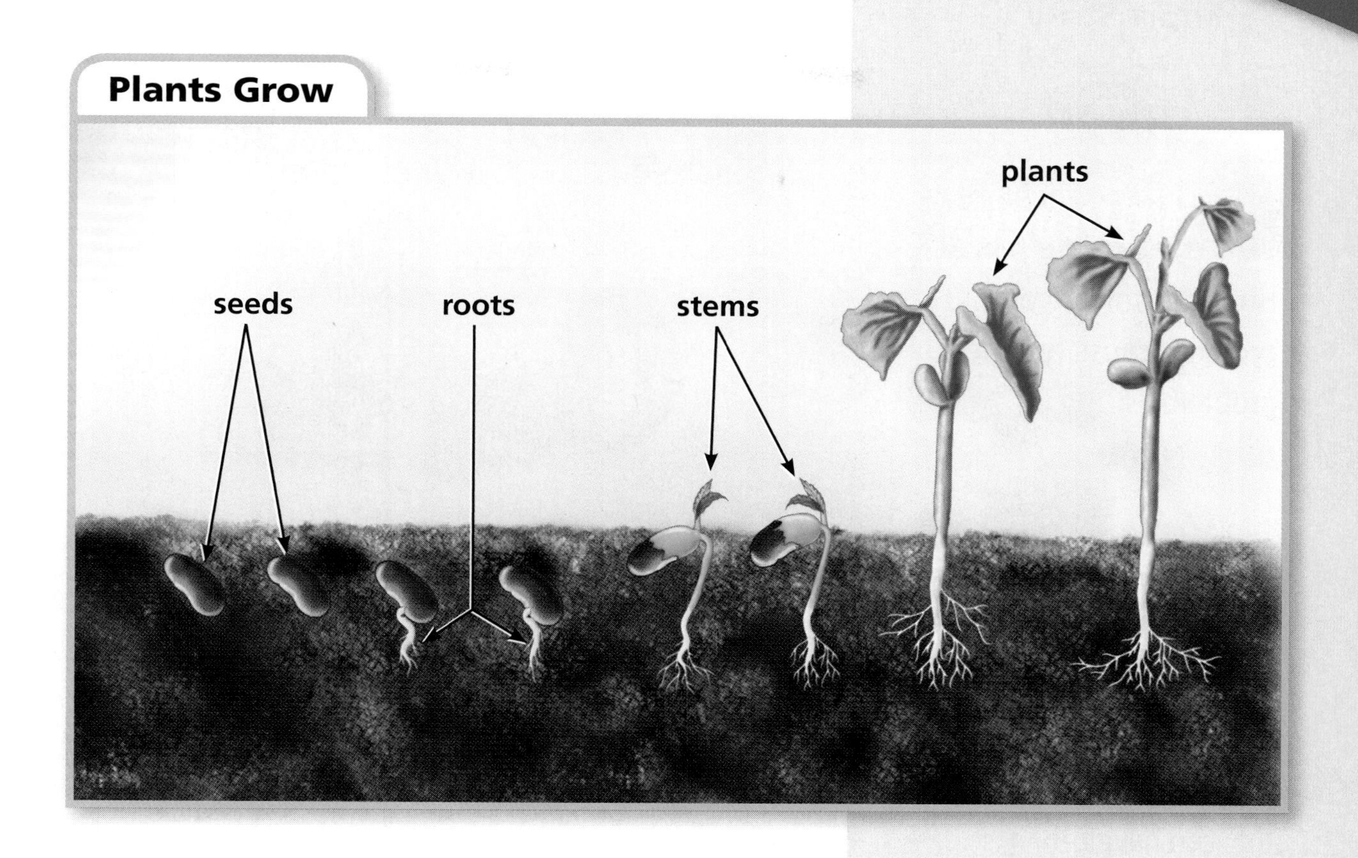

Practice

Use each key word in a sentence.

Make Connections

People can work together in a garden. Have you ever worked together with other people? What did you do? How did you feel?

Academic Words

occur
happen; take place

consequence
result of an action

pages 29–30

Reading 1

LITERATURE

Short Story

How can solving one problem cause another problem?

Reading Strategy

Identify Characters' Conflicts

The characters in a story can have conflicts. **Conflicts** are problems.

- As you read this story, look for the problems.
- Find out how the characters solve the problems.

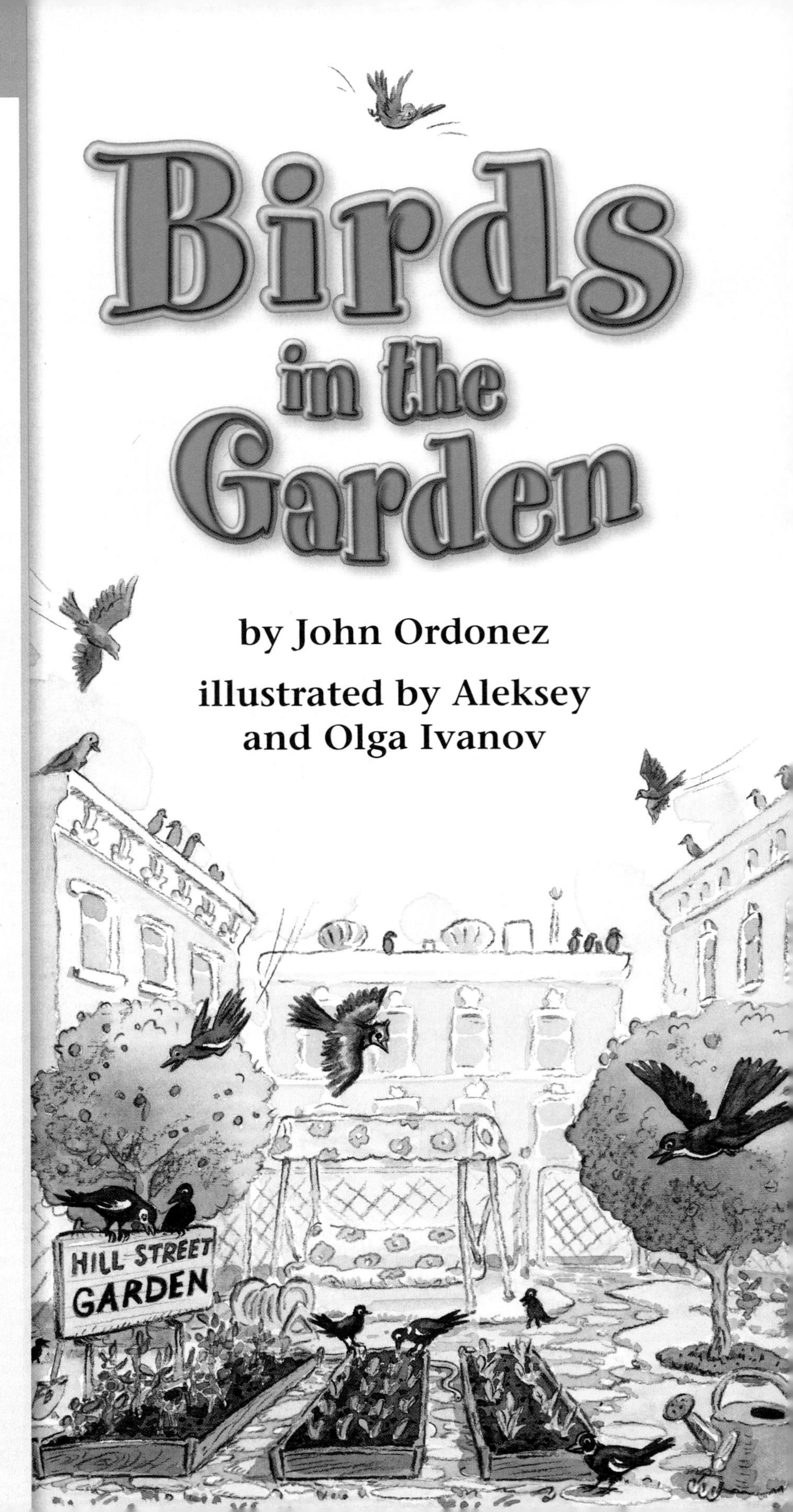

Birds in the Garden

by John Ordonez

illustrated by Aleksey and Olga Ivanov

We have a garden in my neighborhood. We all take care of the flowers and vegetables. We all take care of the trees. But we have a big problem. Birds are eating the seeds! Birds are eating our plants!

My dad says we can fix this problem. We go to the Hill Street Stable. We get a lot of hay. I carry some hay. My mom carries some hay. My dad carries his tools.

---

stable building where horses are kept

hay dry grass used as food for horses and cows

Check Up What is the big problem the family has to solve?

The birds are still in our garden.

"Stop eating our plants," I yell. "Let them grow!"

The birds keep eating. How can we fix the problem? We have hay. We have an old coat and a belt. What can we do with these things?

"We can make a scarecrow," says Dad.

Mom puts hay in the coat. I help make a head. The scarecrow looks like a person!

---

scarecrow object used to scare birds away from plants

"The scarecrow can sit in this chair!" I say. "He has a big job to do."

I look at the scarecrow. I think he needs one more thing. I think he needs a hat.

I put a big hat on the scarecrow. He sits in the chair like a king.

"Now that is a good scarecrow," Mom says. "But I think he needs to look bigger."

Check Up Do you think the scarecrow will solve the problem?

Dad puts the scarecrow on a stick. Then the scarecrow starts his job. The birds do not like the scarecrow. They make loud noises to scare him. But the scarecrow does not move. The birds fly away.

"The birds are scared," I say.

My parents smile at each other.

The birds are sitting on the roof. They are looking at the scarecrow. The birds want him to go away. But the scarecrow does not move.

"Wait!" I say. "The scarecrow saved our garden. But the birds are hungry. Where can they eat now?"

We now have another problem to fix. But Mom has an idea. We can make a bird feeder! We can put bird food in it. Then we can hang the bird feeder in a tree in our yard.

Now the birds eat in our yard. Our neighborhood garden is safe. And the birds are happy, too.

---

bird feeder object that holds food for birds

pages 31–32

Reading Strategy

Identify Characters' Conflicts

- What are the characters' problems?
- How do they solve the problems?
- How did looking for the conflicts help you understand the story?

Think It Over

1. Why are the birds a problem?
2. How does the family make a problem for the birds?
3. How does the family make everyone happy at the end?

Phonics & Fluency

Phonics

Long Vowel Pairs

Long vowel sounds can be spelled with two vowels together making a pair.

Long *a* Pairs		Long *e* Pairs		Long *i* Pair
day	rain	keep	neat	pie

Rule Box

When two vowels are together, the first vowel says its name.

- The letters *ai* or *ay* usually have the long *a* sound.
- The letters *ee* or *ea* usually have the long *e* sound.
- The letters *ie* usually have the long *i* sound.

Read the sentences with a partner. Take turns.

- Is that a bird in the tree?
- What a long tail it has!
- Pass the treat this way.
- We should move the pie!

Long *a*	Long *e*	Long *i*

1. Copy the chart.
2. Find and list the words with long vowel pairs.

page 33

Fluency
Look Ahead

Sometimes readers look for hard words before they read. They then try to figure them out.

Practice

Pick one passage.	Find any hard words.	Practice saying those words.	Read the passage aloud.

1 We have a garden. The birds are eating the plants. We make a scarecrow. But now the birds are hungry. We feed the birds. We solve all the problems!

2 "Wait!" I say. "The scarecrow saved our garden. But the birds are hungry. Where can they eat now?"

We now have another problem to fix. But Mom has an idea. We can make a bird feeder! We can put bird food in it. Then we can hang it in a tree in our yard.

3 We have a garden in my neighborhood. We all take care of the flowers and vegetables. We all take care of the trees. But we have a big problem. Birds are eating the seeds! Birds are eating our plants!

My dad says we can fix this problem. We go to the Hill Street Stable. We get a lot of hay. I carry some hay. My mom carries some hay. My dad carries his tools.

Comprehension

Characters' Conflicts

In most stories, the characters have a problem. The problem is called a **conflict**. They try to find a solution to the problem. A **solution** is a way to solve a problem.

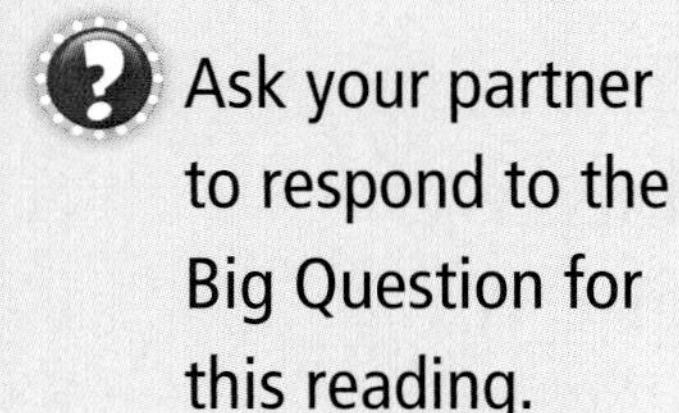

Learning Strategy

Retell

Retell the story to a partner.

Ask your partner to respond to the Big Question for this reading.

Practice

Read these sentences from the story. Tell which sentences describe problems that the characters have.

1. We have a garden in my neighborhood.
2. Birds are eating the seeds!
3. "We can make a scarecrow," says Dad.
4. The birds do not like the scarecrow.
5. "But the birds are hungry. Where can they eat now?"

page 34

Use a Problem and Solution Chart

You can use a Problem and Solution Chart. This will help you see how the characters solve problems.

Practice

Copy the chart. Use the questions below to help you fill in the problems and solutions.

Problem	Solution
1.	
2.	

- What is the first problem in this story?
- How does the family solve it?
- What is the second problem in this story?
- How do they solve the second problem?

Extension

How would you make a scarecrow? What clothes would you put on it? Draw a picture of your scarecrow. Share your picture with the class.

Grammar & Writing

The Verb *Have*

The verb ***have*** means "own." You may have a thing, such as a hat. Or, you may have an idea.

This chart shows how to use different forms of ***have*** with different subjects.

Subject	form of *have*	Subject	form of *have*
I	have	We	have
You (one person)	have	You (more than one)	have
She, He, or It	has	They	have

Practice

Write each sentence. Use the correct form of *have*.

1. I _____ a friend named Pedro.

2. He _____ a new bike.

3. Do you _____ a bike like that?

4. They _____ a dream.

5. We _____ a dream, too.

page 35

Write a Problem and Solution Story

What problem have you faced? How did you solve it?

Andy wrote about a problem he had. He tells how he solved his problem.

I want to have a garden. I want to grow flowers. But we live in the city. We live in an apartment. We do not have a yard.

My mom has an idea. We go to the store. We buy a box to put in the window. We put dirt in the box. We put seeds in the dirt. Now my flowers are growing. I have a window garden.

SPELLING TIP

The letters *ai* and *ay* make the long *a* sound. The letters *eigh* also can make the long *a* sound, as in ***neighbor***.

pages 36

Practice

Think about a problem you had. How did you solve it? Did anyone help you? Write a story about what happened.

- Tell what the problem was.
- Tell how you solved the problem.

Writing Checklist

- ✓ Did you state the problem clearly?
- ✓ Did you explain how you solved it?
- ✓ Did you use the ***have*** verbs correctly?
- ✓ Can a partner understand how you solved your problem?

Vocabulary

In *The Rabbit and the Lion*, a smart rabbit plays a trick on a proud lion.

Key Words

- **dinner**
- **well**
- **roars**
- **reflection**

Words in Context

1 All around the world, people eat different foods for **dinner**.

2 In some places, people cannot get water in their houses. They go to a **well** to get water. A well is a deep hole in the ground. The hole goes down to where there is water.

3 Different animals make different noises. A duck quacks. A horse neighs. A dog barks. A lion **roars**!

4 The **reflection** in this lake is very clear. You can see the mountains, trees, and clouds in the water.

Practice

Use each key word in a sentence.

Make Connections

In this play, animals talk and act like people. If you could be an animal, what animal would you be? Why?

Academic Words

identify
tell what something is

elements
important parts that make up something

pages 37–38

LITERATURE

Play

Sometimes, a character meets a challenge with quick thinking. How can thinking be a good way to meet a challenge?

Reading Strategy

Identify Events in a Plot

As you read, think about the important events.

- Lion catches Rabbit.
- How does Rabbit try to save himself?

by Ed Vuong
illustrated by Tim Haggerty

Characters
Narrator
Rabbit
Lion

characters people or animals in a play or story

narrator person who tells a story

Narrator:	Rabbit is smart. But one night his foe, Lion, catches him.
Rabbit:	Help!
Lion:	I have you now, Rabbit! I am going to eat you for dinner!
Rabbit:	I am too small. You need a big animal to eat.
Lion:	Yes. But you are just the right size for a snack.
Rabbit:	Who are you to go around eating rabbits?
Lion:	I am king of this forest!
Rabbit:	Look at the lion in the well. He says he is king!

---

foe enemy

snack small bit of food to eat

Check Up Why does Rabbit say he is too small?

Narrator:	Lion looks into the well. He sees a lion in the water.
Rabbit:	Ha! Ha! He thinks his own reflection is another lion!
Narrator:	Lion roars at his own reflection in the water in the well.
Lion:	You are a fake! I AM KING OF THIS FOREST!
Narrator:	But a strange voice comes back out of the well.
Voice:	I AM KING OF THIS FOREST!
Rabbit:	Hee! Hee! It is this silly king's own voice. It is an echo.

---

fake someone who is not what they seem to be

echo sound you hear again

Lion:	Fake! You will be sorry for this!
Narrator:	Lion jumps into the well. But the other lion is gone!
Lion:	Where are you? Come out!
Rabbit:	I guess I am king of this forest tonight. See you tomorrow, Lion.

pages 39–40

Reading Strategy

Identify Events in a Plot

- What does Rabbit tell Lion?
- What does Lion do?
- How did identifying the events help you see how Rabbit saves himself?

Think It Over

1. What is the conflict?
2. What does Lion think his reflection is?
3. Why does Rabbit trick Lion?

Phonics & Fluency

Phonics

More Long Vowel Pairs

Long vowel pairs can make the long *o* or long *u* sound.

Long *o* Pairs		Long *u* Pairs	
road	foe	blue	fruit

Rule Box

When two vowels are together, the first vowel says its name.

- The letters *oa* or *oe* usually have the long *o* sound.
- The letters *ue* or *ui* usually have the long *u* sound.

Practice

Read the words below with a partner. Take turns.

1. Write a list of the words that have the long *o* sound.
2. Write a list of the words that have the long *u* sound.

toad	woe	foam	fruit
true	loan	toe	cue
clue	doe	suit	soak

page 41

Fluency

Read with Expression

When you read aloud, use your voice to show feelings.

Practice

Read silently. → Read aloud. → Get comments. → Read aloud again.

Lion:	I have you now, Rabbit! I am going to eat you for dinner!
Rabbit:	I am too small. You need a big animal to eat.
Lion:	Yes. But you are just the right size for a snack.
Rabbit:	Who are you to go around eating rabbits?
Lion:	I am king of this forest!
Rabbit:	Look at the lion in the well. He says he is king!
Narrator:	Lion looks into the well. He sees a lion in the water.
Rabbit:	Ha! Ha! He thinks his own reflection is another lion!
Narrator:	Lion roars at his own reflection in the water in the well.
Lion:	You are a fake! I AM KING OF THIS FOREST!
Narrator:	But a strange voice comes back out of the well.
Voice:	I AM THE KING OF THIS FOREST!
Rabbit:	Hee! Hee! It is this silly king's own voice. It is an echo.

Reading 2

Comprehension

Learning Strategy

Retell

Retell the play to a partner.

Ask your partner to respond to the Big Question for this reading.

page 42

Events in a Plot

Events are the things that happen in a play. The events make up the plot. The **plot** is the main story of a play.

Practice

Read these lines from the play. Tell who says each line. Then tell which are events that show how Rabbit tricks Lion.

1. Help!
2. But you are just the right size for a snack.
3. I am king of this forest!
4. Look at the lion in the well. He says he is king!
5. Ha! Ha! He thinks his own reflection is another lion!
6. Lion jumps into the well.

Use a Sequence Chart

In this play, the events happen in a certain order. One event makes the next one happen.

Practice

Copy the Sequence Chart. Answer the questions to complete it.

1. Which is the best sentence for Number 3 in the chart?
   a. Lion jumps into the well.
   b. Rabbit thinks the reflection in the well is another lion.
   c. Lion thinks his reflection in the well is another lion.
   d. Rabbit runs away.

2. Which is the best sentence for Number 6 in the chart?
   a. Rabbit jumps into the well to fight the reflection.
   b. Lion jumps into the well to fight his reflection.
   c. Rabbit says there is another rabbit in the well.
   d. Lion says that Rabbit is king of this forest.

1	Lion catches Rabbit. Lion says that he is going to eat Rabbit.
2	Rabbit says there is another lion in the well. Rabbit says that lion says he is king of the forest.
3	
4	Lion roars and shouts at the reflection in the well.
5	An echo from the well comes back out at Lion.
6	

Extension

Work with a partner. Make up a skit with two characters. Show how the characters solve a problem. Present your skit to the class.

Grammar & Writing

The Verb *Be*

The verb ***be*** can tell what something is.

I am a rabbit.

The verb ***be*** can tell what something is like.

I am smart.

This chart shows how to use different forms of ***be*** with different subjects.

Subject	Form of *be*	Subject	Form of *be*
I	am	We	are
You (one person)	are	You (more than one)	are
She, He, or It	is	They	are

Practice

Write each sentence. Use the correct form of the verb *be*.

1. They _____ the characters in the play.
2. He _____ king of this forest.
3. _____ you the rabbit?
4. We _____ happy the rabbit is safe.
5. It _____ an echo.

page 43

Write a Scene

A **scene** is one part of a play. Kara wrote this scene.

Ken: My basketball is stuck in the tree branches! How can I get it down?

Marta: Here is another ball. Throw it up there. Maybe it will knock your basketball down.

Ken: I am trying. But the branches are too thick. I can't hit my ball.

Marta: Here is a stick. Maybe you can get the basketball with this stick.

Ken: The stick is not long enough.

Marta: I know! Here is Dad's fishing pole. You can use this.

Ken: The pole is just right! I can push the ball up...and up. Look out! It's coming down! Thank you, Marta.

SPELLING TIP

Some words are easy to mix up, such as ***lion*** and ***line***.

A lion is big. ***Lion*** has two syllables.

A line is thin. ***Line*** has one syllable.

page 44

Practice

Write a scene about two characters who face a problem.

- Use their words to tell what the problem is.
- Use their words to show how they solve the problem.

Writing Checklist

- ✓ Did the characters' words tell what the problem is and how they solved it?
- ✓ Did you use ***be*** verbs correctly?
- ✓ Can a partner understand the problem in your scene?

Reading 3

The Contest

Vocabulary

In *The Contest,* North Wind and Sun find out who is stronger.

Words in Context

Key Words

clouds
stronger
spiders
webs
brighter

1. Some **clouds** are puffy and light. Some clouds are dark and heavy. Which ones do you think bring rain?

2. Which bridge is **stronger**?

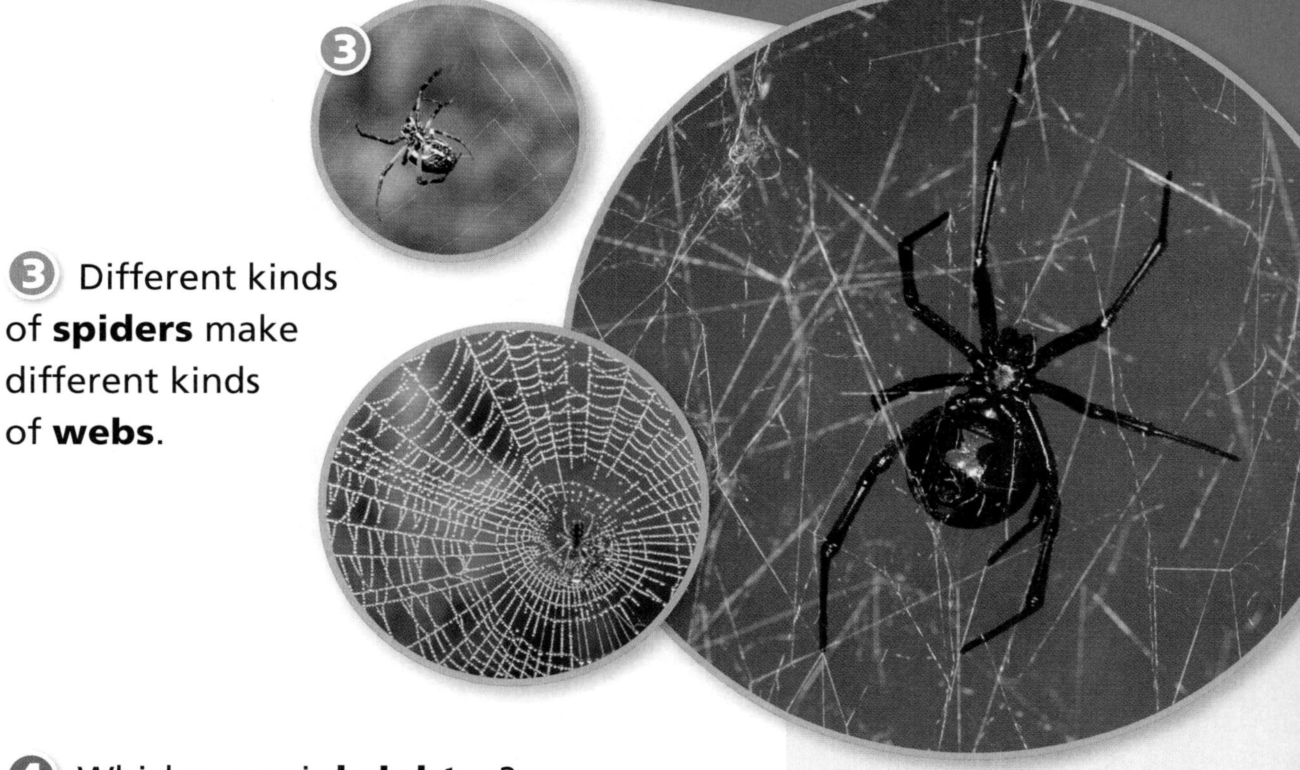

3 Different kinds of **spiders** make different kinds of **webs**.

4 Which room is **brighter**?

Practice

Use each key word in a sentence.

Make Connections

In this story, one character wants to win. Do you think winning is important? Why or why not?

Academic Words

context
things around something that help to explain it

final
coming at the end; last

pages 45–46

Reading 3

LITERATURE

Fable

Do you always need to be strong to meet a challenge?

Reading Strategy

Visualize

As you read, try to make pictures in your head.

- Where are the characters?
- What do the characters look like?
- What are the characters doing?

The Contest

by Matt Aun
illustrated by Stephen Alcorn

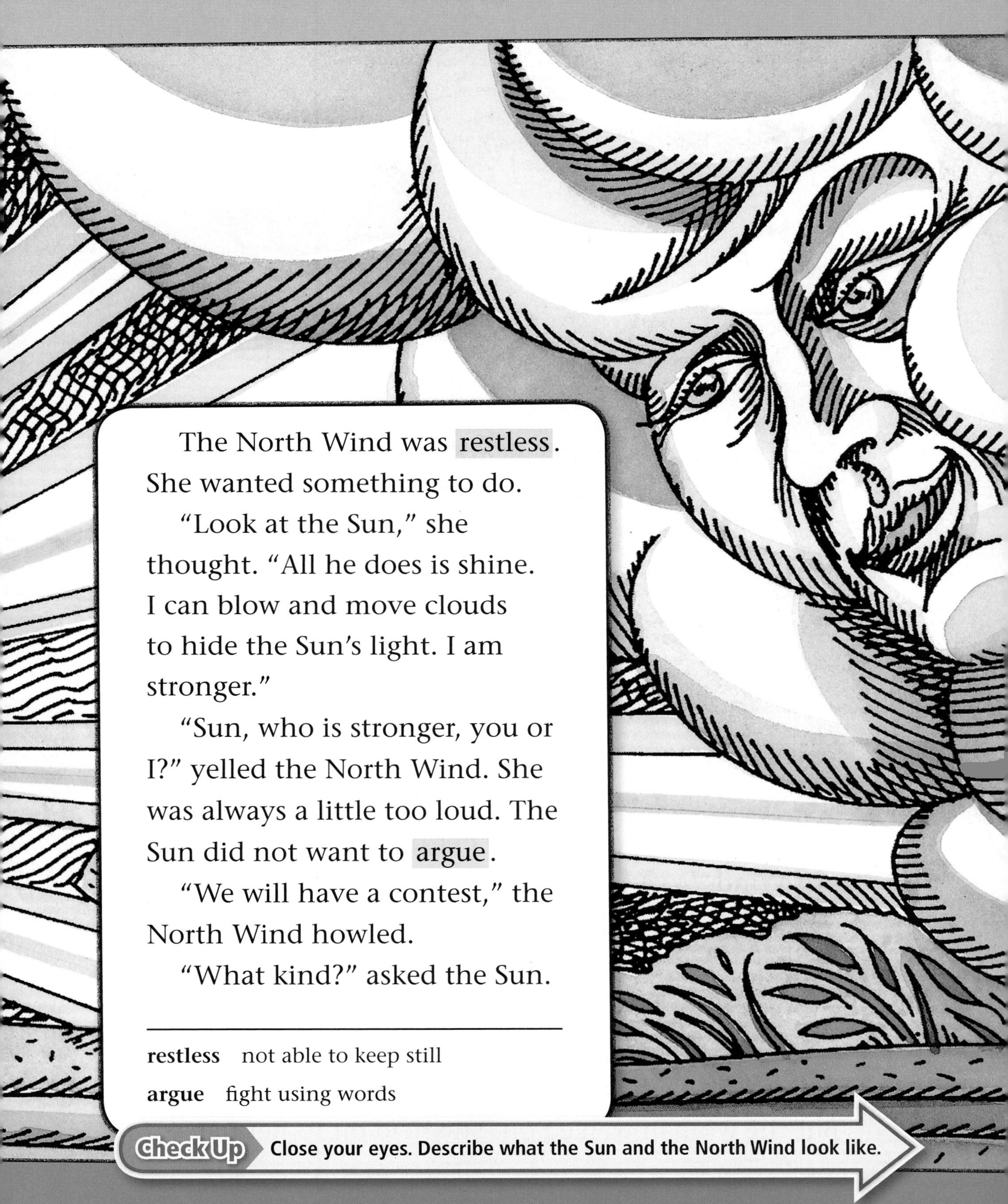

The North Wind was restless. She wanted something to do.

"Look at the Sun," she thought. "All he does is shine. I can blow and move clouds to hide the Sun's light. I am stronger."

"Sun, who is stronger, you or I?" yelled the North Wind. She was always a little too loud. The Sun did not want to argue.

"We will have a contest," the North Wind howled.

"What kind?" asked the Sun.

---

restless not able to keep still

argue fight using words

Check Up Close your eyes. Describe what the Sun and the North Wind look like.

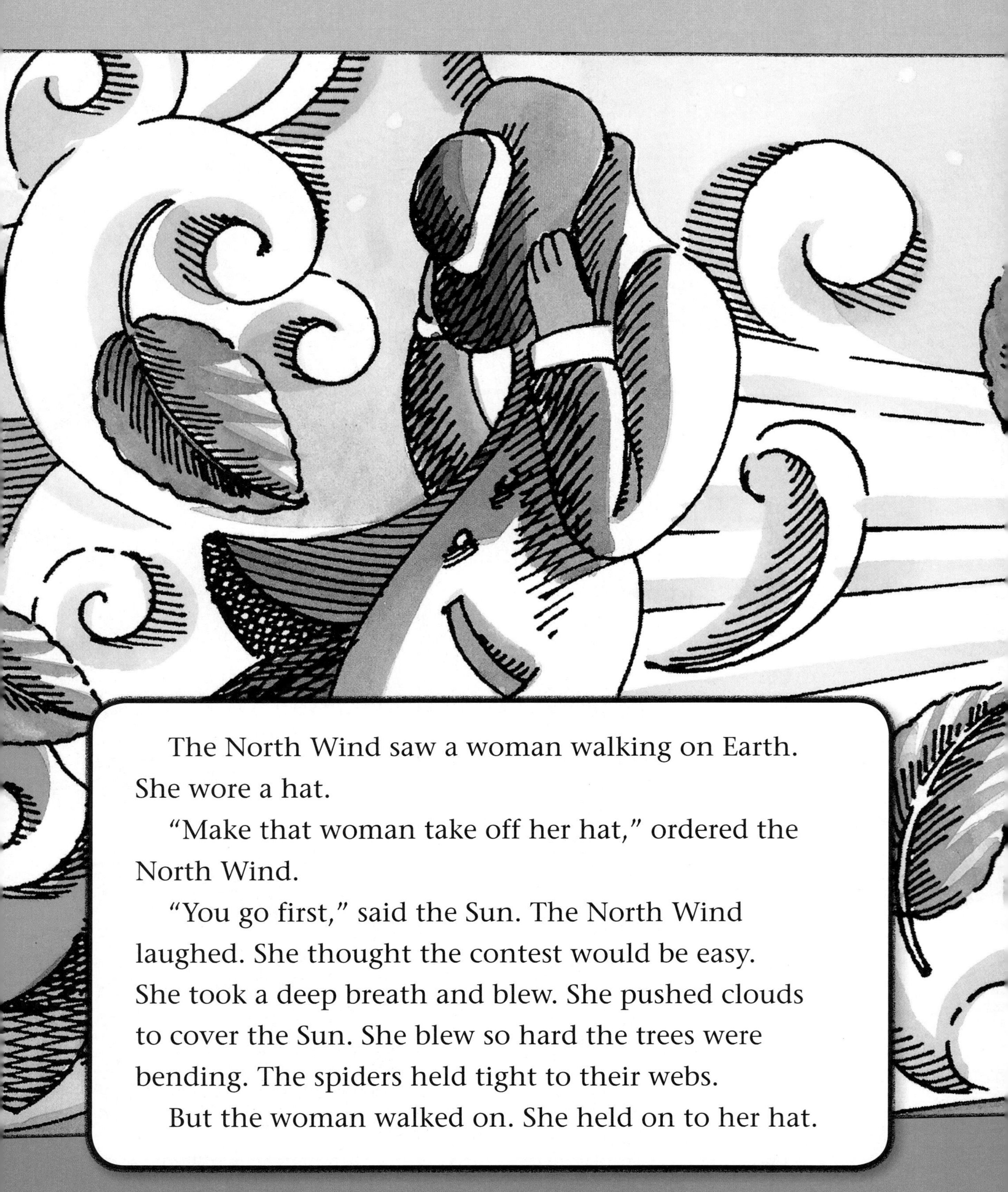

The North Wind saw a woman walking on Earth. She wore a hat.

"Make that woman take off her hat," ordered the North Wind.

"You go first," said the Sun. The North Wind laughed. She thought the contest would be easy. She took a deep breath and blew. She pushed clouds to cover the Sun. She blew so hard the trees were bending. The spiders held tight to their webs.

But the woman walked on. She held on to her hat.

The North Wind took another breath and then she blew very hard. She blew leaves from the trees. She pushed flying birds from the sky. They hid in their nests. The North Wind threw spiders to the ground. She sent their webs flying away.

In the strong wind, it was hard for the woman to stay on her feet. But she never let go of her hat. She held it on her head with both hands.

Check Up Describe what the Sun and the North Wind are doing.

The North Wind gave up. She could not blow any stronger. The great North Wind had been so proud. She had been so sure of her strength. Now she thought, "What good am I? The woman was stronger in the end."

The Sun said, "Can I try now?"

"You can try," said the Wind. "But that woman won't take off her hat."

The North Wind tried not to worry. How could the Sun win the contest? All he could do was shine.

---

strength power that makes someone strong

The Sun turned his face to Earth. He grew brighter. The clouds disappeared. The Sun became even brighter. The birds peeked out of their nests. They started to sing. The spiders crawled back up the trees. They started to make new webs.

The woman stopped walking. She looked up.

Check Up What do you think the woman will do with her hat?

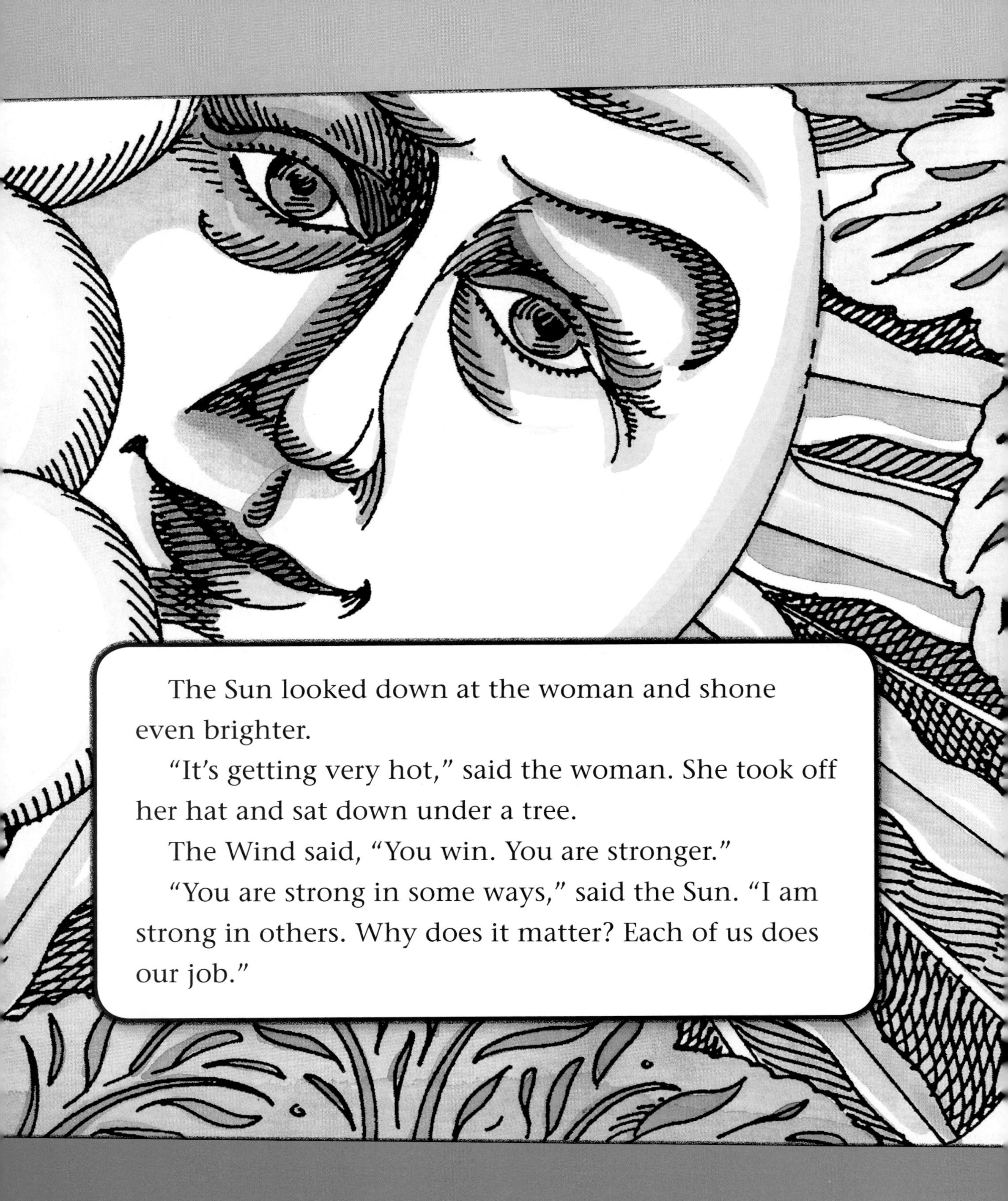

The Sun looked down at the woman and shone even brighter.

"It's getting very hot," said the woman. She took off her hat and sat down under a tree.

The Wind said, "You win. You are stronger."

"You are strong in some ways," said the Sun. "I am strong in others. Why does it matter? Each of us does our job."

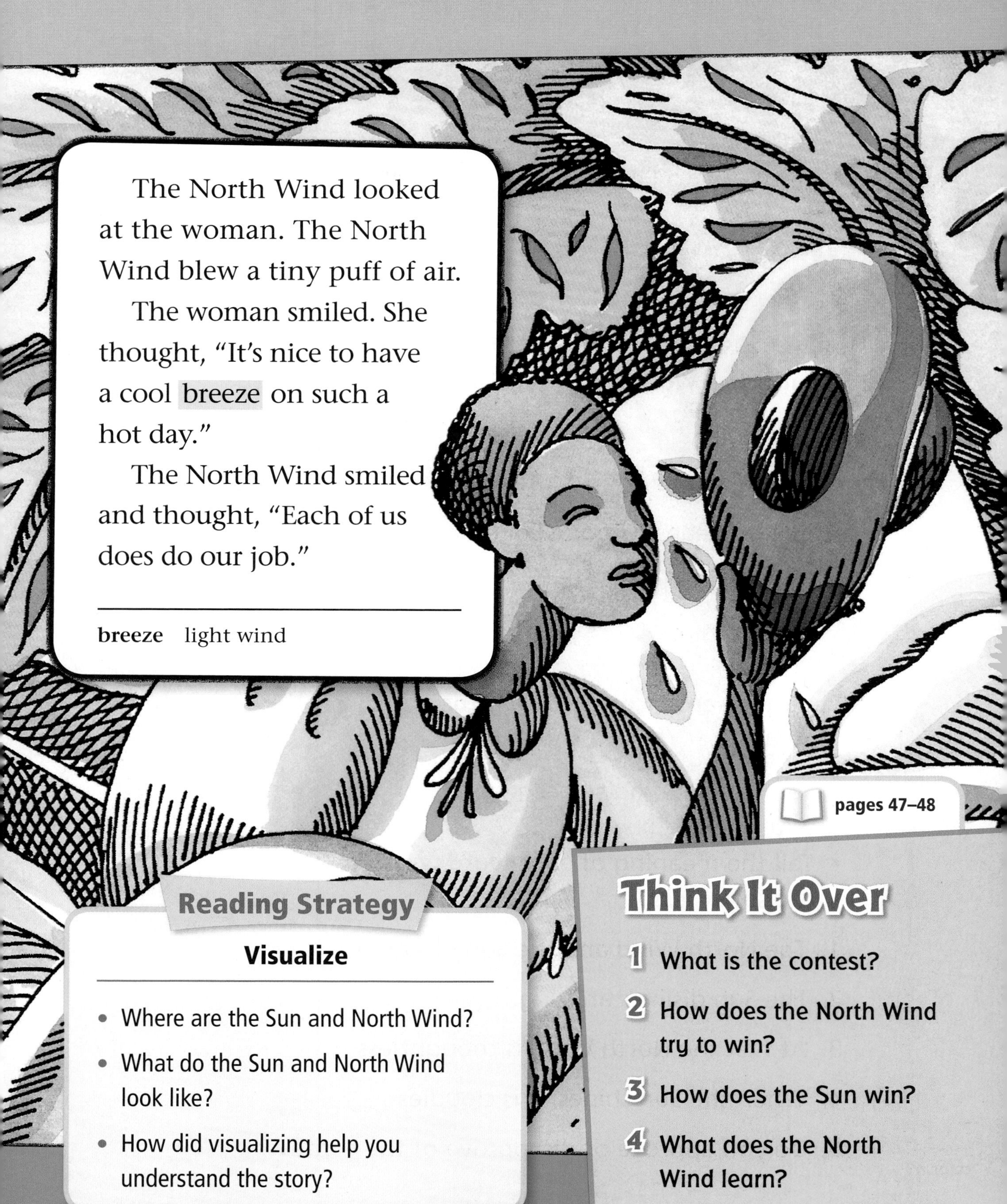

The North Wind looked at the woman. The North Wind blew a tiny puff of air.

The woman smiled. She thought, "It's nice to have a cool breeze on such a hot day."

The North Wind smiled and thought, "Each of us does do our job."

---

breeze light wind

pages 47–48

Reading Strategy

Visualize

- Where are the Sun and North Wind?
- What do the Sun and North Wind look like?
- How did visualizing help you understand the story?

Think It Over

1. What is the contest?
2. How does the North Wind try to win?
3. How does the Sun win?
4. What does the North Wind learn?

Word Analysis & Fluency

Word Analysis

Prefixes and Suffixes

A **prefix** is a word part added to the beginning of a word.
A **suffix** is a word part added to the end of a word.

Rule Box

The prefix *dis* means ***not***. So *disappear* means ***not appear***.

The suffix *less* means ***without***. So *restless* means ***without rest***.

Practice

Read the sentences with a partner. Take turns.

- Tell the meaning of each word with the prefix ***dis***.
- Tell the meaning of each word with the suffix ***less***.

1. The North Wind and the Sun disagree.
2. The Sun dislikes arguing.
3. At first the North Wind is thoughtless.
4. When the Sun shines, it is cloudless.
5. Do you approve or disapprove of the contest?

page 49

Fluency

Read for Speed and Accuracy

You should read quickly. But never read so quickly that you lose your understanding.

Practice

Read for one minute.	Count the words you read.	Study any hard words.	Read and count again.

The Sun turned his face to Earth. He grew brighter.	10
The clouds disappeared. The Sun became even	17
brighter. The birds peeked out of their nests. They	26
started to sing. The spiders crawled back up the trees.	36
They started to make new webs.	42
The woman stopped walking. She looked up.	49
The Sun looked down at the woman and shone	58
even brighter.	60
"It's getting very hot," said the woman. She took off	70
her hat and sat down under a tree.	78
The Wind said, "You win. You are stronger."	86
"You are strong in some ways," said the Sun. "I am	97
strong in others. Why does it matter? Each of us does	108
our job."	110
The North Wind looked at the woman. The North	119
Wind blew a tiny puff of air.	126

Comprehension

Visualizing

As you read, you can **visualize**, or make pictures in your head. You may make pictures of where the characters are. You may make pictures of what the characters look like. You may picture what is happening in the story.

Practice

Read each sentence. Describe the pictures you make in your mind. Choose one sentence and draw it.

1. The North Wind was restless. She wanted something to do.
2. The Sun turned his face to Earth. He grew brighter.
3. In the strong wind, it was hard for the woman to stay on her feet.

Learning Strategy

Retell

Retell the story to a partner.

Ask your partner to respond to the Big Question for this reading.

page 50

Use a Three-Column Chart

A Three-Column Chart can help you compare things. You will compare different types of writing. These are called **genres.**

Practice

Copy the chart. List each of the statements below in the correct column. Some of the genres may have more than one statement.

Story	Play	Poem

- has events in a plot
- uses rhyme
- lists the name of the characters
- tells about conflicts

Work in a group of three to act out *The Contest* as a play. Present your play to the class.

Grammar & Writing

Action Verbs

You can't tell a story without action verbs. **Action verbs** show what the characters do.

The action verbs below are in red.

The Wind **pushed** flying birds from the sky.

The Sun **turned** his face to Earth.

Practice

Work with a partner. Take turns.

- Read each sentence.
- Find the action verbs and write them.

1. The Wind challenged the Sun to a contest.
2. The woman held her hat on her head.
3. The Sun shone brightly.
4. The woman removed her hat.
5. The Wind helped the woman at the end.

page 51

Retell a Story

Many stories are told over and over. David wrote this retelling of a story.

Hare and Tortoise

Hare laughed at Tortoise. "You are so slow," he said. "I could beat you in a race, even if I hopped on one foot." Tortoise challenged, "I will race you. We will see."

They began the race. Hare hopped away. Tortoise walked slowly. She took one step at a time. Hare danced along the path. He sang and chased butterflies. Then he stopped to rest. "I have plenty of time," he thought. Tortoise just kept walking.

Then Hare woke up. It was very late. "I'll have to go fast now," he thought. And he leaped along the path. But when he got to the finish line, Tortoise had already won! With her slow, steady walk she had beaten the leaping Hare.

SPELLING TIP

You know *ue* and *ui* can make a long *u* sound. Another way to make this sound is *ew*. The word ***blew*** has the long *u* sound.

page 52

Practice

Choose a favorite story.

- Retell the story in your own words.
- Use action verbs!

Writing Checklist

- ✓ Did you retell the story in your own words?
- ✓ Did you use action verbs?
- ✓ Can a partner follow your story?

A Year Later

by Mary Ann Hoberman

Last summer I couldn't swim at all
I couldn't even float
I had to use a rubber tube
Or hang on to a boat
I had to sit on shore
While everybody swam
But now it's this summer
And I can!

UNIT 2 Wrap Up

The Big Question

All of us have challenges at times.
How can people meet challenges?

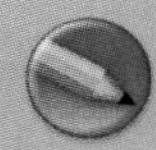 **Written**

Email

Think of a problem you faced. Write an email to a friend or relative. Tell that person what your problem was. Tell how you solved the problem.

T-Chart

Create a T-Chart. Use **Problem** as one heading. Use **Solution** as the other heading. Complete the chart to tell about the selections in this unit.

 **Oral**

Talk and Help

Give a talk to children in first grade. Tell them about challenges you had when you were in first grade. Tell how you met your challenges.

Act It Out

Work with a partner. Think of a problem to solve. Act out a scene about the problem. Show the problem, and then show the solution.

 **Visual/Active**

What If Book

Create a picture book. Show ways that children can solve problems. For example, ask, "What if you don't understand a question?" Show a child raising his or her hand.

Matching Game

Use ten blank cards. Write a problem on five cards. Write a solution on the other five cards. Turn all the cards face down. Have a partner try to match problems and solutions.

✓ Learning Checklist

Word Analysis and Phonics

- ✓ Read words with long vowel pairs.
- ✓ Read words with more long vowel pairs.
- ✓ Identify prefixes and suffixes.

Comprehension

- ✓ Identify characters' conflicts.
- ✓ Use a Problem and Solution Chart.
- ✓ Identify events in a plot.
- ✓ Use a Sequence Chart.
- ✓ Visualize.
- ✓ Use a Three-Column Chart.

Grammar and Writing

- ✓ Recognize and use the verb *have*.
- ✓ Recognize and use the verb *be*.
- ✓ Recognize and use action verbs.
- ✓ Write a problem and solution story.
- ✓ Write a scene.
- ✓ Write a retelling of a story.

Self Evaluation Questions

- You read about people who solve problems. How can this help you solve your own problems?
- What did you like about this unit?
- What are you most proud of? Why?

UNIT 3

Animals at Home

What animals change shape as they grow? What do alligators eat? What animals hide right at home? Read on! You'll find out!

Readings

1 How Do They Grow?

2 Animals at Home

3 Can You See Them?

The Big Question

What can we learn about animals and why is learning about them important?

Listening and Speaking

What do you know about animals? In this unit, you will talk about animals and how they live.

Writing

Which animal do you like best? You will write a poem about an animal.

Quick Write

Which animal do you most want to learn about? Write your reasons.

Bonus Reading

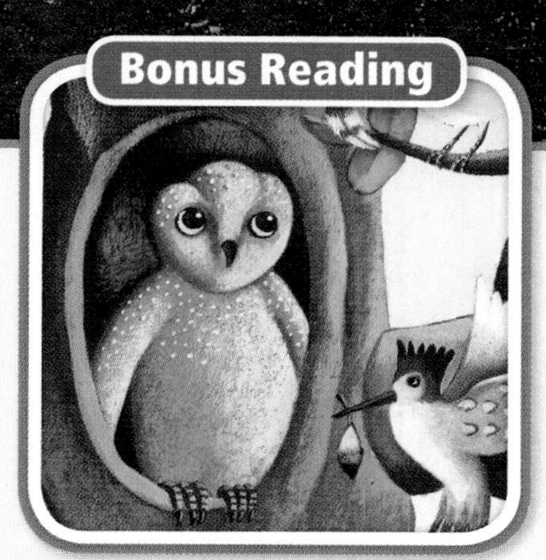

Why Owl Hunts at Night

What Do You Know about Animals at Home?

Words to Know

1. Use these words to talk about animals.

frog

squirrel

monkey

butterfly

raccoon

horse

---

2. Where do animals live?

Animals live ______________ .

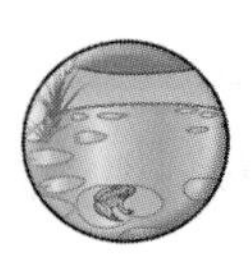
near a pond

in a rain forest

in the woods

in a stable

3. What can animals do?

A ____________ *can* ____________ .

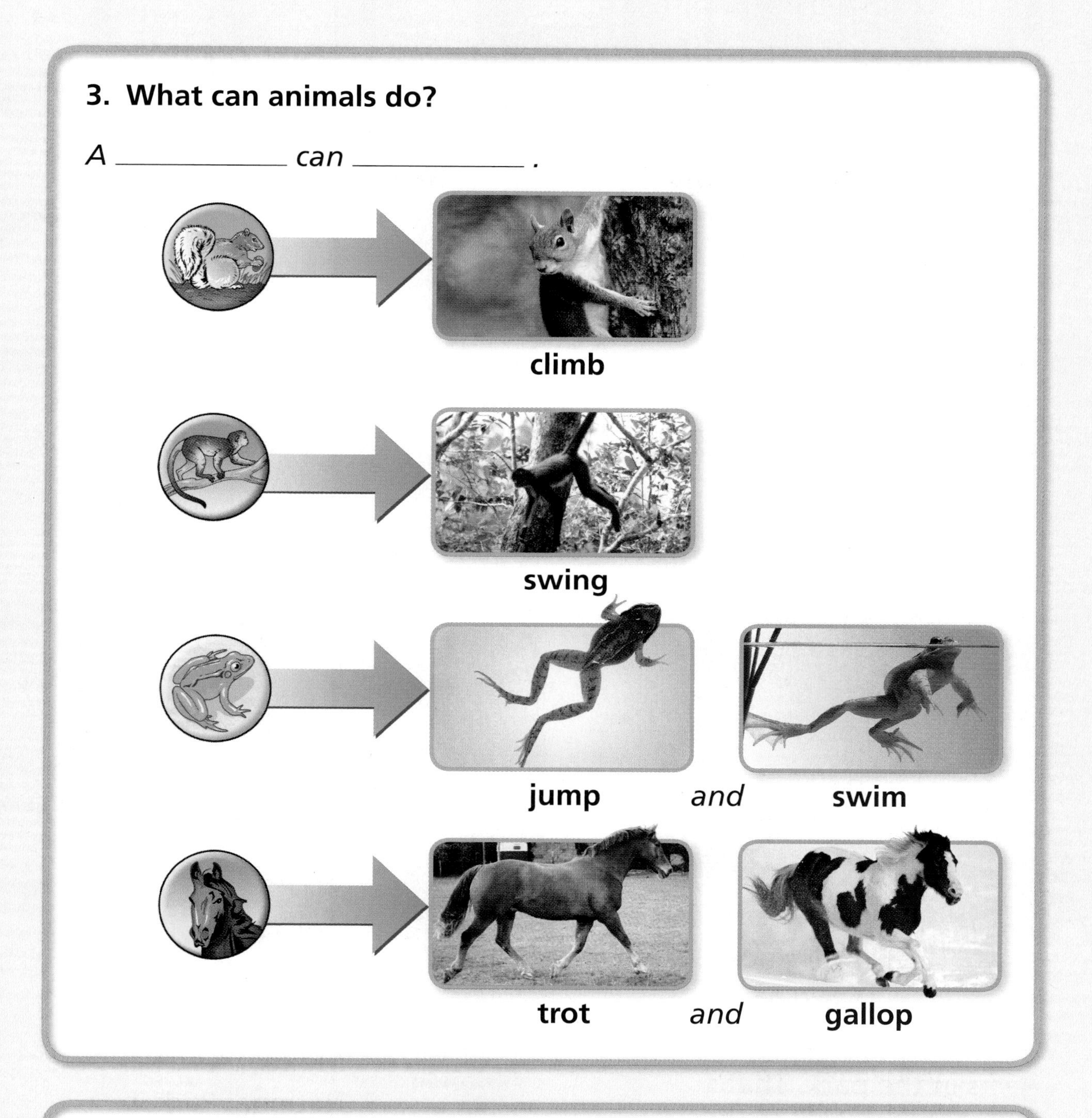

4. Use these words to talk about some other animals.

bear

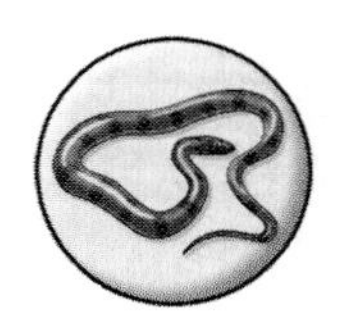

snake

skunk

wolf

Your Stories about Animals at Home

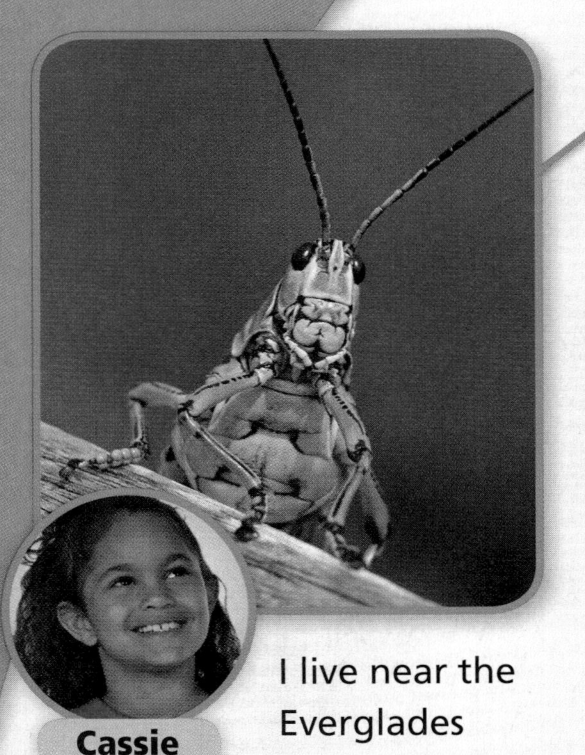

Cassie

I live near the Everglades National Park in Florida. There are lots of insects in the park. That's good, because I like insects. This yellow grasshopper is called an eastern lubber. I see a lot of these grasshoppers in the summer.

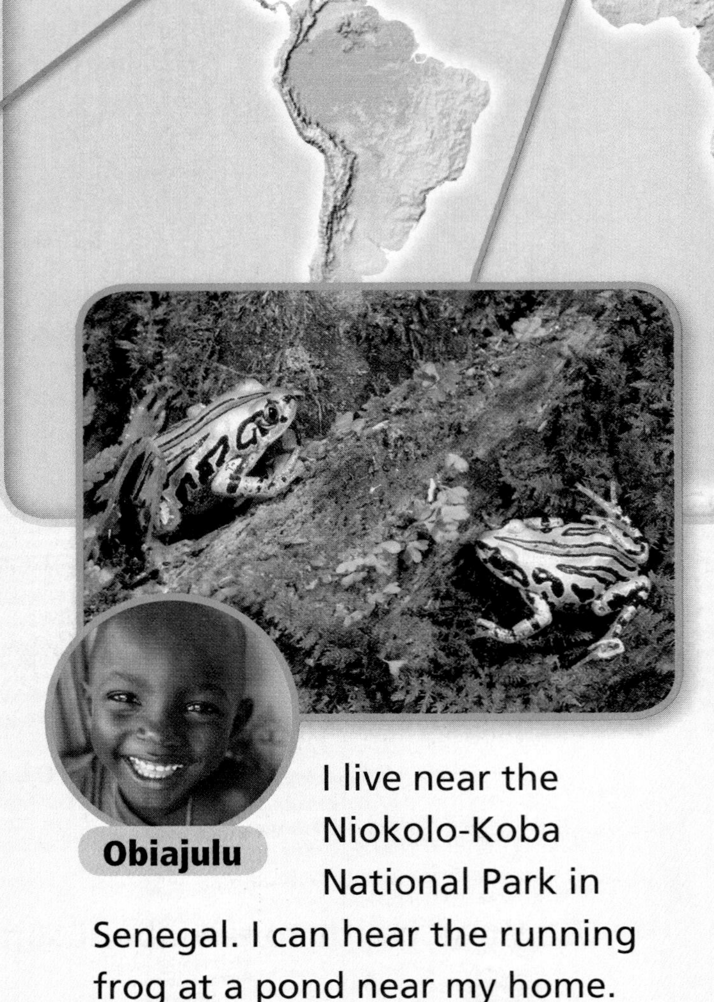

Obiajulu

I live near the Niokolo-Koba National Park in Senegal. I can hear the running frog at a pond near my home. Its voice sounds like water dropping in a pail. The running frog does not hop like other frogs. It runs!

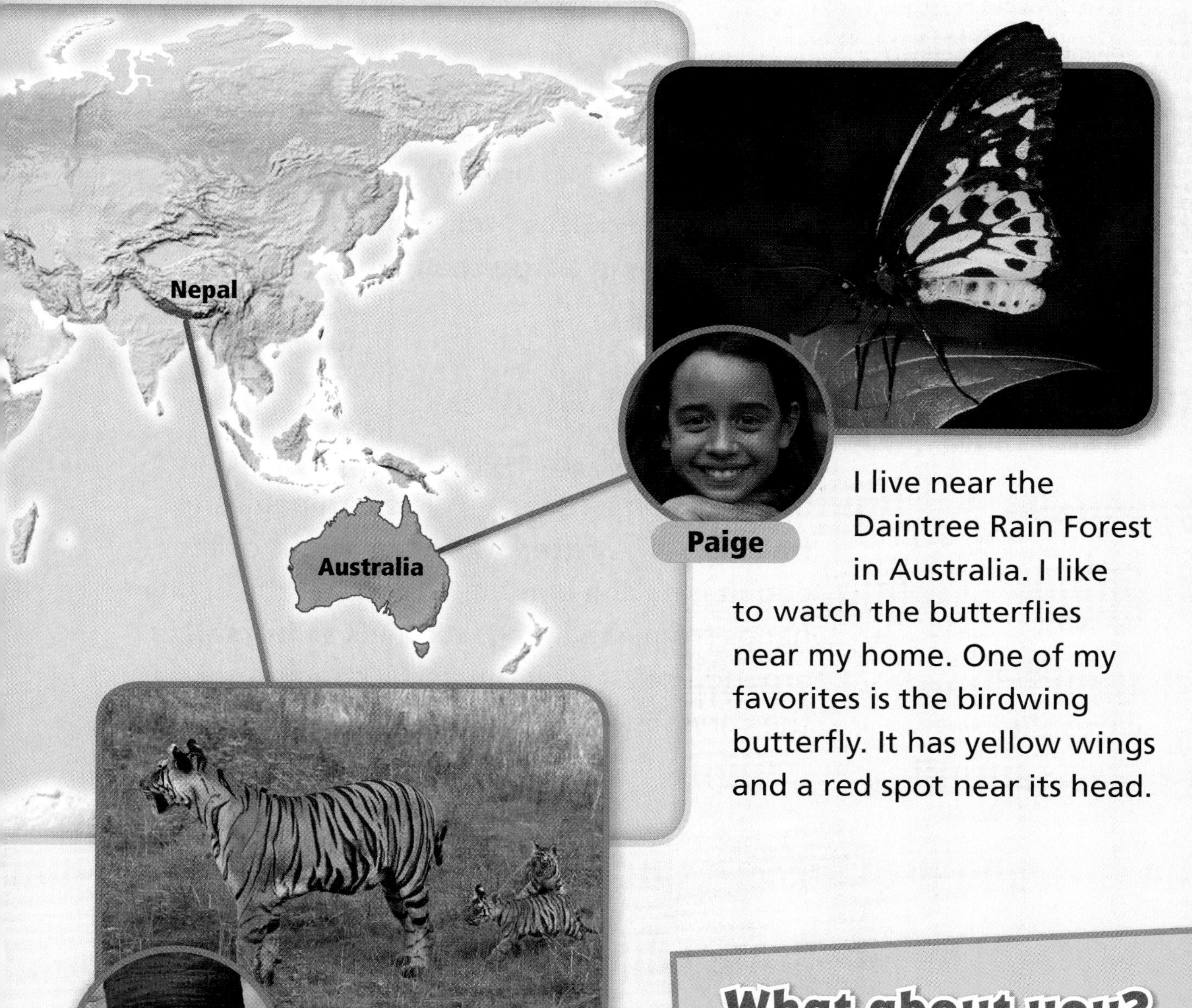

I live near the Daintree Rain Forest in Australia. I like to watch the butterflies near my home. One of my favorites is the birdwing butterfly. It has yellow wings and a red spot near its head.

I live near the Chitwan National Park in Nepal. Tigers live in this park. There are not many tigers left in Nepal. People have hunted them. Today, forest rangers are working hard to protect the tigers.

What about you?

1. What animals do you see where you live?
2. How are these students' stories similar to yours?
3. Do you have other stories about animals and where they live? Tell your story!

Reading 1

Vocabulary

How Do They Grow? tells how a butterfly and a frog change as they grow.

Key Words

butterfly
leaf
hatch
caterpillar
chrysalis
tadpole

Words in Context

A **butterfly** changes as it grows. ① It starts as an egg on a **leaf**. ② The egg begins to **hatch**. ③ A **caterpillar** comes out of the egg. It eats and eats. ④ Then the caterpillar hangs from a leaf. ⑤ It builds a **chrysalis** around itself. ⑥ A butterfly comes out of the chrysalis.

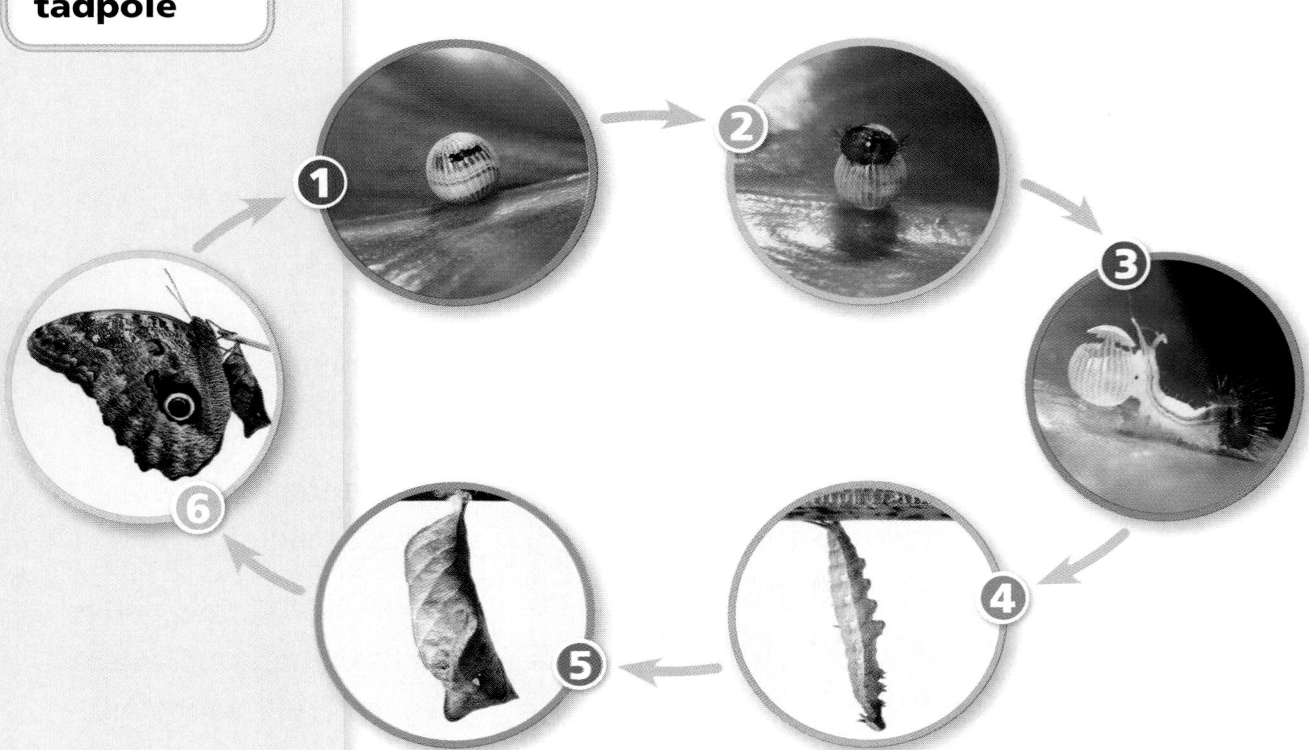

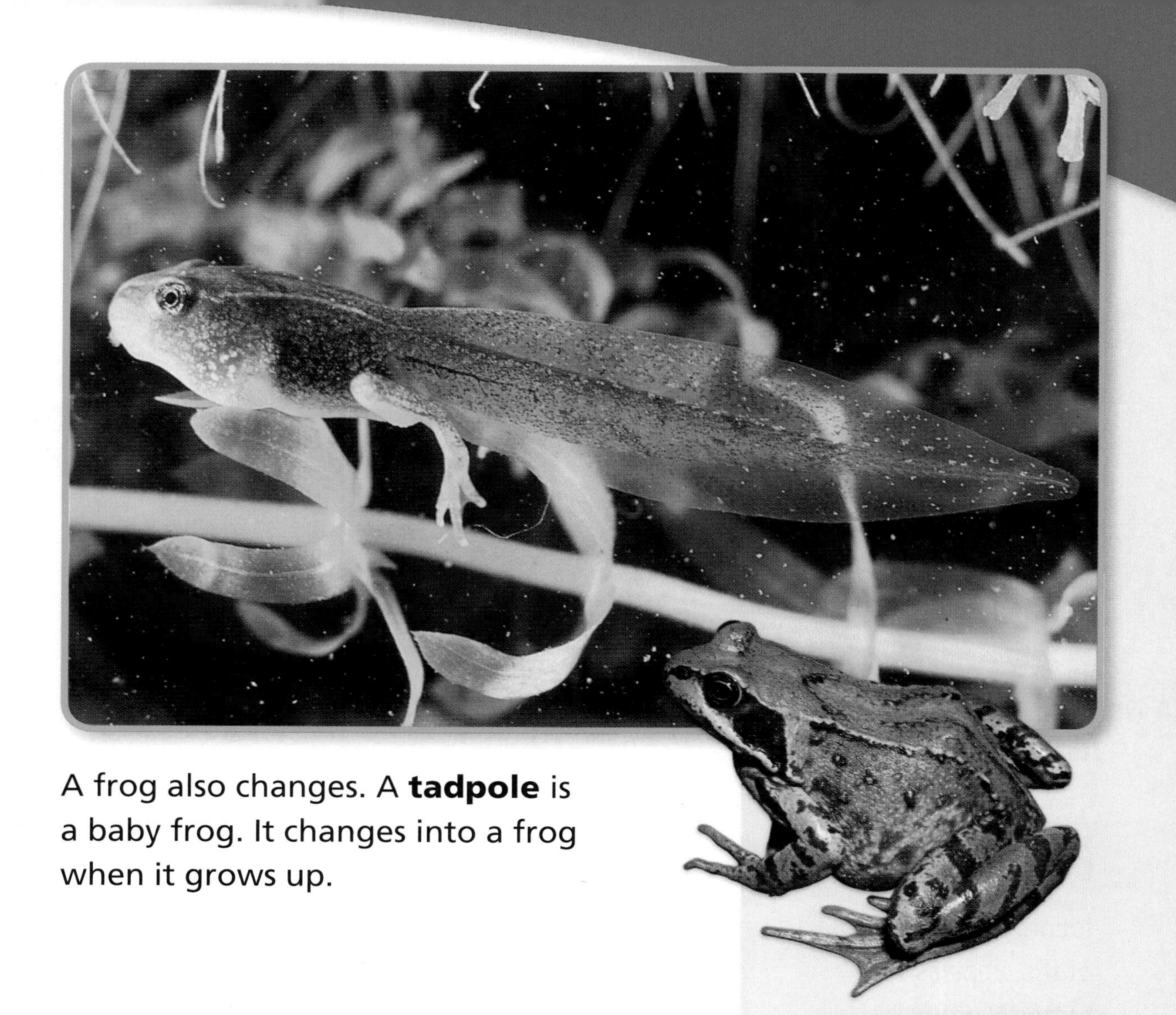

A frog also changes. A **tadpole** is a baby frog. It changes into a frog when it grows up.

Practice

Use each key word in a sentence.

Make Connections

Some animals change as they grow. How do you change as you grow? How do you feel about these changes?

Academic Words

process
set of steps that makes something change

initial
at the beginning; first

pages 55–56

Reading 1

INFORMATIONAL TEXT

Science

Why should people care how animals change as they grow?

Reading Strategy

Identify Steps in a Process

- Look at the pictures.
- Identify the order of the steps as the butterfly grows.
- Identify the order of the steps as the frog grows.

How Do They Grow?

by Leila Han

This frog was not always big and brown. This butterfly did not always have bright wings.

Living things grow and change. They are born one way. Then they become different.

Let's look at how butterflies and frogs grow and change.

Butterfly

A butterfly must find a place to lay eggs. A leaf is a good place.

Soon an egg will hatch. A tiny caterpillar crawls out. The caterpillar starts to eat right away. It munches on plants.

Next, the caterpillar builds a chrysalis around itself. The chrysalis sticks to a tree branch. It hangs there and does not move. But changes happen inside.

Then the butterfly breaks out of the chrysalis. It spreads its wings. It is ready to fly.

munches chews

Check Up What happens inside the chrysalis?

Frog

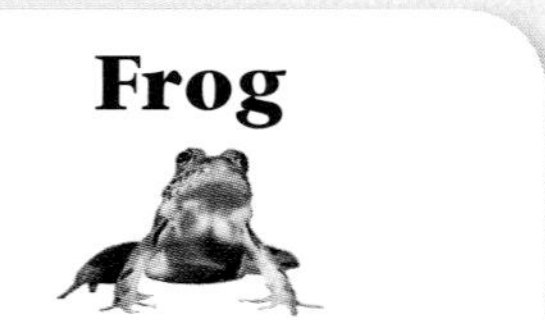

A frog lays eggs in the water. Soon, an egg hatches. A tiny tadpole **wiggles** out.

A tadpole lives in the water. It starts to grow legs.

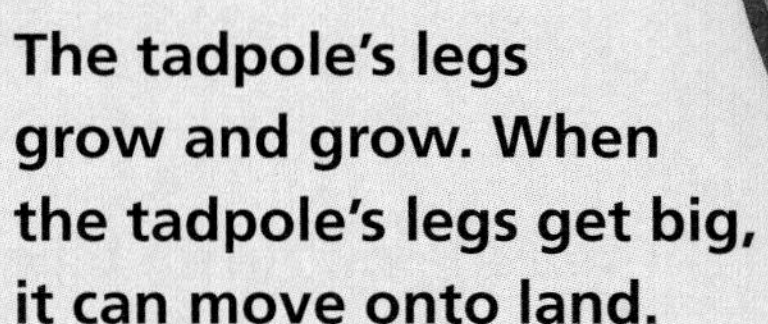

The tadpole's legs grow and grow. When the tadpole's legs get big, it can move onto land.

---

wiggles moves from side to side

Now the tadpole is a frog. The frog can hop on land. It can swim in the water, too.

pages 57–58

Think It Over

1. How are the butterfly and the frog similar?
2. How are the butterfly and the frog different?
3. Do all animals change in steps the way these animals do? How do you know?

Reading Strategy

Identify Steps in a Process

- How does a butterfly change as it grows?
- How does a frog change as it grows?
- Did identifying the order of the steps help you understand the selection? How?

Phonics & Fluency

Phonics

Digraphs: *ch, sh, th*

Digraphs may be at the beginning, middle, or end of a word.

ch	sh	th
change branch	ship wish	then both

Rule Box

The letters *ch*, *sh*, and *th* come together to make one sound.

Practice

Read the sentences with a partner. Take turns.

- Living things may change.
- Fish hatch from eggs.
- Snakes shed their skin.
- Silkworms become moths.
- Children grow into adults.

1. List the words with *ch*, *sh*, or *th.*

2. Circle the letters *ch*, *sh*, or *th* in the words.

page 59

Fluency

Look Ahead

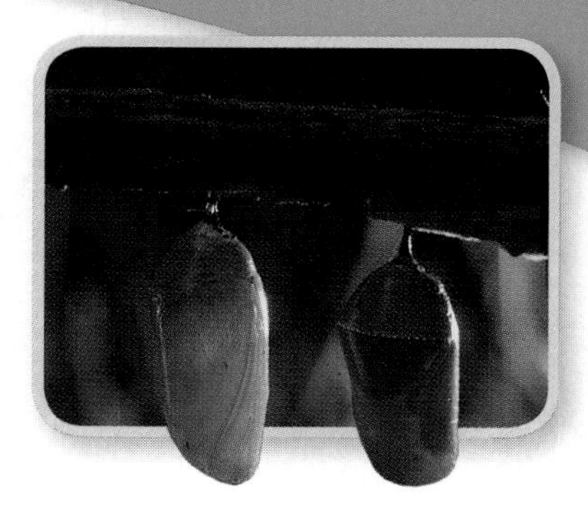

Sometimes readers look for hard words before they read. They then try to figure them out.

Practice

Pick one passage.	Find any hard words.	Practice saying those words.	Read the passage aloud.

1 Some living things change as they grow. A frog goes through different steps. A butterfly goes through different steps, too.

2 A tadpole lives in the water. It starts to grow legs. The tadpole's legs grow and grow. When the tadpole's legs get big, it can move onto land.

Now the tadpole is a frog. The frog can hop on land. It can swim in the water, too.

3 An egg hatches. A tiny caterpillar crawls out. The caterpillar starts to eat right away. It munches on plants.

Soon, the caterpillar builds a chrysalis around itself. The chrysalis sticks to a tree branch. It hangs there and does not move. But changes happen inside.

The butterfly breaks out of the chrysalis. It spreads its wings. It is ready to fly.

Reading 1

Comprehension

Steps in a Process

A **process** is something that happens in order. The parts of a process are called **steps**.

Learning Strategy

Summarize

Summarize the selection for a partner.

? Ask your partner to respond to the Big Question for this reading.

Practice

The list below shows steps in a frog's life. Put the steps in the right order.

- The frog hops on land.
- The frog lays eggs in the water.
- The tadpole wiggles out.
- The egg hatches.
- The tadpole grows legs.

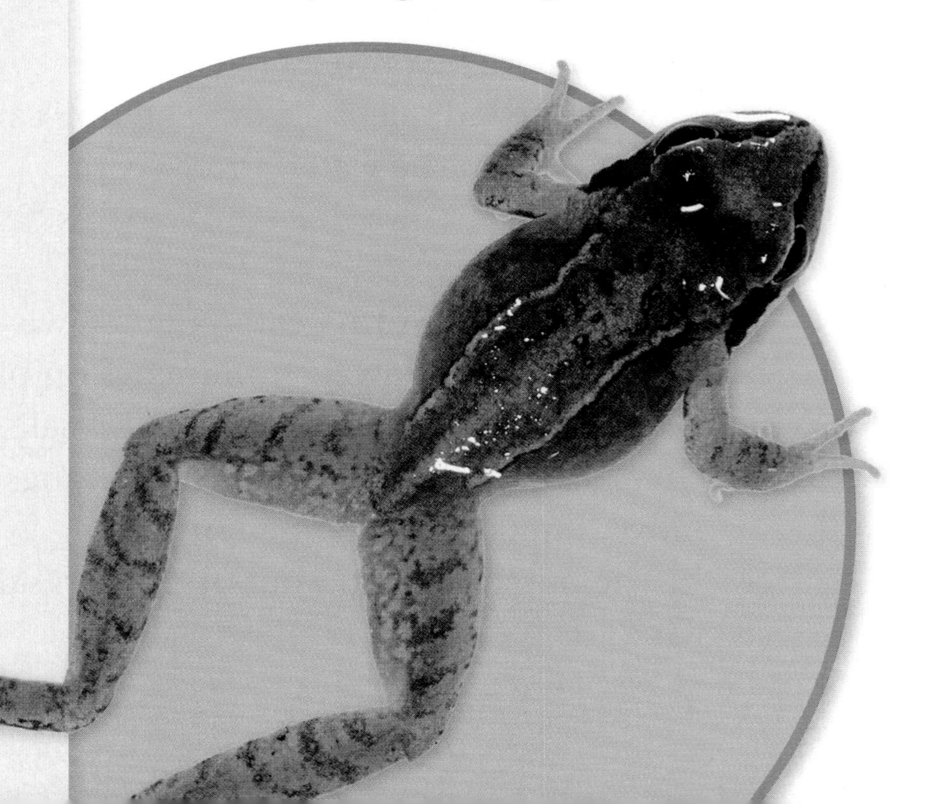

page 60

Use a Sequence Chart

A Sequence Chart can help you put steps in a process in the right order.

Practice

This Sequence Chart shows some steps in the life of a butterfly.

1. Which step should be in Box 3?
   a. A butterfly comes out of the egg.
   b. A tadpole comes out of the egg.
   c. A caterpillar comes out of the egg.
   d. A chrysalis comes out of the egg.

2. If there were a Box 6, which step would it be?
   a. The butterfly becomes a caterpillar.
   b. The butterfly spreads its wings.
   c. The butterfly makes a chrysalis.
   d. The butterfly becomes a tadpole.

1. A butterfly lays an egg.
2. The egg hatches.
3.
4. The caterpillar makes a chrysalis. The chrysalis hangs from a branch.
5. A butterfly breaks out of the chrysalis.

Extension

Think of something you do in steps. It can be tying your shoes or brushing your teeth. Make a Sequence Chart. Show the steps you do. Share your chart with your class.

Grammar & Writing

Subject-Verb Agreement

In a sentence, a verb should agree with the subject. **Agreement** means that they go together.

A **tadpole lives** in the water.

Many **tadpoles live** in the water.

Subject	Verb
one person, place, or thing	Add *-s* to the verb.
more than one person, place, or thing	Do not add *-s* to the verb.
I or *you*	Do not add *-s* to the verb.

Practice

Write each sentence. Use the correct form of the verb *live*.

1. That frog _____ in this pond.
2. The butterfly _____ outdoors.
3. Caterpillars _____ on plants.
4. You _____ in a big city.
5. They _____ in a small town.

page 61

Write a Description

Think about a time when you saw something change. What were the steps in the process? Maria wrote about how her sister changed.

My little sister is Lori. She keeps changing.

At first, Lori just sat. Then, she started to crawl. One day, she crawled to a chair I was sitting in. She wanted to see me, so she pulled herself up. Lori was standing!

Yesterday, Lori tried to follow me across the room. She took three steps. Now she can walk.

The *ch* sound may be spelled *tch* when it is in a one-syllable word with a short vowel.
hatch

page 62

Practice

Write about something that changes.

- First, choose something you have seen change.
- Make a list of the steps. Put the list in the right order.
- Write sentences telling what happened.

Writing Checklist

- ✓ Did you write about something that changed?
- ✓ Did you tell things in order?
- ✓ Did you use correct subject-verb agreement?
- ✓ Can a partner follow the steps in your process?

Vocabulary

Animal at Home tells about animals and where they live.

Words in Context

Key Words
- camels
- amazing
- habits
- caves
- plains

1 **Camels** live in the desert. These camels have two humps on their backs. Some camels have just one hump.

2 The flying squirrel is **amazing**. It does not fly. It jumps and glides through the air.

③ The children in this family each have different **habits**. The oldest, David, sings in the shower. Matt runs everywhere. Grace still sucks her thumb. David and Matt hope she will grow out of this habit.

④ Some bears live in **caves**. This bear looks out from a cave in the side of a mountain.

⑤ Zebras and gazelles live on the wide, flat **plains** of Africa.

Practice

Use each key word in a sentence.

Make Connections

Some animals live in caves. Some live on plains. What animals live near you? Where do they live?

Academic Words

method
plan for doing something

feature
important part of something

pages 63–64

LITERATURE

Poetry

Why should people care where animals live?

Reading Strategy

Make Inferences

- As you read, think about the different animals.
- Think about why each animal has its own type of home.

Animals at Home

by Mario Herrera

Animals do amazing things
and have amazing habits.
Some we like to keep at home,
like cats and dogs and rabbits.

Animals live all over the world
in many kinds of homes.
Bats live in caves, monkeys in trees,
and camels in desert zones.

Hippos live their lives in mud
and polar bears in snow.
Zebras live out on the plains
where lions come and go.

Crocodiles live in lakes and rivers,
and fish and snakes do, too.
Whales and sharks and jellyfish
swim in the ocean blue.

Animals share the world with us,
as pets or wild and free.
Animals living in their homes —
what a beautiful sight to see!

Reading Strategy

Make Inferences

- Why do you think different animals have different kinds of homes?
- What can you infer about crocodiles?

pages 65–66

Think It Over

1. What animals live on the plains?
2. What animals live in the ocean?
3. How do animals share the world with us?

A Closer Look at...

Alligators

▲ Eggs in a nest

A mother alligator lays many eggs in a nest.

▲ Hatching

A baby alligator hatches. It comes out of its shell.

▲ Going to water

The mother alligator takes the baby alligator to water. Babies know how to swim right away by instinct.

▲ Free ride

This baby alligator rests on its mother's head.

▲ Friends

This young alligator shares a log with a painted turtle. But the turtle needs to be careful.

▲ Food

A grown alligator eats turtles. Alligators like to eat fish, too. An alligator uses its teeth to catch food. It does not chew the food. It swallows the food whole.

▲ Sunning themselves

Alligators are usually in or near water. Alligators warm themselves in the sun. This one rests on rocks in a swamp.

---

swamp wet land near a river

Activity to Do!

These two pages use words and pictures to tell you about alligators.

- Choose another animal.
- Find pictures to show that animal.
- Post your pictures and captions in your classroom.

Phonics & Fluency

Phonics

Clusters

Read the words. Listen for the sounds at the beginning.

r-blends	*l*-blends	*s*-blends
frog trees	fly plains	sky swim

Rule Box

Blend the sounds of both letters when a word has

- a consonant followed by the letter *r*
- a consonant followed by the letter *l*
- the letter *s* followed by another consonant

Practice

Work with a partner. Take turns.

- Choose a word from the chart above to answer each question.
- Circle each *r*-blend, *s*-blend, or *l*-blend.

1. Where do monkeys live?
2. Where do zebras live?
3. What do sharks do?
4. What rhymes with sky?

page 67

Fluency

Read with Expression

When you read aloud, use your voice to show feelings.

Practice

Read silently. → Read aloud. → Get comments. → Read aloud again.

Animals do amazing things
and have amazing habits.
Some we like to keep at home,
like cats and dogs and rabbits.

Animals live all over the world
in many kinds of homes.
Bats live in caves, monkeys in trees,
and camels in desert zones.

Hippos live their lives in mud
and polar bears in snow.
Zebras live out on the plains
where lions come and go.

Reading 2

Comprehension

Inferences

You make **inferences** when you figure out something as you read.

Practice

Make inferences about the poem.

- Read the poem.
- Put together what you know and what you read.

> Animals share the world with us,
> as pets or wild and free.
> Animals living in their homes —
> what a beautiful sight to see!

1. How do pets share the world with us?
2. How do wild animals share the world with us?
3. How are the homes of pets and wild animals different?

Learning Strategy

Summarize

Summarize the poem for a partner.

Ask your partner to respond to the Big Question for this reading.

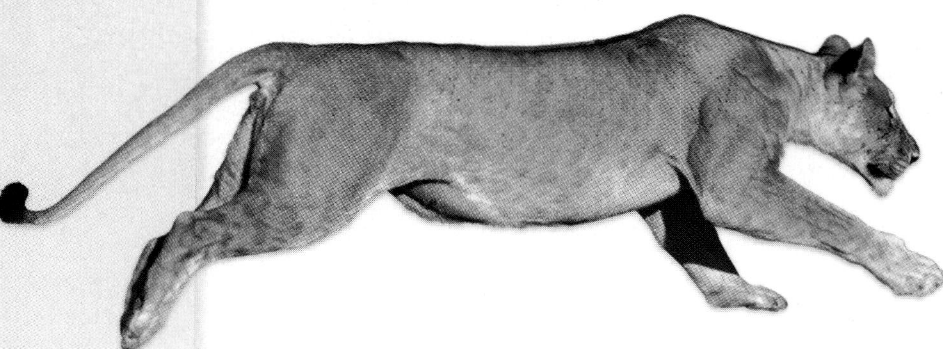

page 68

Use a KWL Chart

You can use a KWL Chart to make inferences. KWL stands for What You **Know**, What You **Want** to Know, and What You **Learned**.

Practice

Read the chart. Answer the questions below. Your answers will help you fill in the chart.

What You Know	What You Want to Know	What You Learned
The poem says "Animals share the world with us."	How do animals and people share the world?	People and animals live on Earth together. People need to take care of Earth so animals have their homes.
The poem says that it is "beautiful" to see animals in their homes.	______	______

1. What is special about animals' homes? Why is it "beautiful" to see them?
2. How does the poet feel about animals in their homes?

Extension

Choose an animal that you like. Make a chart showing the name of the animal, where it lives, and what it eats. Draw a picture of the animal in its home. Share your animal with the class.

Grammar & Writing

Types of Sentences

There are four types of sentences.

Type of Sentence	Purpose	Example
Declarative	tells something	Alligators eat fish.
Interrogative	asks a question	What do alligators eat?
Imperative	tells someone to do something	Be careful.
Exclamatory	shows strong feeling	A grown alligator eats turtles!

Practice

Work with a partner. Read each sentence. Tell what type of sentence each one is.

1. Alligators live near water.
2. How do baby alligators learn to swim?
3. Look at that alligator.
4. That's a really big alligator!
5. Are the alligators sleeping in the sun?

page 69

Write a Poem

Write a poem about an animal. Anji wrote this poem.

What Am I?

Sometimes I crawl.
Sometimes I fly.
Sometimes I stay very still.
What am I?

Practice

Now write your own "What Am I?" poem about an animal.

- Write as if you are the animal talking.
- Give three clues about the animal.
- End your poem with the line "What am I?"

Spelling Tip

Words that end with a silent *e* drop the *e* when you add *-ing*.

amaze → amazing

page 70

Writing Checklist

- ✓ Did you title your poem "What Am I?"
- ✓ Did your poem give three clues about the animal?
- ✓ Share your poem with a partner. Can your partner guess what your animal is?

Vocabulary

Can You See Them? tells how animals use camouflage.

Key Words

- insect
- habitats
- camouflage
- prey
- patterns
- moth

Words in Context

1. This is an **insect.** An insect has three body parts, six legs, and antennae. Insects may also have wings.

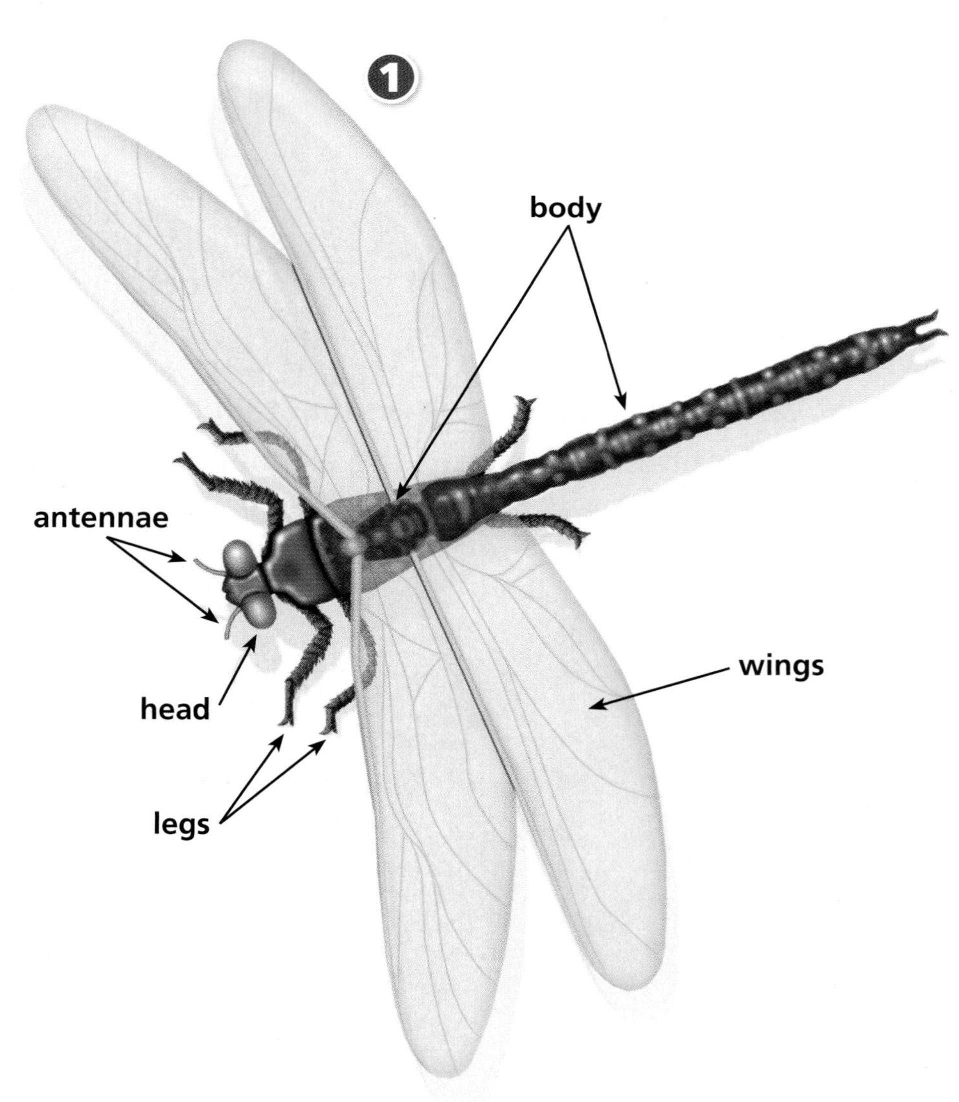

② **Habitats** are where animals live. Animals use **camouflage** to hide in their habitats. They hide from other animals that might eat them. Also, animals hide so they can catch prey. **Prey** is any animal that another animal eats.

③ The **patterns** on the pepper **moth** help it hide on a tree.

Practice

Use each key word in a sentence.

Make Connections

Some animals use camouflage to be safe. People wear seat belts in cars to be safe. What do you do to be safe?

Academic Words

function
purpose

reaction
response

pages 71–72

Reading 3

INFORMATIONAL TEXT

Photo Essay

The Big Question

Why is it important to know how animals use camouflage?

Reading Strategy

Identify Cause and Effect

- As you read, look for things that make other things happen. These are causes.
- Look for things that happen because of something else. These are effects.

Can You See Them?

by Kendra Clay

Can you see the insect in the photograph above? You will need to look carefully.

The insect is called a walking stick. It can hide in a tree because it looks like a small branch, or stick.

Arctic foxes live where the weather is very cold. They can change color. In summer, the foxes are brown. In winter, they are white.

A tawny frogmouth is a bird. It sits very still in a tree. It waits for prey to come near. Then it pounces!

Many animals hide. They may hide to keep safe from predators. Or, they may hide so they can catch prey.

This kind of hiding is called camouflage. When animals have camouflage, they are hard to see in their habitats.

---

pounces jumps suddenly after waiting

predators animals that kill and eat other animals

Patterns help this moth stay safe. Look at the big spots on the moth's wings. They look like a large animal's eyes. Predators stay away from this insect.

Check Up Why does the tawny frogmouth stay very still?

A horned lizard is the color of the ground. The lizard can quickly change from a light color to a dark color. The insects it eats do not know it is there.

A Bengal tiger is a very large cat. It's hard for a big animal to hide. But the tiger has stripes. When it rests in the forest, its stripes blend in with the plants.

Sandhill cranes migrate south from Canada and Alaska. These gray-and-white birds blend in with the snowy lands around them.

migrate move from one area to another as the seasons change

A leaf-tailed gecko is a kind of lizard. It blends in with a tree branch in Africa. It waits for prey to fly by.

This cottontail rabbit hides in some leaves on the ground in the forest. It must hide from predators.

pages 73–74

Reading Strategy

Identify Cause and Effect

- Did you find out why some animals use camouflage?
- How did looking for cause and effect help you understand the selection?

Think It Over

1. Why does the leaf-tailed gecko use camouflage?
2. Why does the cottontail rabbit use camouflage?
3. What are two reasons for animals to use camouflage?

Word Analysis & Fluency

Word Analysis

Compound Words

Compound words are made up of two smaller words.

frogmouth	**sandhill**	**cottontail**
frog + mouth	sand + hill	cotton + tail

Rule Box

Look for the smaller words to help you read compound words.

Practice

Read each sentence with a partner. Take turns.

- Tawny frogmouths are related to nighthawks.
- They live in the woodlands.
- They sleep during daylight hours.
- At nightfall, they wake up.

1. List the compound words.
2. Show the two words that make up each compound word.

page 75

Fluency

Read for Speed and Accuracy

You should read quickly. But never read so quickly that you lose your understanding.

Practice

Read for one minute. → Count the words you read. → Study any hard words. → Read and count again.

The insect is called a walking stick. It can hide in a tree	13
because it looks like a small branch, or stick.	22
Many animals hide. They may hide to keep safe from	32
predators. Or, they may hide so they can catch prey.	42
This kind of hiding is called camouflage. When animals	51
have camouflage, they are hard to see in their habitats.	61
Arctic foxes live where the weather is very cold. They	71
can change color. In summer, the foxes are brown. In	81
winter, they are white.	85
A tawny frogmouth is a bird. It sits very still in a tree.	98
It waits for prey to come near. Then it pounces!	108
Patterns help this moth stay safe. Look at the big spots	119
on the moth's wings. They look like a large animal's	129
eyes. Predators stay away from this insect.	136
A Bengal tiger is a very large cat. It's hard for a big	149
animal to hide. But the tiger has stripes. When it rests in	161
the forest, its stripes blend in with the plants.	170

Comprehension

Cause and Effect

One thing can make another thing happen. The **cause** is the thing that happens first. The **effect** is the thing that happens because of the first thing.

Practice

Match each effect with its cause.

Cause	Effect
1. The Bengal tiger has stripes.	**a.** It can hide in a tree.
2. The Arctic fox lives where there is snow.	**b.** It can hide in the forest.
3. The walking stick insect looks like a small branch.	**c.** It can hide in the winter when its coat turns white.

Learning Strategy

Summarize

Summarize the selection for a partner.

Ask your partner to respond to the Big Question for this reading.

page 76

Use a Cause and Effect Chart

Use a Cause and Effect Chart to show how camouflage helps animals.

Practice

Copy this chart.

- Fill in the effects.
- Add two more causes. Fill in their effects.

Cause	Effect
The Bengal tiger has stripes.	It can hide in the forest.
The Arctic fox lives where there is snow.	______________
The walking stick looks like a branch.	______________
______________	______________
______________	______________

Extension

Draw a picture of yourself as an animal. Label the picture to show how your camouflage helps you to stay safe. Share your drawing with the class.

Grammar & Writing

Complete Sentences

A **complete sentence** tells a complete thought.

Complete	**A tiger is a very large cat.**
Not complete	**A Bengal tiger**

A sentence begins with a capital letter. It ends with a punctuation mark. Use different punctuation marks for different types of sentences.

Type of Sentence	End Punctuation
Interrogative	question mark ?
Declarative	period .
Imperative	period or exclamation mark . or !
Exclamatory	exclamation mark !

Practice

Write each sentence correctly. Start with a capital letter. End with a punctuation mark.

1. the Arctic fox can change color
2. what color is the sandhill crane
3. watch this television show with me
4. that was an amazing sight

page 77

Write a Friendly Letter

You have learned a lot about animals. Miguel wrote this letter to tell his grandmother what he had learned.

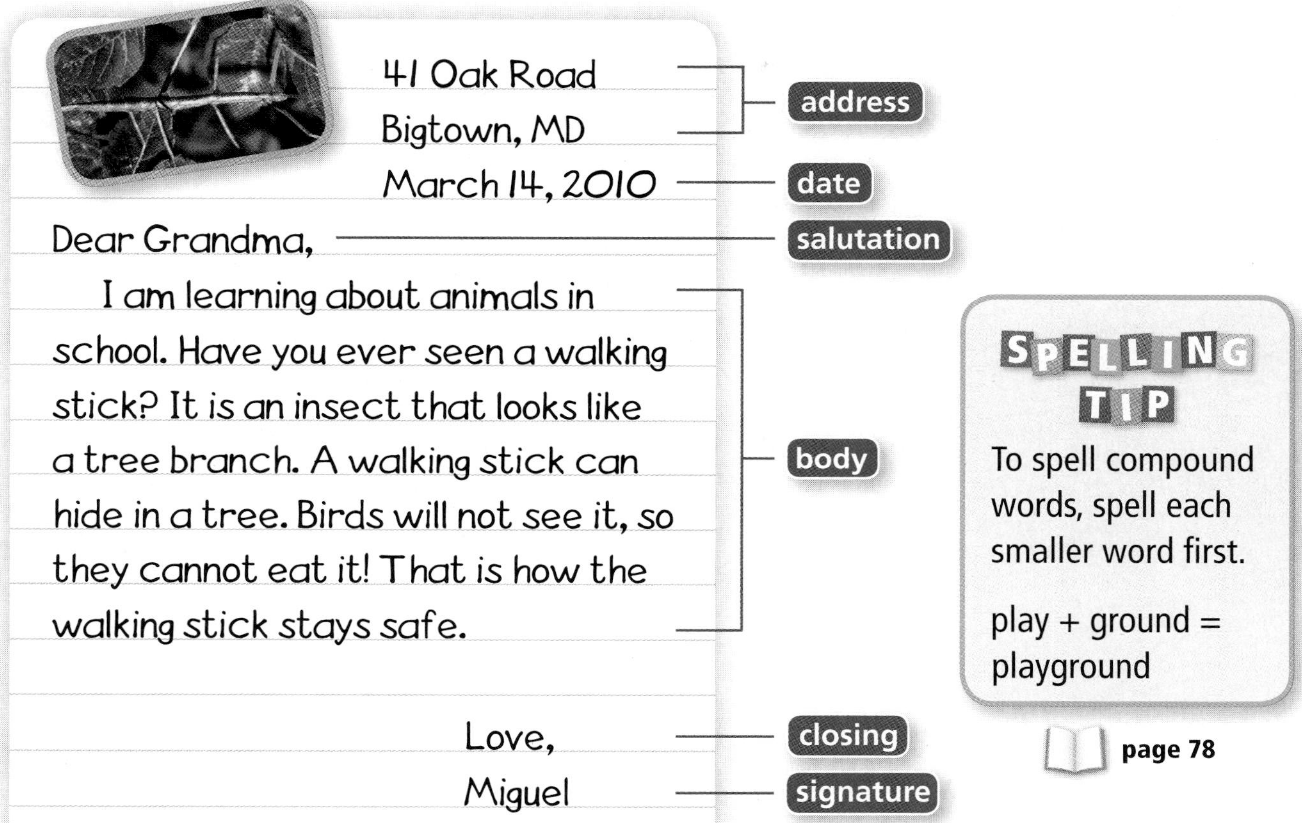

41 Oak Road
Bigtown, MD
March 14, 2010

Dear Grandma,

I am learning about animals in school. Have you ever seen a walking stick? It is an insect that looks like a tree branch. A walking stick can hide in a tree. Birds will not see it, so they cannot eat it! That is how the walking stick stays safe.

Love,
Miguel

SPELLING TIP

To spell compound words, spell each smaller word first.

play + ground = playground

page 78

Practice

Write a letter to a friend or family member. Tell what you have learned about animals.

Writing Checklist

- ✓ Did you tell what you have learned about animals?
- ✓ Did you use the parts of a letter?
- ✓ Did you write the correct punctuation marks?
- ✓ Can a partner understand your letter?

Bonus Reading

LITERATURE

Pourquoi Tale

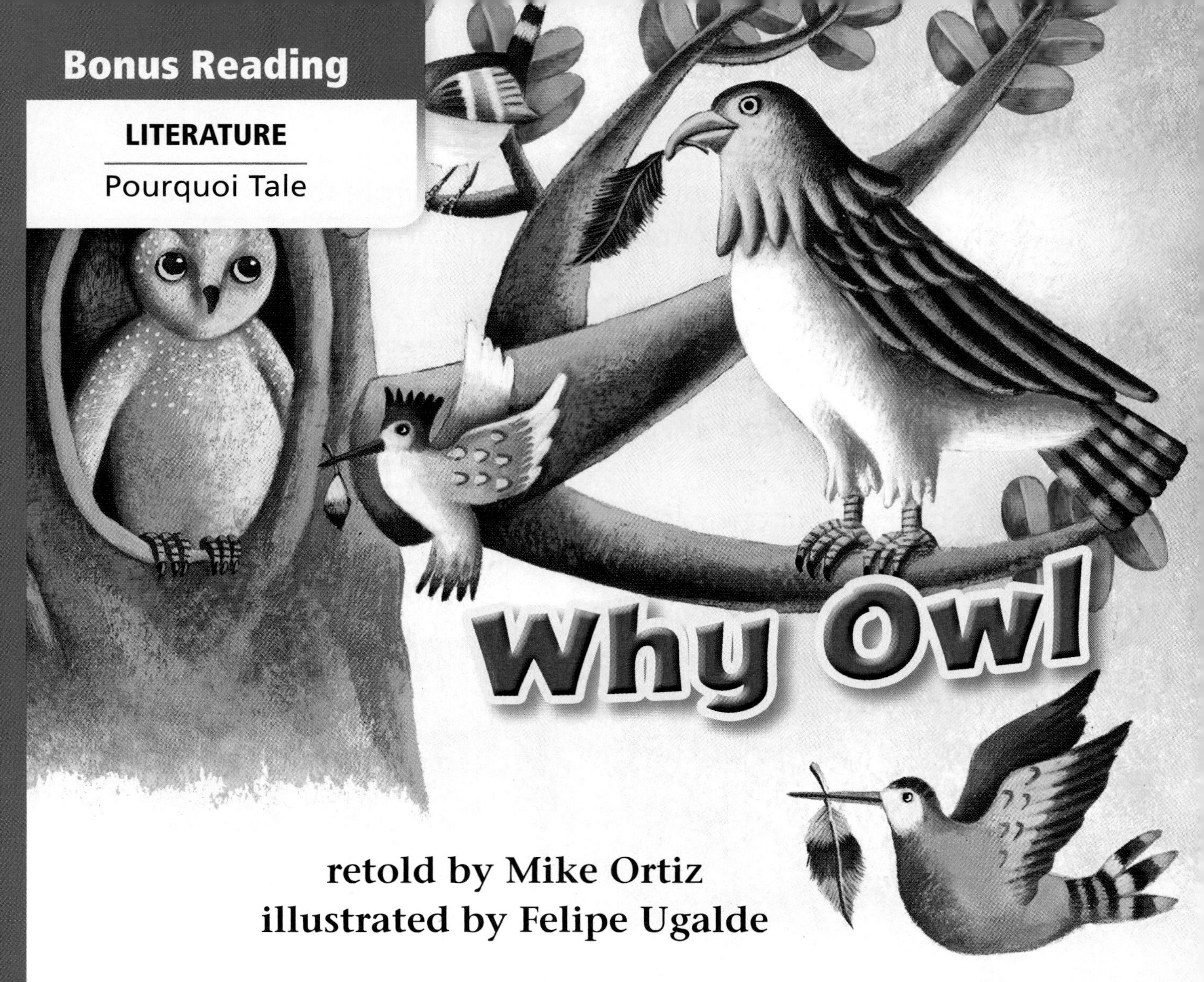

Why Owl

retold by Mike Ortiz
illustrated by Felipe Ugalde

Long, long ago, Owl had no feathers to keep him warm. He could hunt only in the day. He needed the rays of the sun to stay warm.

One night, the birds had a big party. But Owl could not go. Nights in the forest were too cold.

Eagle said, "I have an idea. Each bird can loan you one feather. Then you can be warm."

Each bird loaned Owl one feather.

"Remember," Eagle told him, "you must give the feathers back tomorrow."

Owl came to the party. He looked beautiful in the feathers. He was warm, too. Owl liked the feathers so much he did not want to give them back. He left the party. He hid in the forest.

The next day, the other birds looked for Owl. But they could not find him. The birds are still looking for Owl!

That is why Owl comes out only at night. He knows the other birds hunt in the day. He knows the other birds sleep at night. And Owl does not want to give back the warm, beautiful feathers.

UNIT 3 Wrap Up

The Big Question

What can we learn about animals and why is learning about them important?

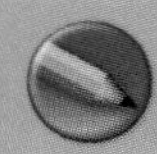 Written	 Oral	 Visual/Active
Animal Facts Choose an animal that you like. Write three facts about that animal. Tell where it lives, what it eats, and what it looks like.	**Guessing Game** Make a list of facts about an animal. Tell what it eats and where it lives. Read the facts aloud. Have a partner guess the animal.	**Diorama** Make a diorama. Show sky, land, and water. Put animals in the places where they live. Share your diorama with the class.
Animal Story Write a story about an animal. Tell about its home. Tell how the animal found its home.	**Talk About It** Find out about an animal that uses camouflage to stay safe. Give a talk about the animal to your class.	**Habitat Mobile** Make a mobile. Show pictures of animals in their homes. On the back of each picture, write a fact about that home. Hang the mobile in your classroom.

pages 79–80

✓ Learning Checklist

Word Analysis and Phonics

- ✓ Read words with digraphs *ch*, *sh*, and *th*.
- ✓ Read words with *r*-, *l*-, and *s*- blends.
- ✓ Identify compound words.

Comprehension

- ✓ Identify steps in a process.
- ✓ Use a Sequence Chart.
- ✓ Make inferences.
- ✓ Use a KWL Chart.
- ✓ Identify cause and effect.
- ✓ Use a Cause and Effect Chart.

Grammar and Writing

- ✓ Recognize subject-verb agreement.
- ✓ Recognize different types of sentences.
- ✓ Recognize complete sentences.
- ✓ Write a description.
- ✓ Write a poem.
- ✓ Write a letter.

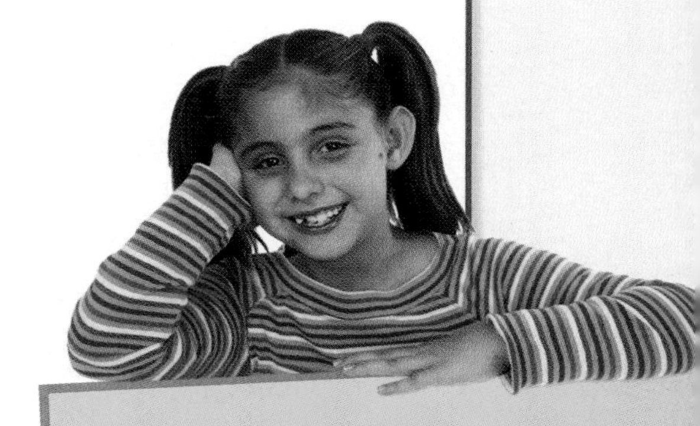

Self-Evaluation Questions

- What are your strengths in learning about animals?
- What questions do you still have about animals in their homes?
- How could you make your work better?

UNIT 4

Great Ideas

Create art. Explore in science. Start with an idea and build on it. That's how we get great ideas.

Readings

1 On Your Bike, Get Set, Donate!

2 Scientists and Crows

3 A Story to Tell

The Big Question

What are some great ideas that make our world a better place?

Listening and Speaking

Think hard! You will talk about great ideas and inventions.

Writing

You will write about a family photograph.

Bonus Reading

A Man with Great Ideas

Quick Write

What is your great idea? Describe something you would like to create.

What Do You Know about Great Ideas?

Words to Know

1. Use these words to talk about people with great ideas.

 **inventor**

 **builder**

 **actor**

 **painter**

 **writer**

 **gardener**

2. What can people with great ideas do?

They can _______________ .

 **invent**

 **build**

 **paint**

 **write**

3. What can people create?

The ____________ *can create a* ____________ *.*

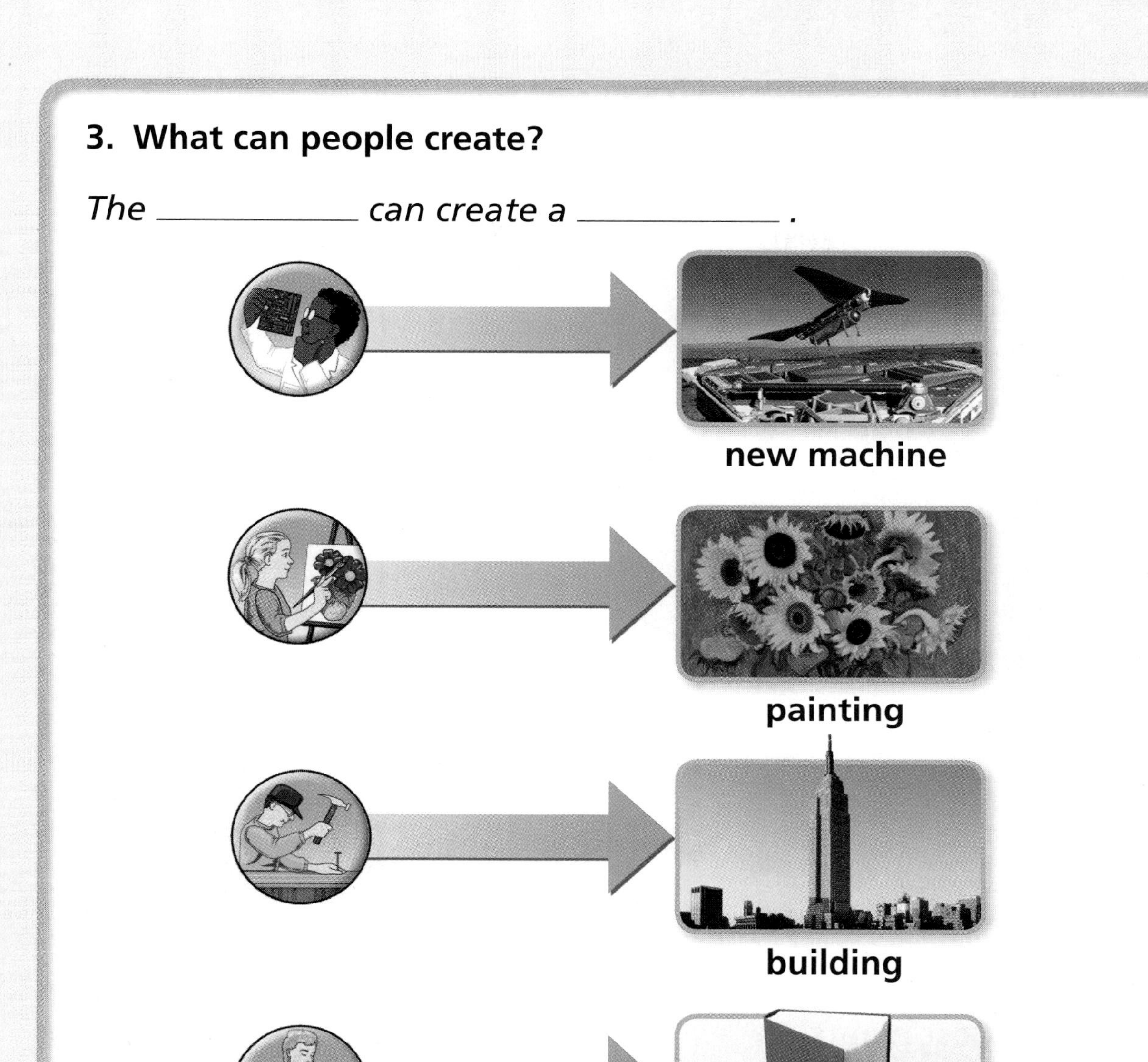

4. Use these words to talk about other great inventions.

Your Stories about Great Ideas

Allison

Most plants grow in dirt. In my school in Vermont, we are learning how to grow plants in water. We put food for the plants in the water. Scientists have grown plants this way. This can help countries that don't have much land. Farmers can use water to help them grow more food.

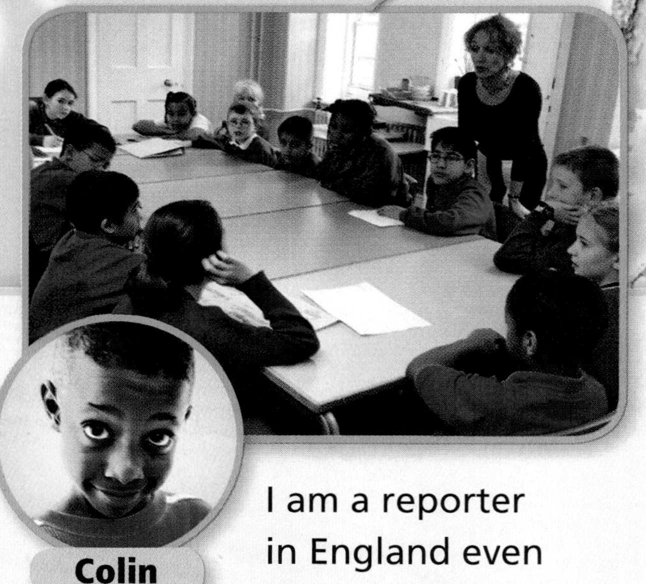

Colin

I am a reporter in England even though I am nine years old! I am part of a news group that is run by young people. We decide what to write about. Then we talk with people. Our stories are in newspapers, on websites, and on the radio.

Zarifa

I live in Azerbaijan. We have a museum of tiny books. There are more than 4,000 books. The biggest book is only 4 inches tall! A woman who loves books opened this museum.

Anton

Many people in my country, France, love to ski. Some schools in France teach people who are physically challenged how to ski. These people can take part in special races, too. This way, everyone can have fun in the snow!

What about you?

1. What great ideas do you know about?
2. How are these students' stories similar to yours?
3. Do you have other stories about great ideas? Tell your story!

Reading 1

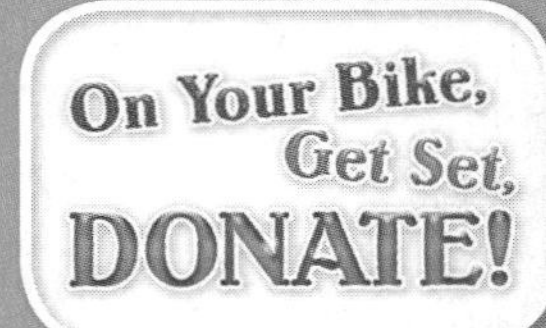

Vocabulary

On Your Bike, Get Set, Donate! **v about groups who fix old bicycles to help people.**

Words in Context

1 Each year, our school has a bake sale to raise money. We make cookies and cupcakes. Then we **donate** them to be sold. My friends and I are **volunteers** at the bake sale.

Key Words

donate

volunteers

bicycles

helmets

2 **Bicycles** are also called bikes. A bicycle has two wheels.

3 This girl and boy are wearing safety **helmets**.

Academic Words

significant
important

benefit
help

Practice

Use each key word in a sentence.

Make Connections

How can you ride a bicycle safely? What should you wear? Where should you ride?

pages 81–82

Reading 1

INFORMATIONAL TEXT

Magazine Article

How can people use a great idea to help others?

Reading Strategy

Identify Problems and Solutions

- As you read, look for the problems.
- Look for solutions that different people have for these problems.

On Your Bike, Get Set, DONATE!

by Jamaila Veglia

People like to ride bicycles. Every year, many Americans buy new bicycles. What happens to the old bikes? People throw away many of them. What a waste!

---

bikes bicycles

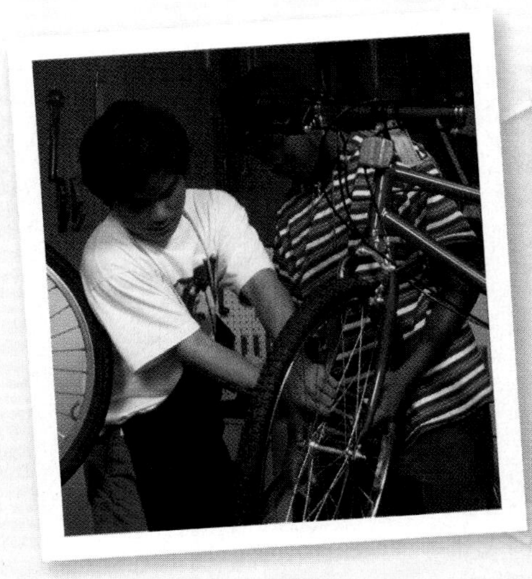

These boys can fix bikes.

A Great Idea

Bicycle riders can donate their old bikes to groups of people who have a great idea. These groups fix the bikes. Then the groups give the bikes to children who don't have bicycles. The groups may give bikes to grown-ups who need them, too. Some groups send bicycles to people in other countries.

---

fix make like new

Some groups donate bicycles to people in other countries.

Check Up What can people do with old bicycles?

New riders learn bicycle safety.

Volunteers Help

Bicycle Exchange is a group that gives away bikes. Each year, people donate their old bikes to this group. People in Bicycle Exchange teach volunteers how to fix bikes. Then, the volunteers work to repair the old bikes. At the end of the year, Bicycle Exchange gives bikes to children. The group also gives helmets to children. People in the group teach children bicycle safety, too. Children need to know how to ride and be safe.

A volunteer works to repair a bike.

repair fix

It can be fun to fix old bikes.

It can be fun to teach others how to fix bikes, too.

A Boy Helps Others

Young people can help, too. Joshua started fixing bikes when he was twelve years old. He gave them to children who did not have families.

Joshua got started when his own bike broke. He had an idea. He would learn how to fix it himself. Soon, neighbors were bringing old bikes to Joshua's house. He repaired them. Now other children have new bikes.

Check Up What was Joshua's idea? What happened because of his idea?

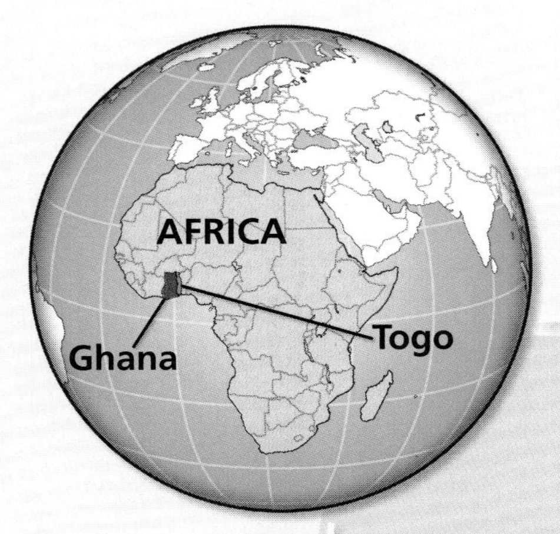

A man rides a bicycle to work in Ghana.

Around the World

Groups send bicycles to countries where it is not easy to buy a bike. One group, Bikes for the World, sent 430 bikes to Togo. Many children must walk ten miles or more to get to school in Togo. Bikes can really help!

Another group, Bike Works, sends bikes to villages in Ghana. Farmers, teachers, and students use the bikes to get to work and to school.

---

villages very small towns in the country

These girls go to school in Ghana. Now they can ride bikes to school.

Riders Write Back

Volunteers love to hear from new bike riders. They like to know that their work makes people happy.

A group called Second Chance got a poem from one rider.

Bike Works got a note from a young girl in Ghana. "I love my bike," she wrote. "It is blue which is my favorite color."

---

favorite one you like best

Bikes are tight.
They make me
Feel all right.

I love my bike.
It is blue which is
my favorite color.
Lakiska

pages 83–84

Reading Strategy

Identify Problems and Solutions

- What problem do people with old bikes have?
- What problem do people without bikes have?
- What solutions do people have for these problems?
- How did looking for problems and solutions help you understand the selection?

Think It Over

1. What do people at the Bicycle Exchange do with bicycles?
2. Why did Joshua start fixing bikes?
3. How do bicycles help people in Togo and Ghana?
4. Why is it a waste to throw away an old bicycle?

A Closer Look at...

Bicycles

▲ **High-Wheel Bicycle**

The high-wheel bicycle was first made in 1871. Riders cannot put their feet on the ground. How do you think that would feel?

Unicycle ▶

It takes a lot of practice to ride this unicycle! Do you think you could ride it?

▲ **Tricycle**

A tricycle has three wheels. Small children can ride tricycles.

BMX Bikes

These girls race on BMX bikes. Riders can do tricks and ride on dirt roads with these bikes.

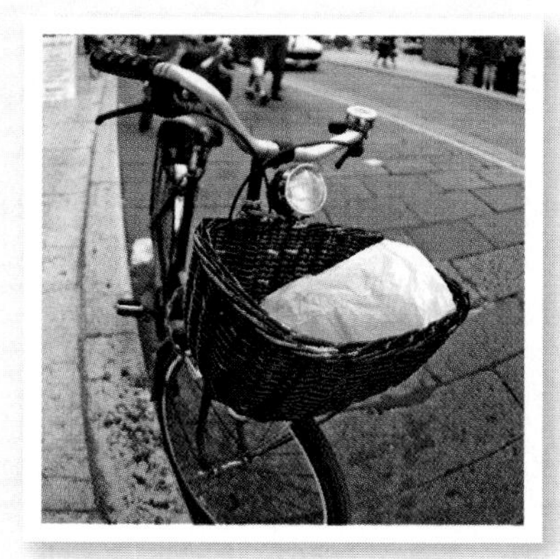

Delivery Bike

The basket on this bike can hold things. A rider could use this bike to take packages to people.

Mountain Bike

This man is riding a mountain bike. These bikes go on dirt trails or bumpy roads. They have wide tires.

Wheelchair Cycle

This man can ride or race on this wheelchair cycle.

Activity to Do!

These two pages use words and pictures to tell about bicycles.

- Choose another machine used for travel.
- Find pictures to show that machine.
- Post your pictures with captions in your classroom.

Word Analysis & Fluency

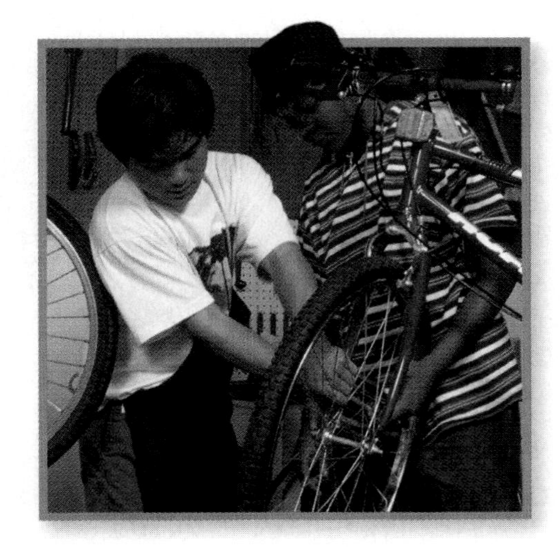

Word Analysis

Ending: *-ed*

Read these sentences.

The children **started** school.
Joshua **repaired** the bikes.

The words **started** and **repaired** both tell about the past. But the ending *-ed* is pronounced differently in each word.

start + ed = start/ed   repair + ed = repaired

Rule Box

If the letter *d* or the letter *t* comes before the *-ed* ending, then *-ed* is pronounced as a separate syllable.

Practice

Work with a partner. Take turns.

- Read each word aloud.
- Add *-ed* to each word. Read the new word aloud.
- Tell if the *-ed* adds a syllable to the word.

1. add

2. help

3. seat

4. play

5. show

page 85

Fluency

Look Ahead

Sometimes readers look for hard words before they read. They then try to figure them out.

Practice

Pick one passage.	Find any hard words.	Practice saying those words.	Read the passage aloud.

1. Some groups had a great idea. These groups get bicycles from people who don't want them. They fix the bicycles. Then they give the bicycles to people who need them.

2. Bicycle riders can donate their old bikes to groups of people who have a great idea. These groups fix the bikes. Then the groups give the bikes to children who don't have bicycles. The groups may give bikes to grown-ups who need them, too. Some groups send bicycles to people in other countries.

3. Bicycle Exchange is a group that gives away bikes. Each year, people donate their old bikes to this group. People in Bicycle Exchange teach volunteers how to fix bikes. Then, the volunteers work to repair the old bikes. At the end of the year, Bicycle Exchange gives bikes to children. The group also gives helmets to children. People in the group teach children bicycle safety, too. Children need to know how to ride and be safe.

Reading 1

Comprehension

Learning Strategy

Summarize

Summarize the selection for a partner.

Ask your partner to respond to the Big Question for this reading.

page 86

Problems and Solutions

A magazine article can tell how people find solutions to problems.

Practice

Read these sentences about the selection. Tell which sentences are problems. Tell which sentences are solutions.

1. Many people throw away old bikes.
2. Many children do not have bicycles.
3. Bicycle Exchange volunteers teach people how to fix old bikes.
4. Groups give repaired bicycles to people who need them.
5. In many countries, it is not easy to buy a bike.

Use a T-Chart

You can use a T-Chart to help you understand the selection.

Practice

Copy the chart. Use the steps below to see how each group or person solved the problem.

Group or Person	Solution
Bicycle Exchange	______
Joshua	______
______	______
______	______

- List two or more things Bicycle Exchange does to solve the problems.
- List two or more things Joshua does to solve the problems.
- List two more groups. Tell one thing each group did to solve the problems.

Extension

Choose one thing that you could give away. Draw a picture of it. Write about why someone else might want it. Present your idea to the class.

Grammar & Writing

Pronouns

Pronouns take the place of nouns.

The group sends bikes to children.
It sends helmets, too.

Joshua fixes bikes.
Joshua fixes **them** for other children.

The pronoun ***It*** takes the place of ***The group***.
The pronoun ***them*** takes the place of ***bikes***.

Pronouns	
I, you, he, she, it, we, they	me, you, him, her, it, us, them

Practice

Use pronouns to take the place of the underlined words. Write each sentence.

1. People can donate bicycles.
2. Mr. Garza can teach Ella and me.
3. The group will help the boy.
4. Joshua and I fixed the bike.
5. A girl in Ghana wrote the letter.

page 87

Write a Story

It feels good to help someone! Sometimes you need help, too. Read Jaime's story.

I lost my red backpack. I looked at home. I looked at school. I could not find it.

My friend Ramón wanted to help. He had an idea. He asked me, "When did you last have it? What were you doing? Where were you going?"

I thought and thought. Then I remembered. I had it when I went to my karate class. Maybe I left it there! Ramón came with me to the karate classroom. There was my red backpack.
I was so happy!

To make verbs agree with a singular subject, add *-s*. For verbs hat end in *x*, *s*, *ch*, *sh*, and *z*, add *-es*.

page 88

Practice

Think of a time when you helped someone or when someone helped you. Write a story about it.

- Tell what the problem was.
- Tell how you solved it together.
- Tell how you felt after you solved the problem.

Writing Checklist

- ✓ Did your story state the problem?
- ✓ Did your story tell what happened?
- ✓ Did you use pronouns correctly?
- ✓ Can a partner understand your story?

Reading 2

Scientists and Crows

Vocabulary

In *Scientists and Crows*, you will read about how scientists study crows.

Words in Context

Key Words
- **instinct**
- **proof**
- **tool**
- **scientists**
- **lab**

1 Babies cry when they are hungry or tired. They cry to show they need help. No one teaches babies how to cry. They know by **instinct**.

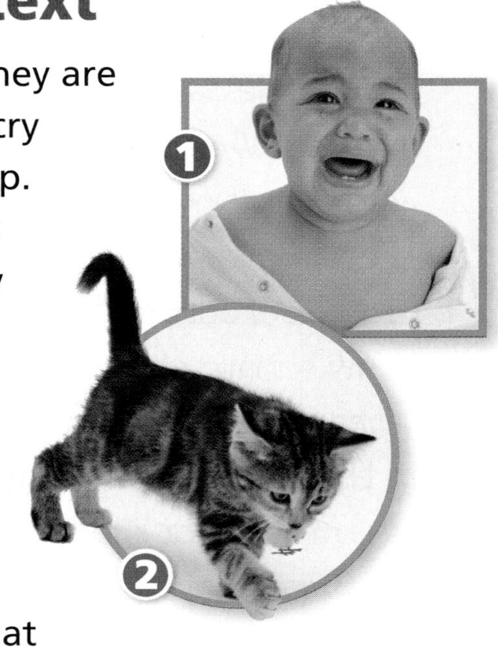

2 How do I know the kitten took the toy bird? This photo is the **proof**.

3 A rake is a **tool** that people use in a garden.

◀ Jane Goodall studied chimpanzees in their habitat.

George Washington Carver was a famous scientist. In this picture, he is working in a lab. ▼

④ **Scientists** work in different places. Some work outside in nature. Others work inside, in a laboratory. A laboratory may be called a **lab**.

Practice

Use each key word in a sentence.

Make Connections

Think of a pet that you know. It could belong to you or someone else. How smart do you think the pet is? Why do you think so?

Academic Words

conclude
decide something is true based on what you know

theory
idea that explains something

pages 89–90

Reading 2

INFORMATIONAL TEXT

Science

The Big Question

How can people try out their ideas to learn new things?

Reading Strategy

Identify Main Idea and Details

- The main idea is the most important idea in a selection.
- As you read, look for the main idea of the selection.
- Look for details that tell about the main idea.

Scientists and Crows

by Remore Williams
illustrated by Laura Jacobsen

Do you ever watch crows? You may see crows fly over trees. You may see a crow sit on a power line. Maybe you hear crows call, "Caw! Caw! Caw!"

Scientists watch crows, too. They watch what crows do in their habitat. They also study crows in labs. Scientists study crows to learn more about them.

Crows and Clams

Crows eat clams. Clams are small animals that live inside a shell. The shell is hard. How can a crow eat an animal inside a shell? Scientists found out by watching.

The crow picks up a clam with its beak. It carries the clam high in the air and drops it to the ground. The shell breaks. Then the crow eats the clam.

---

shell hard outer part

Check Up How do crows open clams?

Crows and Walnuts

Crows eat walnuts, too. Walnuts are nuts that have very hard shells. How can a crow break the shell? Scientists learned by watching.

In Japan, some crows drop walnuts on a street. Cars drive over the shells and crack them. Then the crows can eat the nuts.

Sometimes the crows do not drop the walnuts. Sometimes a crow carries a walnut and puts it down in a crosswalk. The crow flies away. Cars drive over the walnut and crack the shell. Then the crow comes back and eats the walnut.

---

nuts dry fruit inside shells

crack break the outside part to get what is inside

crosswalk a marked place to cross a street

Scientists know that birds do many things by instinct. For example, they learn to fly by instinct. But the crows in Japan seem to solve a problem. How can scientists find out if the crows are using instinct or are solving a problem?

Scientists had a great idea. They would test crows in a lab. They would try to learn if a crow can solve a problem. They would find the proof.

Check Up How do crows open walnuts?

A crow lifts a bucket with a bent wire.

Crows in a Lab

Scientists studied crows in a lab. They wanted to find out if crows could solve a problem.

Scientists gave crows this problem. Scientists put food in a tiny bucket with a handle. The bucket was at the bottom of a tube. The crows could not reach the bucket without using a tool.

Scientists gave the crows two wires. One wire was straight. The other wire was bent, like a hook. A crow could lift the bucket with the bent wire.

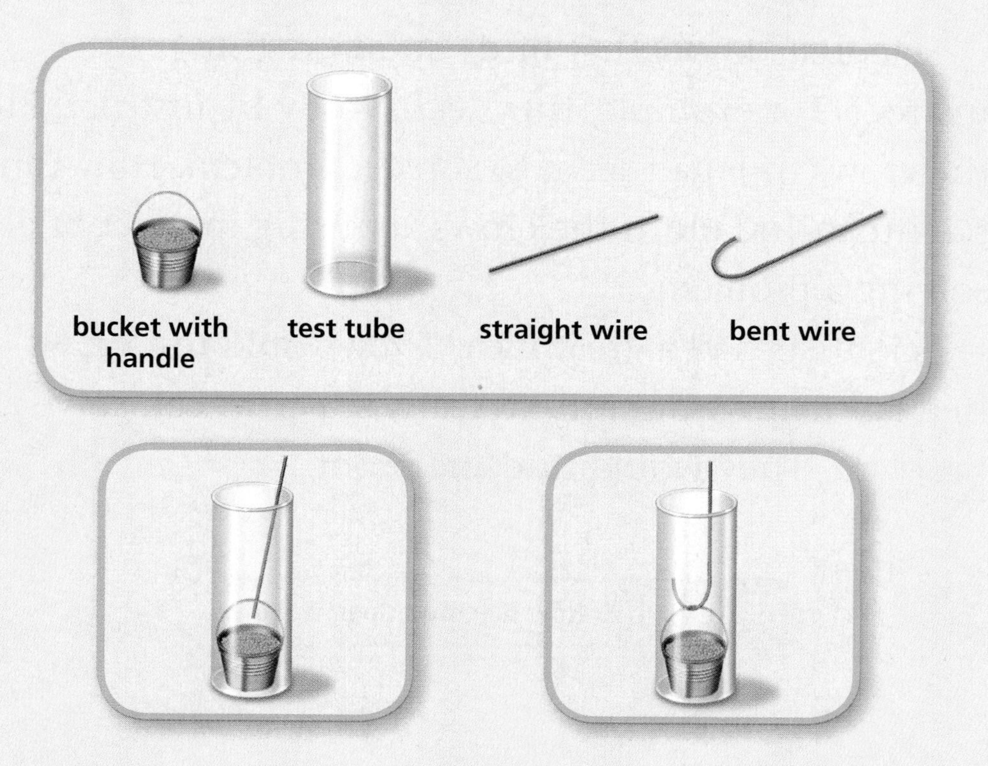

This crow pokes a stick into a rotting log to find insects to eat.

A crow named Betty used the bent wire to lift the bucket four times.

Then, the scientists took away the bent wire. Betty tried to use the straight wire to lift the bucket. It didn't work. Betty needed a hook.

Then, Betty bent the wire herself. She lifted the bucket out of the tube with her new tool. Betty had made the right tool for the job!

Scientists learned that Betty the crow can solve a problem. This is not proof that all crows can solve problems. Scientists have to do more tests. They have to study other crows. But scientists used a great idea to learn something new about crows.

pages 91–92

Reading Strategy

Identify Main Ideas and Details

- What is the main idea?
- What details tell about the main idea?
- How did looking for the main idea help you understand the selection?

Think It Over

1. How do crows open clams?
2. How do crows in Japan open walnuts?
3. What did Betty do in a lab?
4. Why do scientists study crows in a lab?

Phonics & Fluency

Phonics

R-Controlled Vowels: *ir, er, ur*

The letter ***r*** after a vowel gives the vowel a new sound.

bid	gem	hut
bird	germ	hurt

Rule Box

The letters ***ir***, ***er***, and ***ur*** usually have the same vowel sound.

Practice

Work with a partner.

- Sort the words in the box into three lists:
  words with *ir*
  words with *er*
  words with *ur*
- Read the words in your lists aloud.
- Add a word to each list.

dirt	curb	herd
fern	her	perch
first	hurt	third
fur	girl	turn

page 93

Fluency

Read with Expression

When you read aloud, use your voice to show feelings.

Practice

Read silently. → Read aloud. → Get comments. → Read aloud again.

Do you ever watch crows? You may see crows fly over trees. You may see a crow sit on a power line. Maybe you hear crows call, "Caw! Caw! Caw!"

Scientists watch crows, too. They watch what crows do in their habitat. They also study crows in labs. Scientists study crows to learn more about them.

Crows and Clams

Crows eat clams. Clams are small animals that live inside a shell. The shell is hard. How can a crow eat an animal inside a shell? Scientists found out by watching.

The crow picks up a clam with its beak. It carries the clam high in the air and drops it to the ground. The shell breaks. Then the crow eats the clam.

Crows and Walnuts

Crows eat walnuts, too. Walnuts are nuts that have very hard shells. How can a crow break the shell? Scientists learned by watching.

In Japan, some crows drop walnuts on a street. Cars drive over the shells and crack them. Then the crows can eat the nuts.

Comprehension

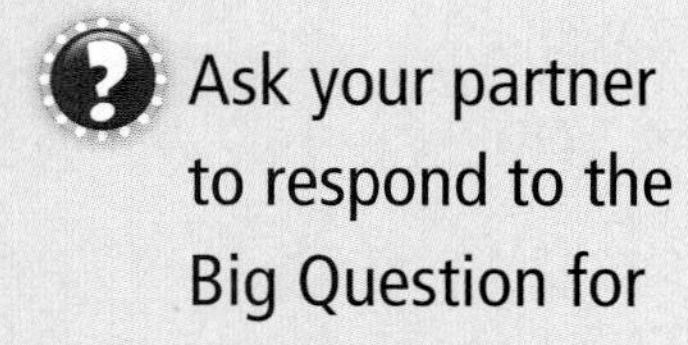

Learning Strategy

Summarize

Summarize the selection to a partner.

Ask your partner to respond to the Big Question for this reading.

Main Idea and Details

The **main idea** is the most important idea in a selection. **Details** give important information to support the main idea. **Support** means to help show something is true.

Practice

Read these sentences about the selection.

- Tell which one is the main idea.
- Tell which ones are details that support the main idea.

1. Crows crack walnuts by putting them in the street.
2. Crows break clams by dropping them on the ground.
3. Scientists study crows in their habitat and in labs.
4. In a lab, a crow bent a wire to get food.

page 94

Use a Main Idea and Details Chart

This chart can help you figure out the main idea of the selection. You can show the details that support the main idea.

Practice

Copy the chart. Fill in the main idea and details.

- What is the main idea of *Scientists and Crows*?
- Reread the selection. Find three details that support the main idea.

Main Idea		
Supporting Detail	Supporting Detail	Supporting Detail

Extension

What animal would you like to study? What would you like to learn about the animal? Talk with a partner. Share what you would do, if you were a scientist.

Reading 2

Grammar & Writing

Possessives

Possessives show what someone or something has. They can be nouns or pronouns.

Rules	Examples
For one person, place, or thing: add an apostrophe (') and *s*.	scientist → scientist's crow → crow's
For more than one person, place or thing: add just an apostrophe (').	scientists → scientists' crows → crows'

Possessive pronouns do not use an apostrophe: ***my, your, his, her, its, our, their***.

Practice

Read each sentence with a partner. Take turns.

- Crows carry clams in their beaks.
- Scientists watched the birds' actions.
- Betty's tool was a piece of wire.
- Now I will watch crows in my neighborhood.
- A clam's body is soft, but its shell is hard.

1. List the possessive nouns.
2. List the possessive pronouns.

page 95

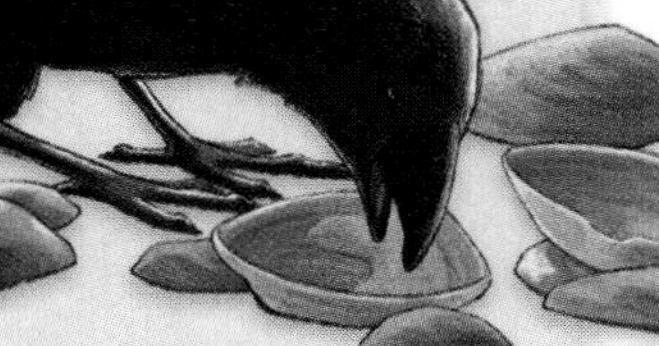

Write a Description

Watch an animal for a while. You might learn something new! Read Erin's description of a squirrel.

The squirrel sits on a branch. It swishes its tail. It has a nut in its mouth. Then it runs down the tree, leaps across the grass, and stops. It sits up and swishes its tail again. Next, it digs with its front paws. It drops the nut into the hole. The squirrel uses its front paws to cover the nut with dirt. It swishes its tail once more. Then it chases another squirrel.

Keep a personal word list. Write words that are hard for you to spell.

page 96

Practice

Watch an animal. It could be a pet or an outside animal that you can watch safely. Tell what the animal does.

Writing Checklist

- ✔ Did you name the animal?
- ✔ Did you tell what the animal did?
- ✔ Did you use possessives correctly?
- ✔ Can a partner understand your description?

Reading 3

A Story to Tell

Vocabulary

In *A Story to Tell*, you will learn about objects Native Americans have made.

Words in Context

Key Words

- **costume**
- **robe**
- **painting**
- **teepee**
- **mask**
- **quilt**

1 Joey wore a lion **costume** in the class play.

2 Queen Elizabeth I of England lived from 1533 to 1603. She wore a **robe** over her dress.

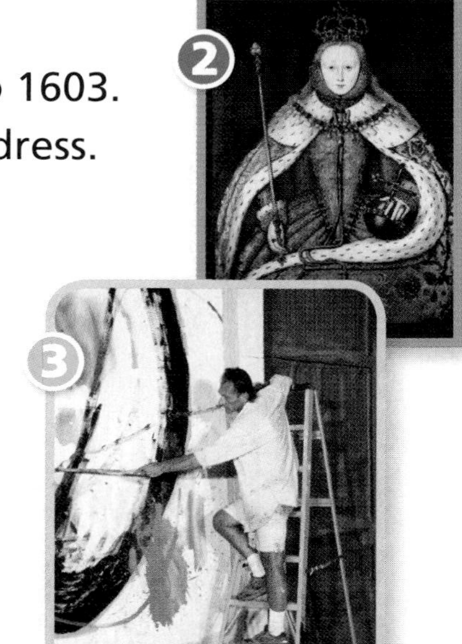

3 This artist stands on a ladder to work on his large **painting**.

4 A **teepee** is a kind of tent. Some Native Americans made teepees. They used poles and the skins of animals.

5 A Japanese actor wears this **mask** to play a young woman.

6 My grandmother made a **quilt** using different pieces of cloth. It shows a little town.

Practice

Use each key word in a sentence.

Make Connections

Have you ever made a mask? What did you use to make it? Describe a mask you would like to make. Tell where you would wear it.

Academic Words

respond
answer

tradition
custom of a group

pages 97–98

Reading 3

INFORMATIONAL TEXT

Photo Essay

How do the things people make show their ideas?

Reading Strategy

Ask Questions

- Read the captions and look at the photographs.
- Ask questions to be sure you understand what you read.
- Ask what story each object tells.

A Story to Tell

by Marta Rosas

How do you catch a dream? You need a dream catcher. A dream catcher is just one of the beautiful objects Native Americans have made.

From early times, Native Americans made the things they needed. They made clothing and costumes. They created paintings and pottery. Many of these objects have a story to tell. They show what was important to the people who made them.

---

objects things you can touch or see

pottery objects made out of baked clay

The Mayan people act out events that are part of their history. This girl is wearing a costume of the Dance of the Conquest. The dance tells the story of the last Mayan king.

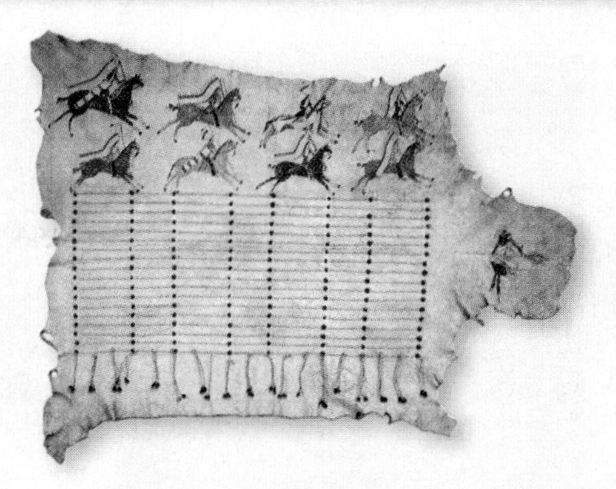

▲ One of the Sioux people wore this warm robe. Notice the painting of riders and horses on the robe. This painting tells us that horses and **warriors** were important to the Sioux.

▲ This photo shows pictures on a teepee. There are buffaloes, people, and horses. What story do you think these pictures tell?

▲ Lakota people made this dream catcher using string, beads, and feathers. Lakota legends say that Spider Woman made the first dream catcher. She told them that the web would catch bad dreams and keep them away. Good dreams could come in through the hole in the center.

---

warriors fighters

Check Up What is a teepee?

▲ An artist carved this wooden mask in Oaxaca, Mexico. A dancer might have worn the mask in a special celebration.

◀ Native Americans carved this famous image into a rock. It is called She-Who-Watches. Can you see why?

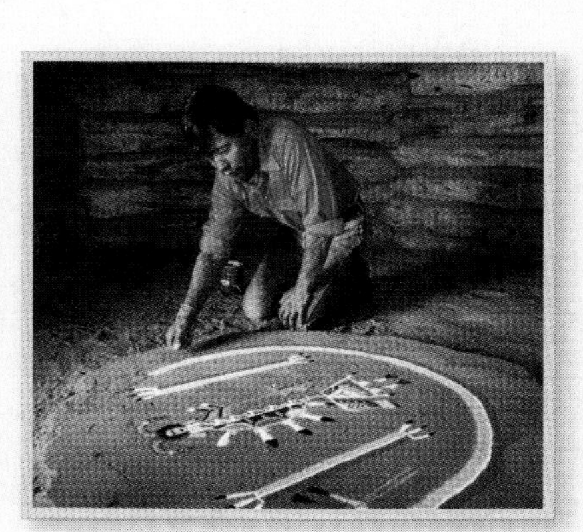

A Navajo artist ▶ creates a colorful sand painting. He uses black, blue, white, and red sand. For hundreds of years, the Navajo have made sand paintings.

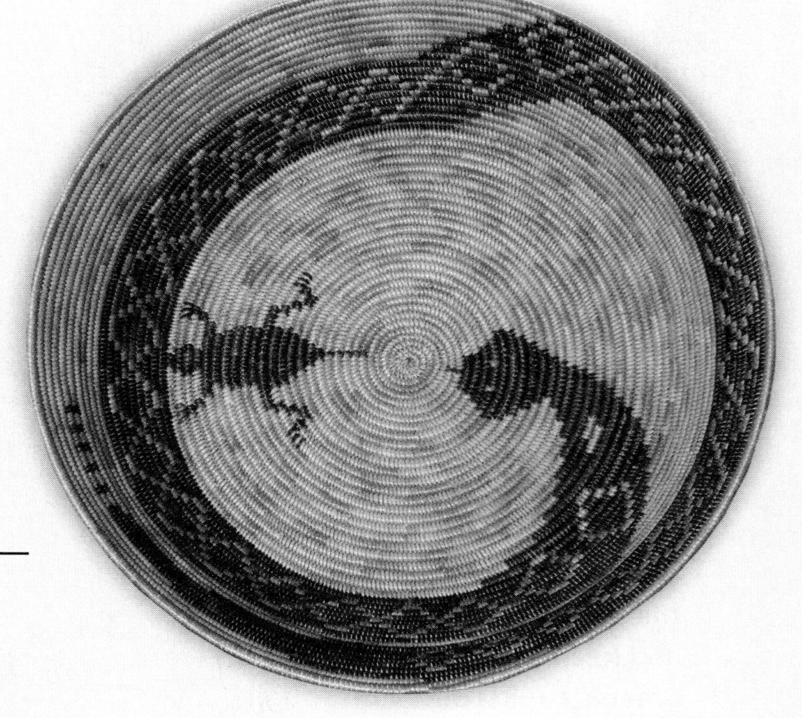

Native people of ▶ California made this basket out of grass. It shows a rattlesnake trying to catch a toad.

---

carved cut a pattern on a surface

famous known by many people

◀ Artists worked together to create this quilt. Each person made one of the squares. The finished work is called a Gathering Quilt. *Gathering* means "bringing together."

This artist is named Mateo. ▶ She weaves a rug on a loom. She uses brown, green, blue, white, and red yarn.

weaves makes threads into cloth

loom frame or machine to weave on

pages 99–100

Reading Strategy

Ask Questions

- What questions did you ask as you read?
- What story did each object tell?
- How did asking questions help you understand the selection?

Think It Over

1. Name three objects that Native Americans have created.
2. What is a dream catcher?
3. How did artists make a Gathering Quilt?
4. What do the pictures on the robe and the teepee tell you?

Phonics & Fluency

Phonics

Hard and Soft *c*

A **hard c** sounds like the *k* in ***kite***.
Catcher has a hard *c*.

A **soft c** sounds like the *s* in ***sun***.
Center has a soft *c*.

A dream **catcher** has a hole in the **center.**

Rule Box

The letter *c* is soft when it is followed by *e*, *i*, or *y*.
The letter *c* is hard when followed by *a*, *o*, or *u*.

Practice

Read each sentence with a partner. Take turns.

- An artist carved this mask. He cut into the wood.
- The dance is part of a celebration.
- The fancy dress has many colors.
- The Mayans built large cities.

1. List the words with a soft *c* sound.

2. List the words with a hard *c* sound.

page 101

Fluency

Read for Speed and Accuracy

You should read quickly. But never read so quickly that you lose your understanding.

Practice

Read for one minute. → Count the words you read. → Study any hard words. → Read and count again.

How do you catch a dream? You need a dream catcher.	11
A dream catcher is just one of the beautiful objects Native	22
Americans have made.	25
From early times, Native Americans made the things	33
they needed. They made clothing and costumes. They	41
created paintings and pottery. Many of these objects have	50
a story to tell. They show what was important to the	61
people who made them.	65
The Mayan people act out events that are part of their	76
history. This girl is wearing a costume of the Dance of the	88
Conquest. The dance tells the story of the last Mayan king.	99
One of the Sioux people wore this warm robe. Notice	109
the painting of riders and horses on the robe. This	119
painting tells us that horses and warriors were important	128
to the Sioux.	131
This photo shows pictures on a teepee. There are	140
buffaloes, people, and horses. What story do you think	149
these pictures tell?	152

Comprehension

Ask Questions

As you read, ask yourself questions. Make sure you understand what you are reading. Try these steps.

- Read part of the selection.
- Look at the key words.
- Look at the pictures for clues.
- Look at the word meanings at the bottom of the page.
- Use what you already know.

Practice

Read this passage. List three questions you could ask to be sure you understand it. Then answer the questions below.

Artists worked together to create this quilt. Each person made one of the squares. The finished work is called a Gathering Quilt. ***Gathering*** means "bringing together."

1. What is a quilt?
2. What is the quilt called?
3. Why is it called a Gathering Quilt?

Learning Strategy

Summarize

Summarize the selection to a partner.

Ask your partner to respond to the Big Question for this reading.

page 102

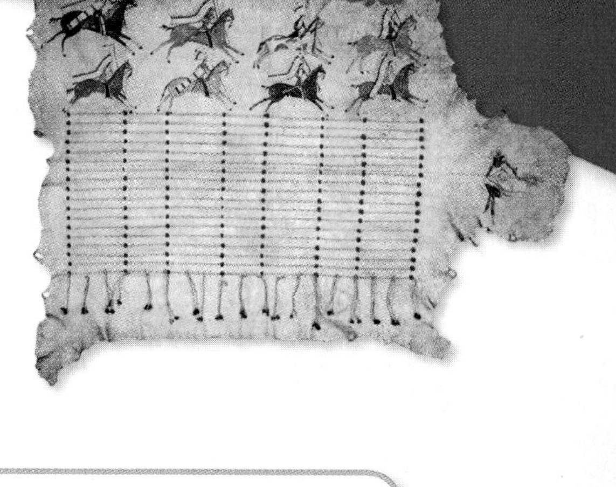

Use a T-Chart

Use a T-Chart to help make sure you understand what you are reading.

Practice

Read this passage from the selection.

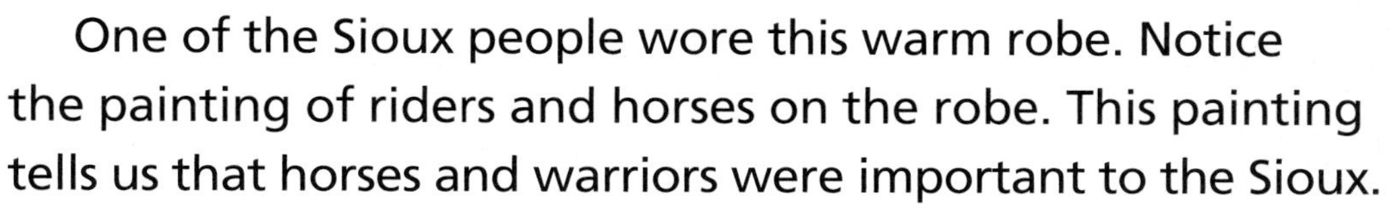

One of the Sioux people wore this warm robe. Notice the painting of riders and horses on the robe. This painting tells us that horses and warriors were important to the Sioux.

- Copy the T-Chart.
- Fill in how to find the answer to the question.
- Add your own question. Tell how you can answer it.

Question	How to Find Answers
1. What was important to the Sioux?	I could reread the passage.
2. What is a robe?	I could look back on the vocabulary page.
3. What is the Sioux tribe?	

Extension

You learned about some of the beautiful objects that Native Americans have made. Which object do you like best? Draw a picture of that object. Present your drawing to the class.

Grammar & Writing

Adjectives and Articles

Adjectives describe or tell more about a noun.

The adjectives are shown in red.
The nouns are shown in blue.

She makes **beautiful baskets**.

The **baskets** are **strong**.

The words ***the***, ***a***, and ***an*** are articles. These special adjectives point out nouns.

Rule Box

Use ***the*** to point out a certain noun or thing. Use ***a*** or ***an*** to point out any noun.

Practice

Write each sentence.

- Draw one line under each adjective.
- Draw two lines under each article.

1. Look at the beautiful costume.
2. The robe is warm.
3. An artist carved the wooden mask.
4. A famous image is carved in the rock.

page 103

Write a Family Story

You may have a story to tell, too. Read Tupac's story about his uncle.

This is my uncle Quizo from long ago. Quizo's family lived in Peru. They made special hats and ponchos.

When Quizo was a young man, he came to the United States. He brought colorful hats and ponchos. People thought they were beautiful. Quizo sold many hats and ponchos.

He had an idea. He built one store. Then he built another one. My family still has these stores.

SPELLING TIP

The letter *q* is usually followed by the letter *u*.

page 104

Practice

Write a story about your family.

- Choose a photo of your family.
- Think about what the photo tells about your family.
- Write a story about what is happening in the photo.

Writing Checklist

- ✓ Did you tell what is happening in the photo?
- ✓ Did you use adjectives and articles correctly?
- ✓ Can a partner understand your story?

A Man with Great Ideas

by Christine Lee

Leonardo da Vinci painted this portrait of himself. A portrait is a picture of a person.

Leonardo da Vinci was a painter. He lived more than 500 years ago. He painted some of the most beautiful paintings in the world. These paintings made him famous.

But Leonardo was also an inventor. He had a lot of ideas. He drew plans for flying machines. Leonardo had ideas for a boat that could go under the water. He drew plans for bridges.

These drawings show Leonardo's plans for a flying machine.

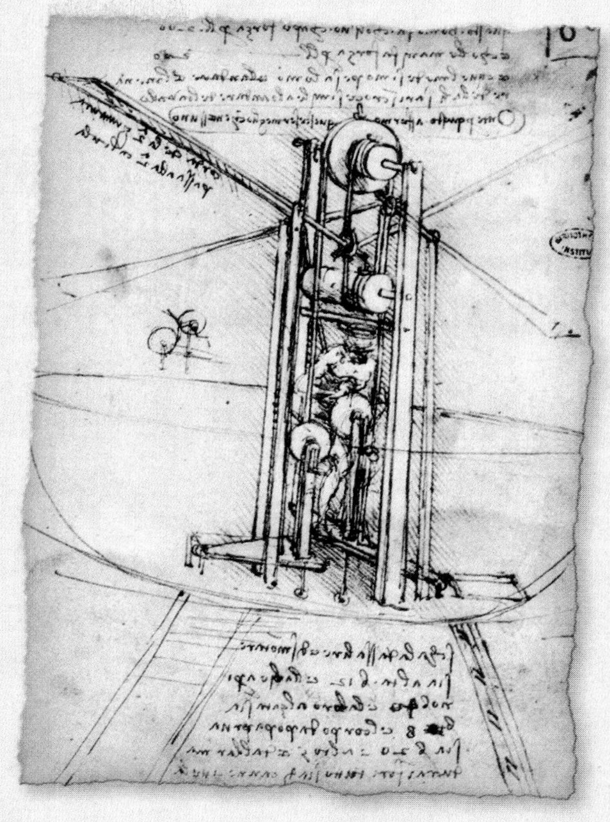

These things were not built while Leonardo was alive. But many of them are part of our lives today.

Leonardo da Vinci asked questions all the time, such as: How do machines work? How does the human body work? How can people move across water?

Leonardo wrote his questions in notebooks. He had hundreds of notebooks. They were full of ideas and plans.

Leonardo watched birds. He drew pictures of flying birds in his notebooks. The things Leonardo learned from watching birds helped him plan flying machines.

Leonardo da Vinci was both an artist and an inventor. He was a man with great ideas.

UNIT 4 Wrap Up

The Big Question

What are some great ideas that make our world a better place?

 Written	 Oral	 Visual/Active
Invent It Think of a new invention. Describe what it might look like and what it could do. You may also want to include a labeled diagram.	**Show and Tell** Think about something important that you use every day. How does it help you? Show and tell why this thing is so important to your life.	**Robes** You saw a picture of a Sioux robe. Draw a robe. Then draw pictures on the robe to show things that make your world a better place.
Poem A good poem can start with just one idea. Think of a great idea you want to share. Write about it in a poem.	**Group Plan** Work with a group. Talk about ways to help some younger children. Choose one idea. Make a plan. Explain your idea and plan to the class.	**Mime** Think of some great inventions. Act out how to use one invention. Do not talk. Can other students guess what the invention is? Act out more inventions.

pages 105–106

✓ Learning Checklist

Word Analysis and Phonics

- ✓ Identify when *-ed* adds a syllable to a word.
- ✓ Read words with *r*-controlled vowels: *ir*, *er*, *ur*.
- ✓ Read words with hard and soft *c*.

Comprehension

- ✓ Identify problems and solutions.
- ✓ Use a T-Chart.
- ✓ Identify main idea and details.
- ✓ Use a Main Idea and Details Chart.
- ✓ Ask questions.
- ✓ Use a T-Chart.

Grammar and Writing

- ✓ Identify pronouns.
- ✓ Use possessive nouns and pronouns.
- ✓ Identify adjectives and articles.
- ✓ Write a story about helping.
- ✓ Write a description of an animal.
- ✓ Write a family story.

Self-Evaluation Questions

- How does what you've learned about great ideas connect to other subjects?
- How has what you've learned changed how you think?
- What are you most proud of?

UNIT 5

Neighbors in Space

The sun, moon, stars, and planets are Earth's neighbors in space.

READINGS

Earth and Beyond

Franklin's Dream

One Moon, Many Myths

? The Big Question

What can we know about our neighbors in space?

Listening and Speaking

You will talk about stars, planets, and astronauts.

Writing

You will create your own myth about the moon.

The Phases of the Moon

Quick Write

Why does the moon change size and shape? Write what you think.

What Do You Know about Neighbors in Space?

Words to Know

1. Use these words to talk about our neighbors in space.

 **Earth**

 **sun**

 **moon**

 **stars**

 **planets**

 **asteroid**

---

2. What neighbors in space will you learn about?

I will learn about ______________ .

 **Earth**

 **stars**

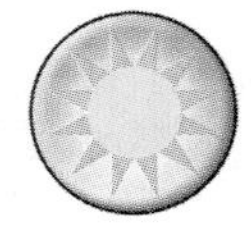 **the sun**

 **planets**

 **the moon**

 **an asteroid**

3. **What can you see in space?**

During the ______________, I can see ______________ .

stars

the sun

the moon

Earth

Your Stories about Neighbors in Space

Rodel

We have star parties here in the Philippines. We go to the best places to see the stars. People bring telescopes. We look at the moon and planets, too. Some people take pictures of the night sky.

Fiona

When I grow up, I want to be an astronaut. I just came back from Space Camp in Alabama. There, we learned how it feels to travel in space. We trained like real astronauts. We got to eat space food. We even met an astronaut!

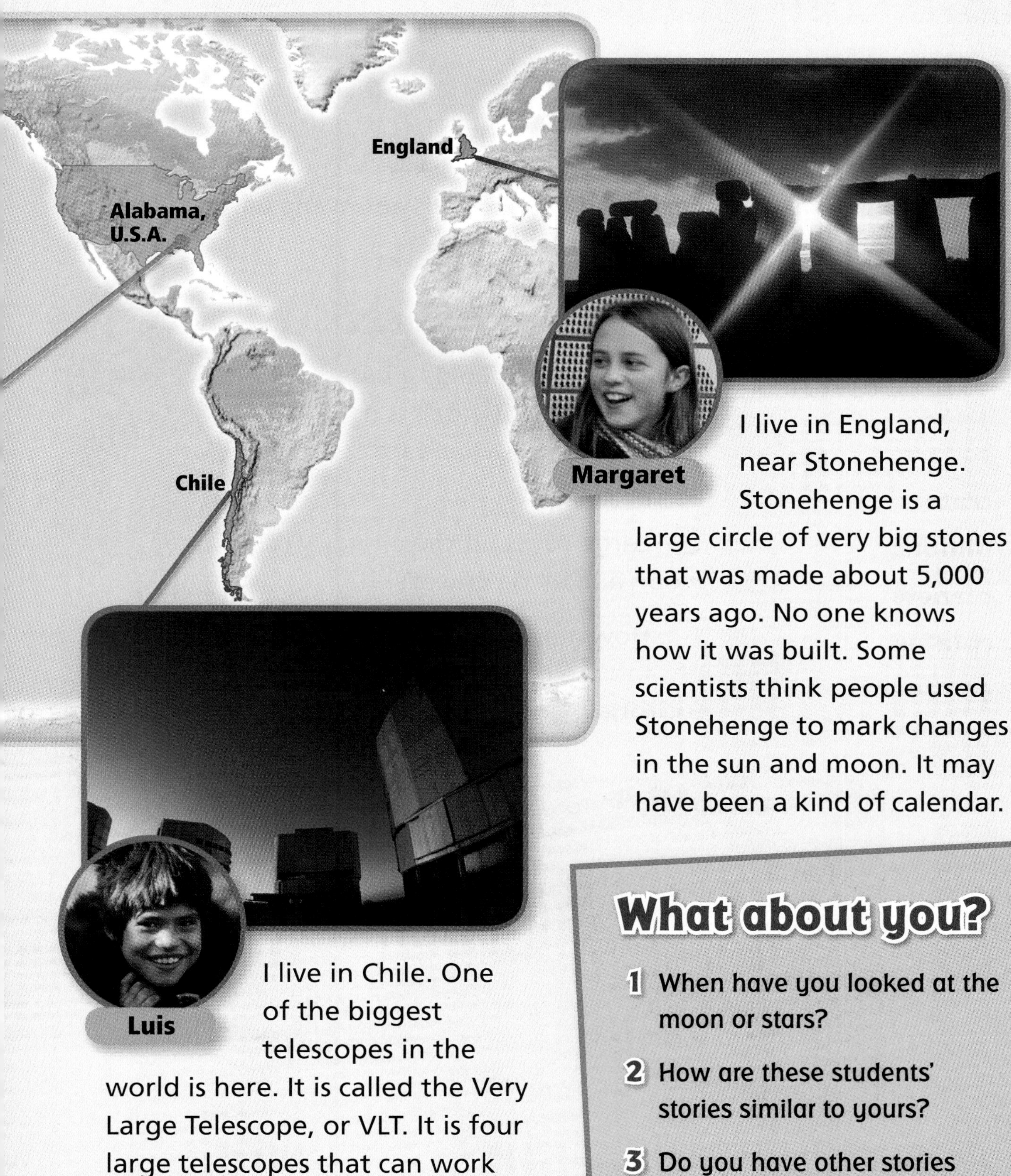

I live in England, near Stonehenge. Stonehenge is a large circle of very big stones that was made about 5,000 years ago. No one knows how it was built. Some scientists think people used Stonehenge to mark changes in the sun and moon. It may have been a kind of calendar.

I live in Chile. One of the biggest telescopes in the world is here. It is called the Very Large Telescope, or VLT. It is four large telescopes that can work together. The VLT is on a high mountain in the desert.

What about you?

1. When have you looked at the moon or stars?
2. How are these students' stories similar to yours?
3. Do you have other stories about what you have seen in the sky? Tell your story!

Vocabulary

Earth and Beyond **tells about the Earth, moon, sun, and stars.**

Key Words

- **sphere**
- **craters**
- **billions**
- **planets**
- **rotates**
- **continents**

Words in Context

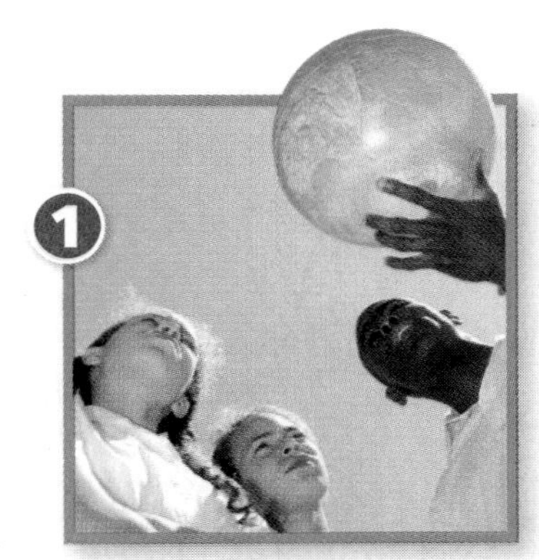

1. The teacher holds a blue **sphere** in one hand. It is a globe. It shows what Earth looks like.

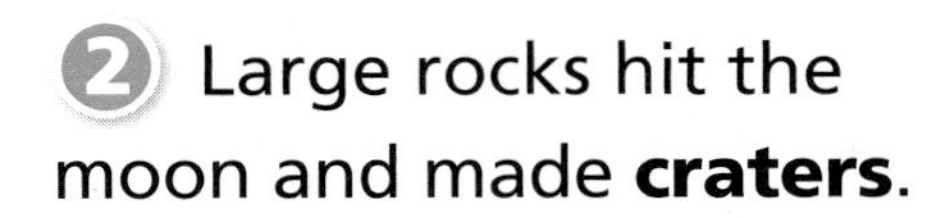

2. Large rocks hit the moon and made **craters**.

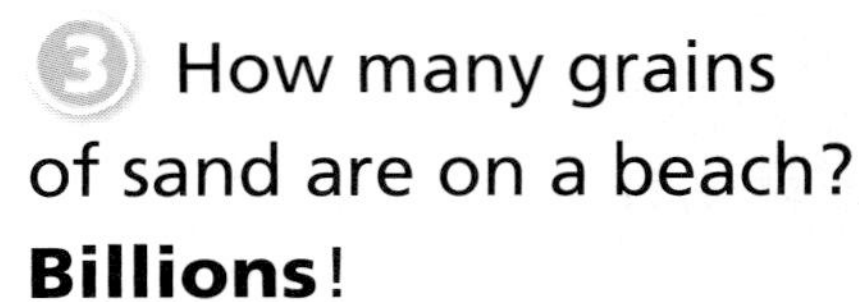

3. How many grains of sand are on a beach? **Billions**!

4 Earth is one of eight **planets** in our solar system. All eight planets travel around the sun.

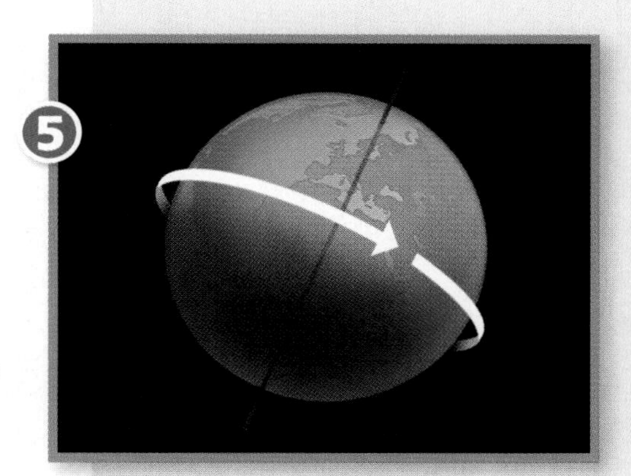

5 Earth **rotates**, or turns, on its axis as it travels around the sun.

6 Do you recognize these **continents**? Which one is Australia? Which one is Africa? Which one is South America?

6

Practice

Use each key word in a sentence.

Make Connections

Some people say they feel small when they look at the stars. How do you feel when you look at the night sky? What does it make you think about?

Academic Words

label
word or phrase that describes something

location
particular place or position

pages 107–108

Reading 1

INFORMATIONAL TEXT

Science

The Big Question

What can we learn about Earth and its neighbors?

Reading Strategy

Review

- As you read, stop after each paragraph to review.
- What questions do you have?
- Reread the paragraph. Look for the answers to your questions.

Earth and Beyond

by Maya Hightower
illustrated by Johnnee Bee

We live on Earth. Earth is a sphere. It is a large, round ball in space. But Earth is not alone.

Look up at the night sky. What do you want to learn? What are stars made of? Do people live on the moon?

Look up at the sky in the day. What do you want to learn? How big is the sun? Why can't you see stars during the day?

The more you look, the more questions you will have. Let's travel through space to find some answers.

What do we know about the moon?

The moon is our nearest neighbor in space. It is 239,000 miles (384,833 kilometers) from Earth.

The moon is a sphere, like Earth. The surface of the moon is dusty. It has mountains and plains. Many craters cover the moon's surface.

Do people live on the moon?

No! The moon does not have air or water. The temperature can change from very hot to very cold. No plants, animals, or people can live on the moon.

Have people ever visited the moon?

Yes! Twelve astronauts have walked on the moon. They wore special suits so they could breathe. They brought back moon rocks.

---

surface top or outside

temperature measure of how hot or cold something is

astronaut someone who travels and works in space

Can people live on the moon? Why not?

What are stars?

Stars look like tiny lights in the sky. But they are giant balls of hot gas.

How many stars are there?

There are billions of stars in space. But we can't see all of them. On a clear night, we can see thousands of stars.

Why do stars look so small?

Stars look small because they are so far away.

What is a constellation?

A constellation is a group of stars that looks like a picture. Long ago, people looked up at the night sky. They saw shapes made by the stars. People named these shapes for things they knew, such as animals.

What is the sun?

The sun is a star. Earth and the other planets orbit the sun.

Why does the sun look so big and bright?

It looks big and bright because it is closer than any other star. The sun is so bright that we can't see other stars during the day.

The sun is always glowing. So why is the sky dark at night?

Earth rotates every 24 hours. When our side of Earth faces the sun, we have day. When our side faces away from the sun, we have night.

Why is the sun so important?

The sun warms and lights Earth.

Can people visit the sun?

No! The sun is too hot.

---

orbit travel in a circle in space around a larger object

Check Up How did people name constellations in the night sky?

What is the solar system?

The solar system is like a large neighborhood. It is made up of the sun and all the things that orbit the sun. Earth and its moon are part of the solar system. So are other planets and their moons. The solar system also has billions of asteroids and meteors.

What is a planet?

A planet is a large sphere that rotates in space as it orbits the sun. Some planets are made of rock. Others are made of gas. Some have rings around them. Some have many moons.

What are the planets in the solar system?

Mercury, Venus, Earth, Mars, Jupiter, Saturn, Uranus, and Neptune are the planets.

---

asteroids small, rocky objects that move around the sun

meteors pieces of rock or metal that float in space

What is special about the planet Earth?

Earth has water and air. It is the only planet where people, animals, and plants can live.

What does Earth look like from space?

Earth looks like a beautiful ball with many colors. From space, the oceans look blue. The continents are brown and green.

Reading Strategy

Review

- What questions did you have as you read?
- Did you find the answers?
- How did reviewing help you understand the selection?

pages 109–110

Think It Over

1. What are stars?
2. What causes day and night?
3. Why do you think the title of the selection is *Earth and Beyond*?

Word Analysis & Fluency

Word Analysis

Synonyms and Antonyms

Synonyms are words that mean the same thing.
Antonyms are words that have opposite meanings.

Practice

Work with a partner. Choose a synonym or an antonym for each underlined word.

Synonyms		
sphere	**large**	**surface**

1. Earth is a big ball in space.
2. Like Earth, the moon is a ball.
3. The outside of the moon is dusty.

Antonyms		
cold	**bright**	**night**

4. Look up at the day sky.
5. The sun is very dim.
6. The temperature on the moon can be very hot.

page 111

Fluency

Look Ahead

Sometimes readers look for hard words before they read. They then try to figure them out.

Practice

Pick one passage.	Find any hard words.	Practice saying those words.	Read the passage aloud.

1. We live on Earth. Earth is a planet. The moon is our neighbor. The sun is a star. There are other planets and stars in the sky.

2. A constellation is a group of stars that looks like a picture. Long ago, people looked up at the night sky. They saw shapes made by the stars. People named these shapes for things they knew, such as animals.

3. The solar system is like a large neighborhood. It is made up of the sun and all the things that orbit the sun. Earth and its moon are part of the solar system. So are other planets and their moons. The solar system also has billions of asteroids and meteors.

Comprehension

Review

You may not understand a selection the first time you read it. You can review it. When you **review** a selection, you read it again.

Learning Strategy

Summarize

Summarize the selection for a partner.

Ask your partner to respond to the Big Question for this reading.

page 112

Practice

Look back in the selection for the answers to these questions. Give the answer and the page on which you found the answer.

1. Why don't people live on the moon?
2. Why do stars look so small?
3. Why does the sun look so big and bright?
4. Why is the sun so important?
5. What is the solar system?
6. What is special about Earth?

Use a KWL Chart

What did you already know about space? What did you want to learn? A KWL Chart can help you see what you have learned.

Practice

Copy the chart. Fill in the last column. Show at least four things you learned by reading the selection.

What I Know	What I Want to Know	What I Learned
I know the moon is in the night sky.	Do people live on the moon?	1. No. There is no air and no water on the moon. 2. No plants, animals, or people can live there.

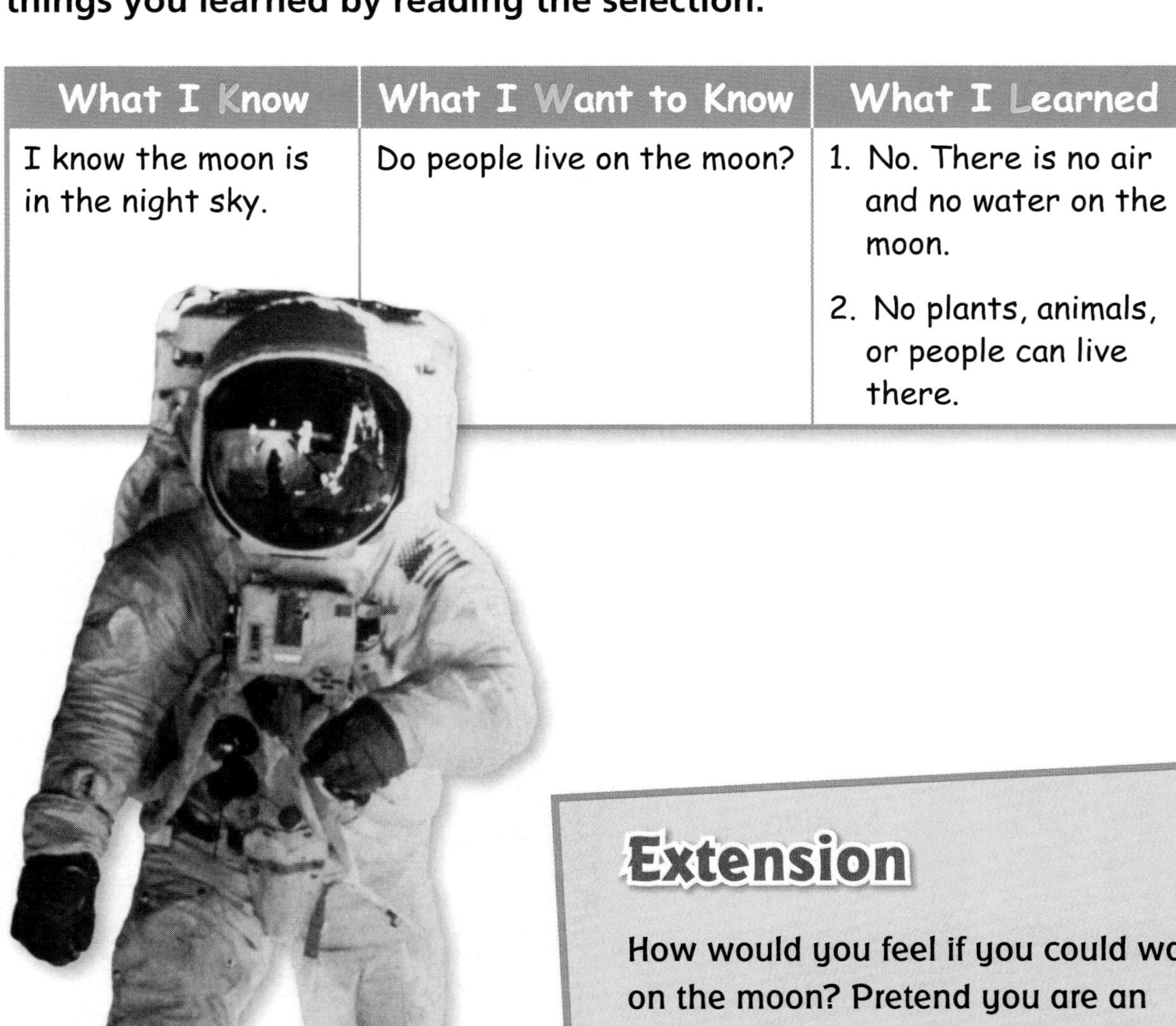

Extension

How would you feel if you could walk on the moon? Pretend you are an astronaut. Describe to a partner how you felt on the moon.

Grammar & Writing

Present Tense Verbs

A **verb** can name an action. A verb can also tell when the action happens.

Present tense verbs name actions that happen now.

The moon **orbits** Earth.	The planets **orbit** the sun.
She **sees** the sun.	I **see** the moon.

Practice

Write a sentence with each verb. Tell about an action that is happening now.

1. live
2. see
3. look
4. walk
5. give

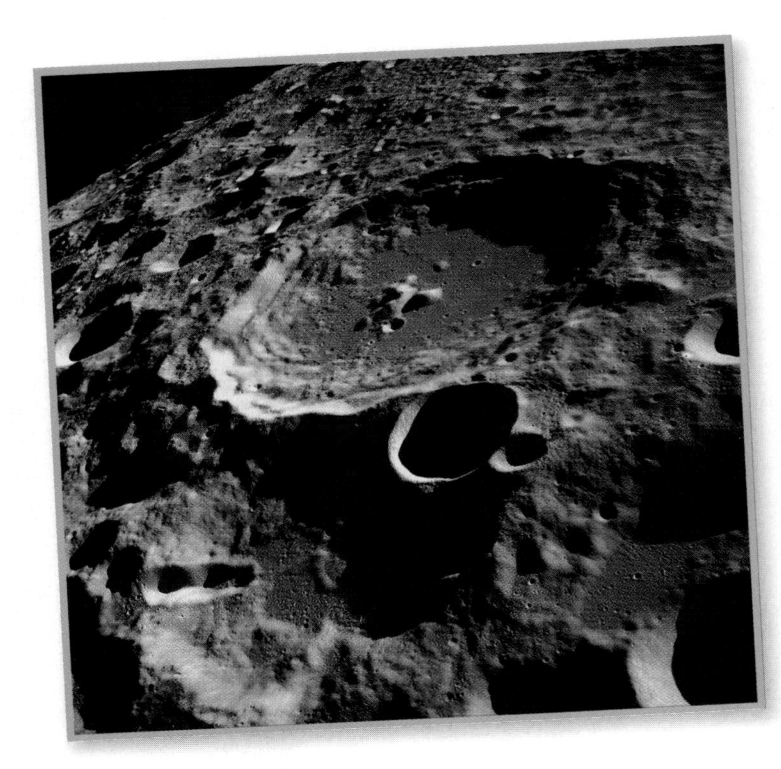

page 113

Write a Report

You write a report to give information. Sami wrote what she learned about Earth.

From space, Earth looks like a big ball. The water is blue. The land is brown and green. Earth is one planet in the solar system. It orbits the sun. Seven other planets orbit our sun, too. Only Earth has air and water. It is the only planet where things can live.

SPELLING TIP

In some words, the /f/ sound is spelled *ph*.

sphere, telephone, photograph, pharmacy

page 114

Write a report.

- Choose one: the moon, the sun, or stars.
- Use a KWL Chart to think about what you know and what you learned.
- Write the information that you learned.

Writing Checklist

- ✓ Did you describe the moon, the sun, or stars?
- ✓ Did you write what you learned?
- ✓ Did you use present tense verbs?
- ✓ Can a partner understand your report?

Reading 2

Franklin's Dream

Vocabulary

Franklin's Dream **tells about a boy who grew up to become an astronaut.**

Key Words

- **space shuttle**
- **flight**
- **satellite**
- **observe**
- **spacewalks**

Words in Context

1. Astronauts ride a **space shuttle** to go into space and come back to Earth. A trip in space is called a space **flight**.

2. The space shuttle may take a **satellite** into space. A satellite orbits Earth. Satellites help telephones and televisions work.

3 Scientists **observe** the stars through a telescope.

4 Astronauts take **spacewalks** to go outside the space shuttle.

Practice

Use each key word in a sentence.

Make Connections

Would you like to be an astronaut? Why or why not?

Academic Words

challenge
something hard to do

achieve
succeed in doing something

pages 115–116

INFORMATIONAL TEXT

Biography

The Big Question

How can someone become an astronaut?

Reading Strategy

Summarize

Think about what is important in the selection.

- Identify the main idea.
- Identify the important details.

Franklin's Dream

by Mirna Cepeda
illustrated by Nathan Hale

It is 1986. The space shuttle *Columbia* lifts off. Franklin Chang-Diaz is on the shuttle. This is his first space flight. His dream has come true.

Franklin was born in San José, Costa Rica. When he was a boy, he heard about *Sputnik*. *Sputnik* was the first satellite to orbit Earth.

Franklin climbed a mango tree. He watched the sky for hours.

"I was seven years old," he said, "when I decided to become an astronaut."

Franklin never let go of his dream.

Check Up What made Franklin want to be an astronaut?

Franklin was a good student in school. But that was not all. He was a curious child. He liked to observe the things around him. He tried to learn more about them. Sports and music were his hobbies. Science and reading were the subjects he liked best. He planned to study science.

---

curious wanting to know or learn things

hobbies favorite things to do in your free time

subjects main things you study in school

Franklin liked to repair things. He found out how they worked. Then he tried to make them work better.

Franklin hoped to become an astronaut. He knew that a good education would help him. He also knew that he needed to learn English. So he moved to the United States. His parents helped him.

Franklin kept working hard. He learned English, and he studied science. His teachers helped him. He went to college. Franklin became a scientist.

---

college school after high school

scientist someone who works in science

Check Up What subjects did Franklin like best in school?

In 1980, Franklin was chosen to become an astronaut. He started to train in classrooms and in labs. After six years of training, he was ready. It was 1986, the year of *Columbia*'s flight.

Franklin would go on six more space flights. As an astronaut, he did experiments. He made spacewalks and repaired things. Franklin went on more space flights than anyone had ever gone on before.

---

train learn skills for a job

experiments scientific tests

Flying in space is exciting. But for Franklin, the sight of Earth from outer space is the best part. He says that it is very beautiful. He says that we must take care of Earth.

"Earth is humanity's spaceship and the only one we have," says Franklin. "We must protect it."

---

humanity's belonging to all people

Summarize

- What was the main idea of the selection?
- What were the main events in Franklin's life?
- How did summarizing the selection help you understand it?

Think It Over

1. Where was Franklin born?
2. How many space flights did Franklin make in all?
3. What does Franklin say is the best part about being an astronaut?

A Closer Look at...

Space Exploration

▲ **Blast off!**
A space shuttle begins its flight into space.

▲ **Docking**
Astronauts ride the space shuttle to get to the space station. The space shuttle docks, or links, to the space station.

▲ **Spacewalk**
An astronaut goes on a spacewalk to work outside the space shuttle.

▲ **Space station**
This is the International Space Station. People from many countries work here.

▲ Robot on Mars

People have not walked on Mars — yet! But scientists sent this robot there. The robot helped scientists study rocks.

▲ Red planet

A robot took this picture of the surface of Mars. Mars is often called the red planet. Can you tell why?

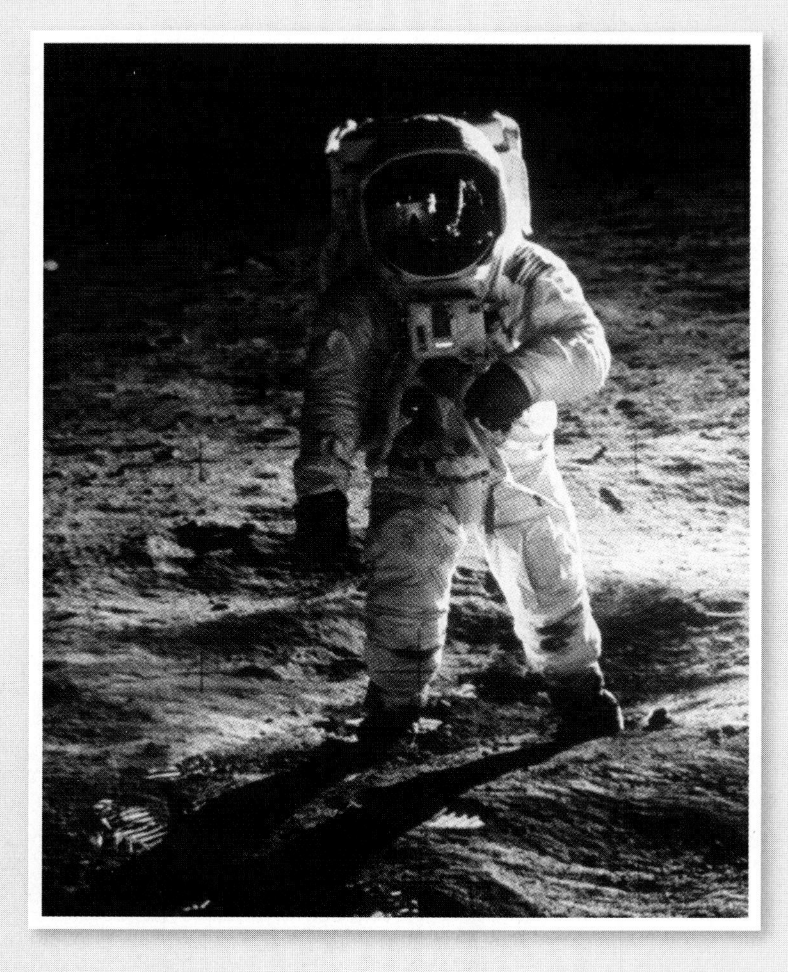

◀ Moon walk

Buzz Aldrin was an astronaut on the first trip to the moon in 1969.

Activity to Do!

These two pages use words and pictures to tell about space exploration.

- Choose another type of exploration.
- Find pictures to show that exploration.
- Post your pictures and captions in your classroom.

Phonics & Fluency

Phonics

R-Controlled Vowels: *ar, or, ore*

The letter *r* changes vowel sounds.

am	ton	toe
arm	torn	tore

Rule Box

The letters *ar* usually have the vowel sound heard in ***art***. The letters *or* and *ore* usually have the vowel sound heard in ***born*** and ***more***.

Practice

Read the sentences with a partner. Take turns.

- His story starts in Costa Rica.
- That is where he was born.
- He was a smart child.
- He enjoyed sports.
- He wanted to explore space.

1. List the words with *ar*.
2. List the words with *or* and *ore*.

page 119

Fluency

Read for Speed and Accuracy

You should read quickly. But never read so quickly that you lose your understanding.

Practice

Read for one minute.	Count the words you read.	Study any hard words.	Read and count again.

Franklin was a good student in school. But that was not	11
all. He was a curious child. He liked to observe the things	23
around him. He tried to learn more about them. Sports	33
and music were his hobbies. Science and reading were the	43
subjects he liked best. He planned to study science.	52
Franklin liked to repair things. He found out how they	62
worked. Then he tried to make them work better.	71
Franklin hoped to become an astronaut. He knew that	80
a good education would help him. He also knew that he	91
needed to learn English. So he moved to the United States.	102
His parents helped him.	106
Franklin kept working hard. He learned English, and	114
he studied science. His teachers helped him. He went to	124
college. Franklin became a scientist.	129
In 1980, Franklin was chosen to become an astronaut.	138
He started to train in classrooms and in labs. After six	149
years of training, he was ready. It was 1986, the year of	161
Columbia's flight.	163

Comprehension

Learning Strategy

Summarize

Summarize the selection for a partner.

Ask your partner to respond to the Big Question for this reading.

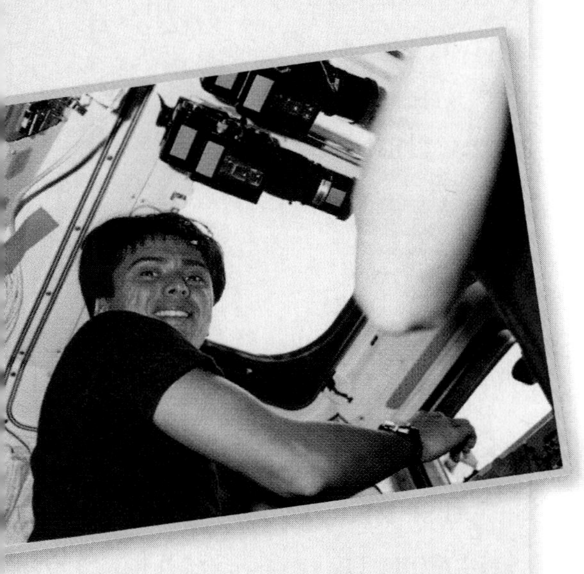

page 120

Summarize

To **summarize**, tell only the main idea and the most important details.

Practice

Read these details from the selection. Choose three important details.

1. Franklin was born in Costa Rica.
2. Franklin climbed a mango tree.
3. Franklin moved to the United States and learned English.
4. Franklin's hobbies were sports and music.
5. Franklin worked hard in school. He became a scientist.
6. Flying in space is exciting.
7. Franklin flew on more space flights than anyone had flown before.

Use a Main Idea and Details Chart

A Main Idea and Details Chart can help you summarize what you read.

Practice

Copy the chart.

Main Idea
Franklin's dream was to become an astronaut. He achieved his goal.

Detail:	Detail:	Detail:
Franklin was born in Costa Rica.		

1. Choose two details that support the main idea. Add them to the chart.
   - **a.** Franklin climbed a mango tree.
   - **b.** Franklin worked hard in school. He became a scientist.
   - **c.** Flying in space is exciting.
   - **d.** Franklin flew on more space flights than anyone had flown before.
2. Use your chart to summarize *Franklin's Dream*.

Extension

Franklin Chang-Diaz had a dream. Think of a time when you had a special dream. Tell a partner what you did to make your dream come true.

Grammar & Writing

Past Tense Verbs

Past tense verbs name actions that already happened.

Franklin **climbed** a mango tree.

Rules	Examples
For most verbs, add *-ed*.	climb → climbed
For verbs ending in *-e*, drop the *e* and add *-ed*.	hope → hoped
For verbs ending in a consonant and *-y*, change the *y* to *i* and add *-ed*.	cry → cried

Practice

Rewrite each sentence. Change the underlined verb to the past tense.

1. Franklin live in Costa Rica.
2. He want to become an astronaut.
3. Franklin's parents help him.
4. He always try his best.

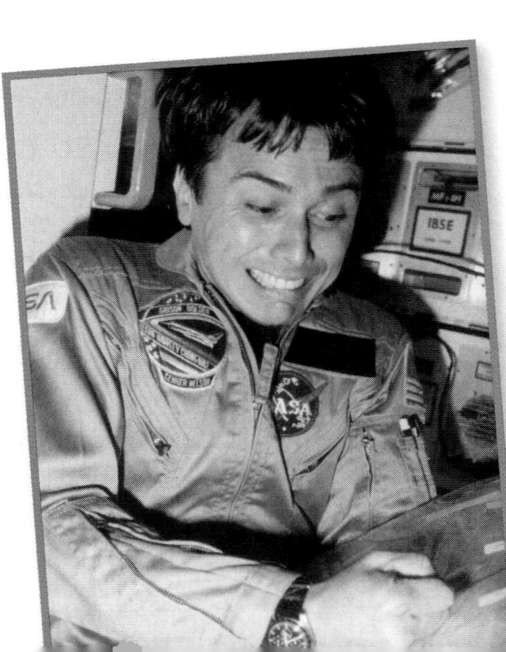

page 121

Write an Autobiography

You write an **autobiography** to tell about your own life. Joey told about something that happened when he was five years old.

When I was five years old, I played outside a lot. I liked to be outside in the day. But I was scared of the dark. I did not like to be outside at night.

One night my dad and I went outside. He showed me constellations in the sky. I looked at all the stars. After that, I was not scared outside at night.

The /i/ sound can be spelled with the letters *igh*.

flight, high, light

page 122

Practice

Tell a story about something you did when you were younger.

- Be sure to use verbs in the past tense.
- Indent each paragraph.

Writing Checklist

- ✔ Did you tell about your own life?
- ✔ Did you tell how old you were when the story happened?
- ✔ Did you use past tense verbs?
- ✔ Can a partner understand your story?

Reading 3

One Moon, Many Myths

Vocabulary

In *One Moon, Many Myths,* you will read different myths about the moon.

Key Words
- **bark**
- **rainbow**
- **canoe**
- **handprints**

Words in Context

1. The **bark** of a tree is its outer covering. Different trees have different kinds of bark.

2. You can see a **rainbow** when the sun shines through drops of water. This can happen in the sky. It can also happen close to you.

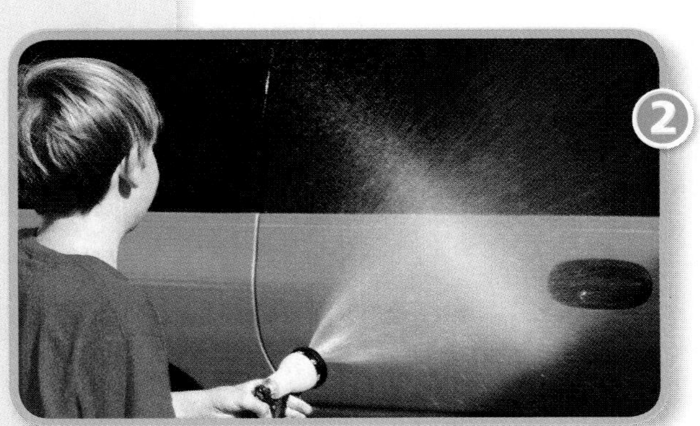

③ These boys paddle a **canoe**. They wear life jackets to be safe.

④ Native Americans made these **handprints** on a cave wall long ago.

Practice

Use each key word in a sentence.

Make Connections

What do you look at in nature? Do you look at the bark on trees? Have you ever seen a rainbow? Describe what you like to look at when you are outside.

Academic Words

summary
short statement that tells the main points

link
join things or pieces together

pages 123–124

Reading 3

LITERATURE

Myths

The Big Question

Why did people make up stories to explain things in space?

Reading Strategy

Compare and Contrast

- To compare, look for ways the myths are the same.
- To contrast, look for ways the myths are different from one another.

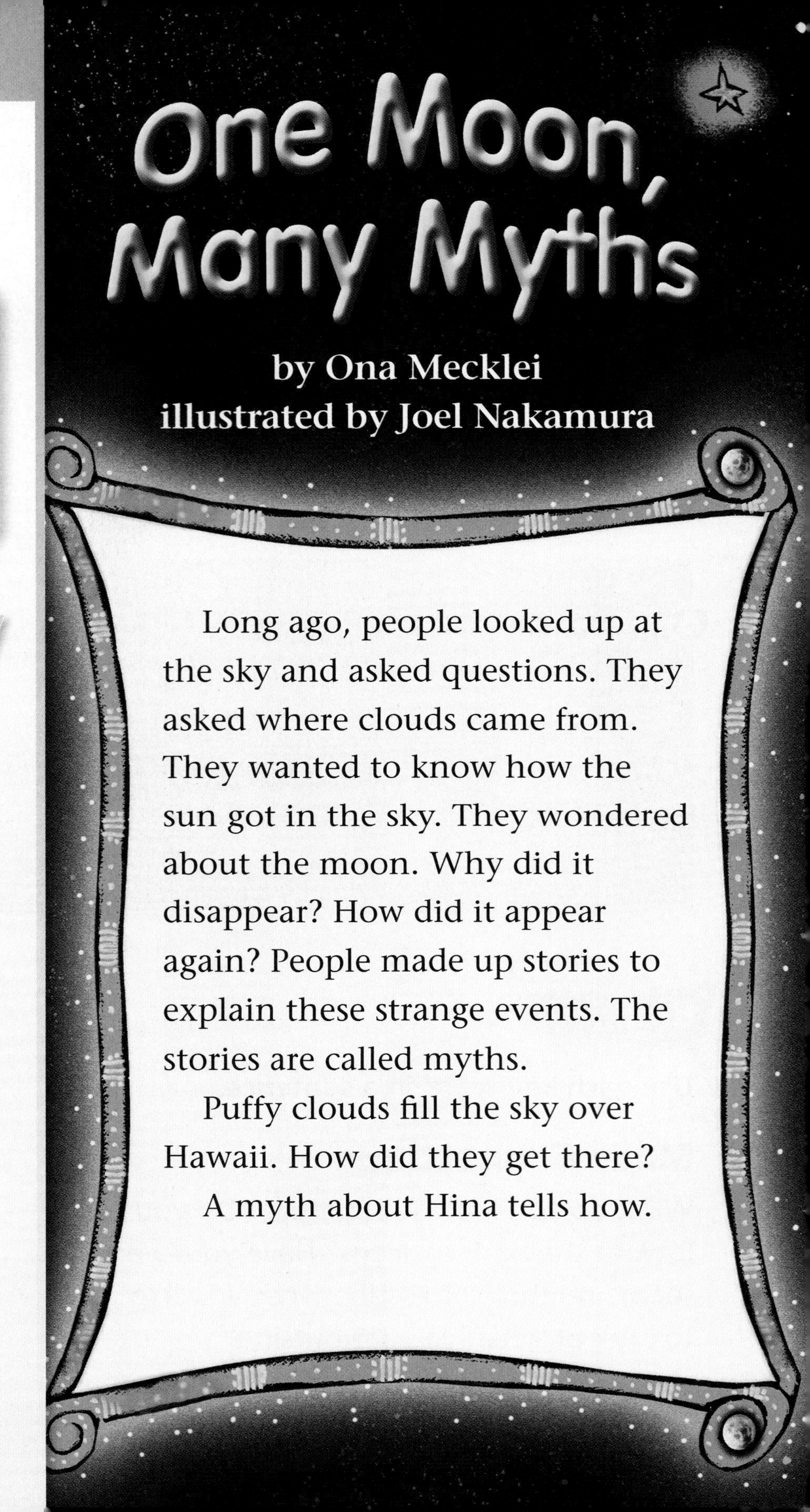

One Moon, Many Myths

by Ona Mecklei
illustrated by Joel Nakamura

Long ago, people looked up at the sky and asked questions. They asked where clouds came from. They wanted to know how the sun got in the sky. They wondered about the moon. Why did it disappear? How did it appear again? People made up stories to explain these strange events. The stories are called myths.

Puffy clouds fill the sky over Hawaii. How did they get there?

A myth about Hina tells how.

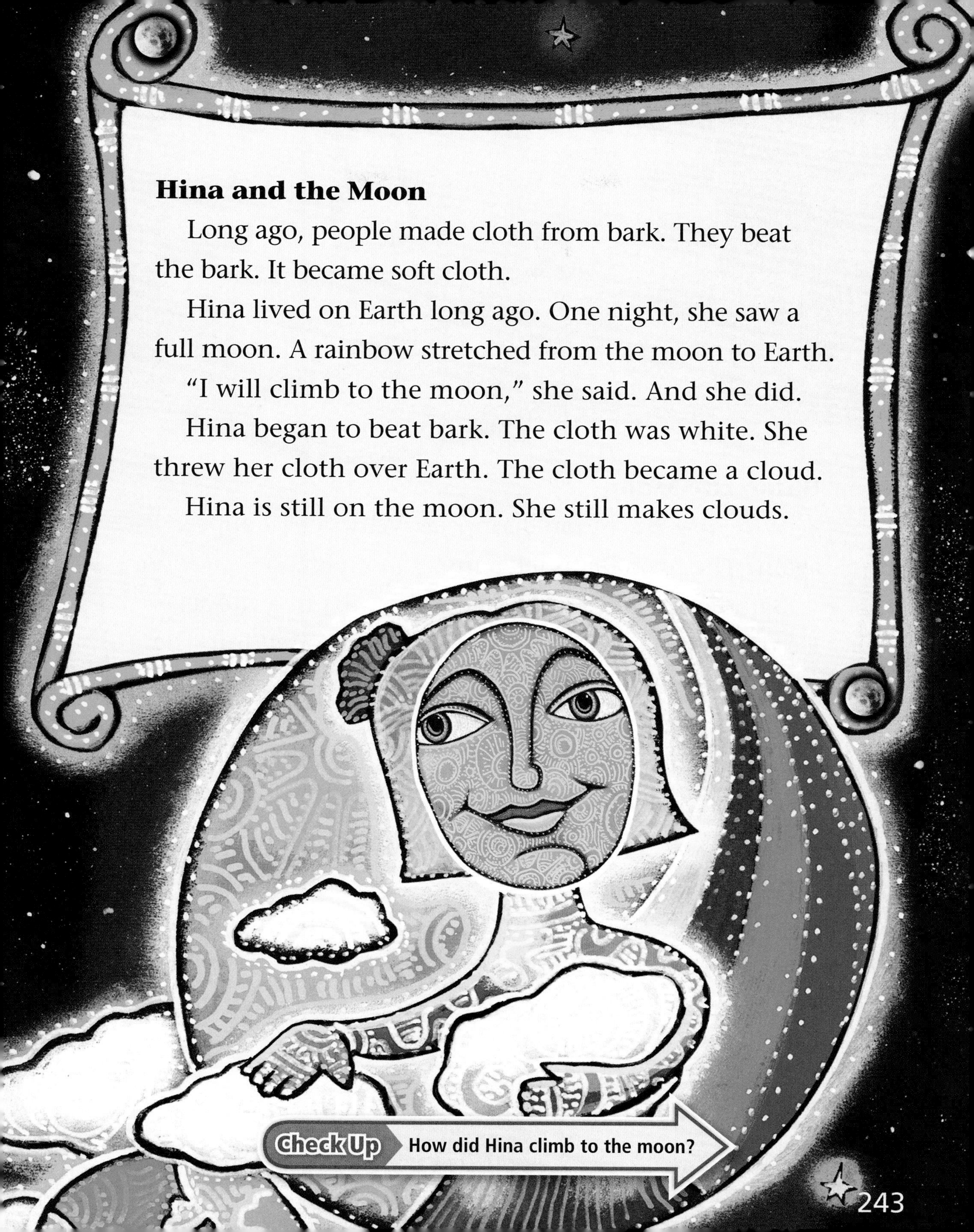

Hina and the Moon

Long ago, people made cloth from bark. They beat the bark. It became soft cloth.

Hina lived on Earth long ago. One night, she saw a full moon. A rainbow stretched from the moon to Earth.

"I will climb to the moon," she said. And she did.

Hina began to beat bark. The cloth was white. She threw her cloth over Earth. The cloth became a cloud.

Hina is still on the moon. She still makes clouds.

Check Up How did Hina climb to the moon?

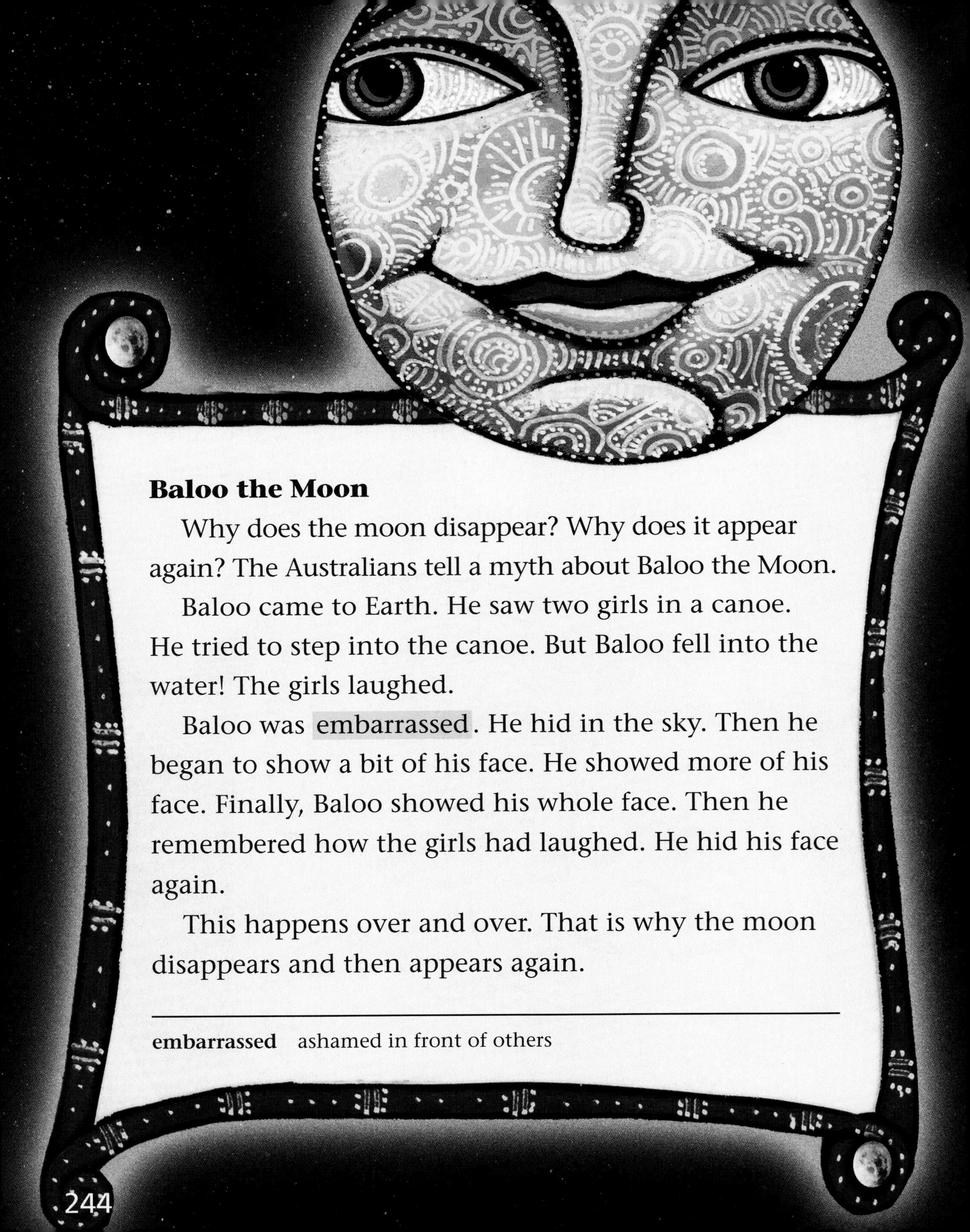

Baloo the Moon

Why does the moon disappear? Why does it appear again? The Australians tell a myth about Baloo the Moon.

Baloo came to Earth. He saw two girls in a canoe. He tried to step into the canoe. But Baloo fell into the water! The girls laughed.

Baloo was embarrassed. He hid in the sky. Then he began to show a bit of his face. He showed more of his face. Finally, Baloo showed his whole face. Then he remembered how the girls had laughed. He hid his face again.

This happens over and over. That is why the moon disappears and then appears again.

---

embarrassed ashamed in front of others

Handprints on the Moon

A myth from India tells about the sun and the moon.

Earth Mother had two children. She loved them very much. She wanted them to live forever. So she sent her children into the sky. Her son became the sun. Her daughter became the moon.

The daughter rose into the sky. Earth Mother wanted to hug her one last time. But it was too late. She could only touch her daughter's cheek. Earth Mother left her handprints on the moon.

pages 125–126

Reading Strategy

Compare and Contrast

- How are the myths the same?
- How are the myths different?
- How did comparing and contrasting help you understand the myths?

Think It Over

1. Where does the myth about Hina come from?
2. Why is Baloo embarrassed?
3. Why does Earth Mother send her children into the sky?

Word Analysis & Fluency

Word Analysis

Multiple-Meaning Words

The word ***bark*** has more than one meaning.

1. Hina makes cloth from tree bark.
2. The dogs bark.

bark[1] outer covering of a tree
bark[2] make a short, loud sound

Practice

Work with a partner. Read each sentence. Choose the best meaning for the underlined word.

1. One night Hina saw a full moon.

   saw[1] looked at

   saw[2] a tool with a sharp blade

2. Baloo began to show a bit of his face.

   bit[1] took a bite of

   bit[2] small amount

page 127

Fluency

Read with Expression

When you read aloud, use your voice to show feelings.

Practice

Read silently. → Read aloud. → Get comments. → Read aloud again.

Why does the moon disappear? Why does it appear again? The Australians tell a myth about Baloo the Moon.

Baloo came to Earth. He saw two girls in a canoe. He tried to step into the canoe. But Baloo fell into the water! The girls laughed.

Baloo was embarrassed. He hid in the sky. Then he began to show a bit of his face. He showed more of his face. Finally, Baloo showed his whole face. Then he remembered how the girls had laughed. He hid his face again.

This happens over and over. That is why the moon disappears and then appears again.

Comprehension

Learning Strategy

Retell

Retell the selection to a partner.

? Ask your partner to respond to the Big Question for this reading.

page 128

Compare and Contrast

When you **compare** things, you tell how they are alike. When you **contrast** things, you tell how they are different.

Practice

Read these sentences about the selection. Tell whether the sentences compare or contrast the myths.

1. All three myths tell about things in the sky.
2. Characters in all the myths do impossible things.
3. Hina climbs on a rainbow. Baloo the moon comes to Earth. Earth Mother's children become the sun and moon.
4. All three myths explain something in nature.
5. Hina makes the clouds. Baloo makes the moon appear and disappear. Earth Mother made handprints on the moon.

Use a Venn Diagram

A Venn Diagram can help you compare and contrast. The outside of the circles tells what is different. The part where the circles link tells what is alike.

Practice

1. **Copy and complete the diagram. Compare and contrast the two myths.**
2. **Then make another Venn Diagram. Compare and contrast the Indian myth with one other myth.**

Baloo myth	(both)	Hina myth
1. Tells why the moon disappears and appears again	1. Explains something in nature	1. Tells where clouds come from
2. Comes from Australia	2. Tells about things in the sky	2. Comes from Hawaii
3. ____________	3. ________	3. ____________

Extension

Make up a myth that tells why there are so many stars in the sky. Draw pictures for your myth. Share your myth with the class.

Reading 3

Grammar & Writing

Future Tense Verbs

Hina says, "I will climb to the moon." She uses the future tense of a verb. **Future tense** verbs name actions that are going to happen.

To form the future tense of a verb, use the helping verb ***will***.

tell → will tell	find → will find

Practice

Rewrite each sentence. Change the underlined verb to the future tense.

1. Olga find more myths about the moon.
2. She look in the library.
3. I choose one myth.
4. Then I read it aloud for the class.
5. I hope that everyone enjoy the myth.

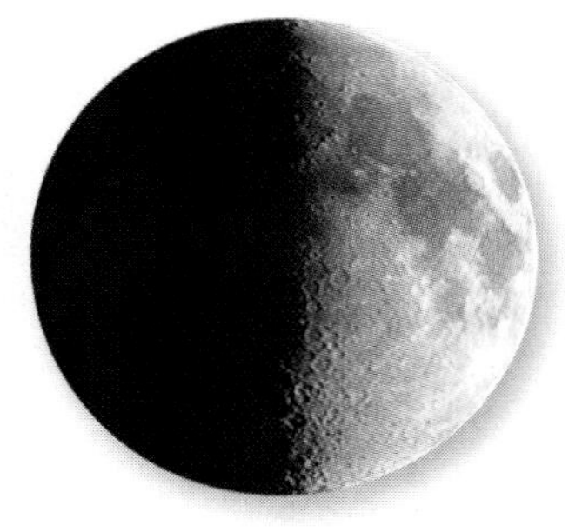

page 129

Write a Myth

A **myth** can tell a story to explain a fact of nature. Read Jesse's tale about how the sun came to be.

It was dark. The animals were cold. They made a fire to keep warm. The animals all tried to get close to the fire.

Bear thought, "I will take some of this for myself." He grabbed a chunk of burning wood.

"OW!" yelled Bear. He threw the burning hot wood as hard as he could. He threw it high in the sky. It stayed there. And so we have the sun.

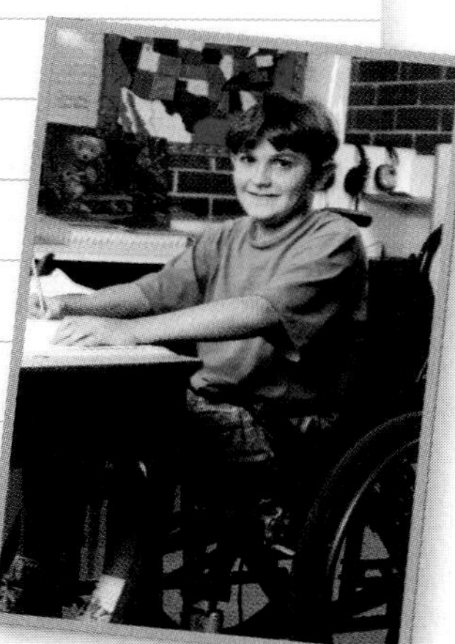

SPELLING TIP

Here are some tips to spell *two, too,* and *to*.

Two = 2

Too has too many *o*'s!

To is spelled like ***go***. I will ***go to*** the store.

page 130

Practice

Write your own myth.

- Look at the moon or at pictures of the moon.
- Tell why the moon looks the way it does.

Writing Checklist

- ✓ Did your myth tell why the moon looks the way it does?
- ✓ Did you use verbs in the future tense?
- ✓ Can a partner understand your story?

Bonus Reading

INFORMATIONAL TEXT

Science

The Phases of the MOON

by Leah Davis

Look at the moon several days in a row. Does it seem to change its shape? Sometimes you can see only a small part of the moon. At other times the moon is a big bright circle. Still other times you can't see it at all! What happens? Does the shape of the moon change?

The moon's shape does not change. It is always a sphere. The moon does not make its own light. Its light is really light from the sun. The sun's light makes the moon shine.

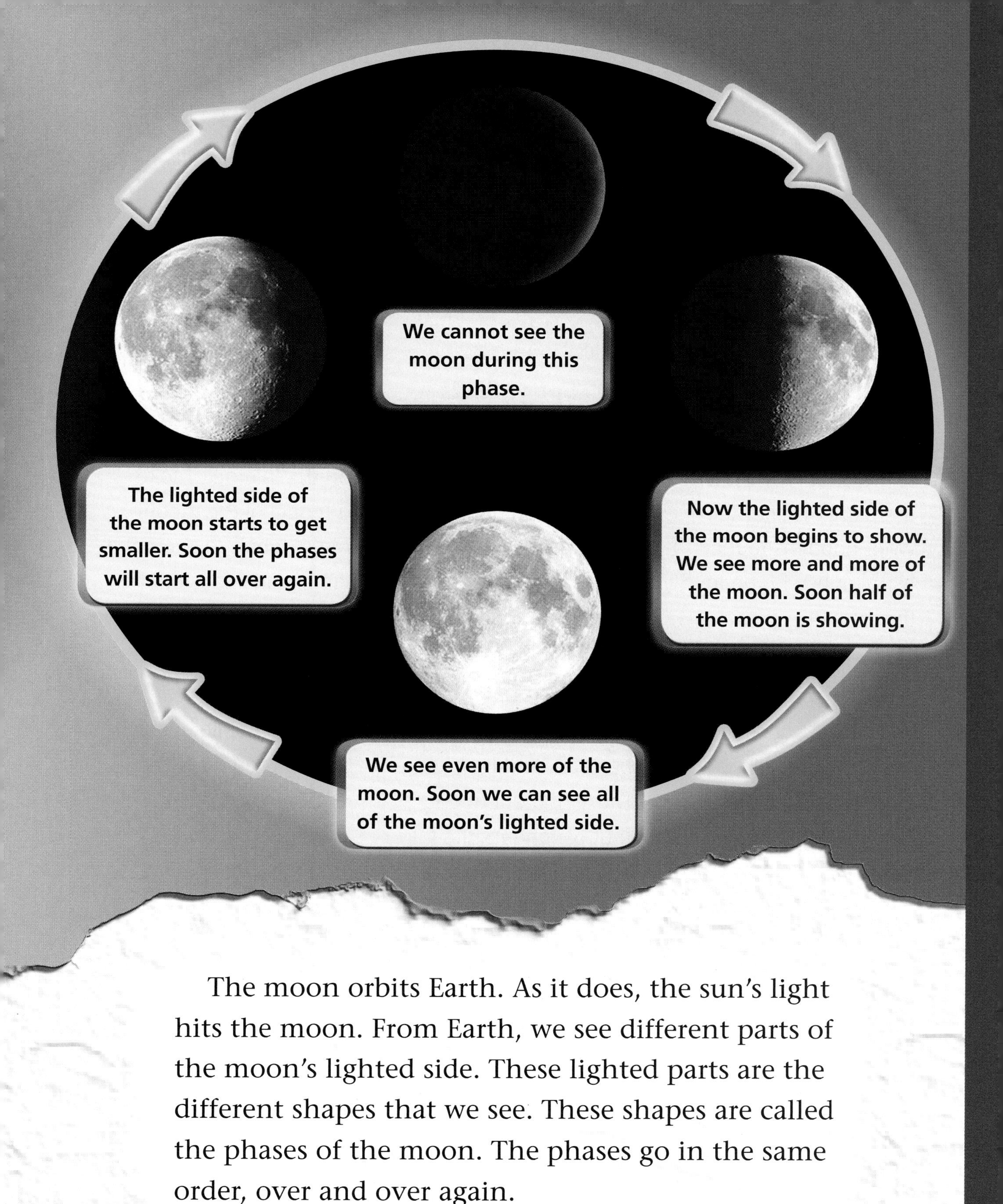

The moon orbits Earth. As it does, the sun's light hits the moon. From Earth, we see different parts of the moon's lighted side. These lighted parts are the different shapes that we see. These shapes are called the phases of the moon. The phases go in the same order, over and over again.

UNIT 5 Wrap Up

The Big Question

What can we know about our neighbors in space?

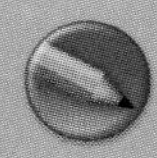 Written	 Oral	 Visual/Active
Space Story Write a story about a trip to a planet. Tell what the planet is like. Tell what happens to the astronauts who go to that planet.	**Space Facts** List three facts about one of Earth's neighbors in space. Read your facts aloud. Have a partner guess which neighbor goes with your list.	**Moon Map** Find a map of the moon on the Internet. Make a model of the moon. Make labels to show the craters and seas on the moon.
Planet Song Write a song about the planets. Name all the planets. The song should help you learn the order of the planets from the sun.	**Biography Lesson** Pick an astronaut besides Franklin Chang-Diaz. Find out about that astronaut's trip into space. Tell what he or she has done in space.	**Space Mobile** Make a mobile of our solar system. On the back of each picture, write a fact about it. Hang the mobile in your classroom.

pages 131–132

✓ Learning Checklist

Word Analysis and Phonics

✓ Identify synonyms and antonyms.

✓ Read words with *r*-controlled vowels: *ar*, *or*, and *ore*.

✓ Use multiple-meaning words correctly.

Comprehension

✓ Review.

✓ Use a KWL Chart.

✓ Summarize.

✓ Use a Main Idea and Details Chart.

✓ Compare and contrast.

✓ Use a Venn Diagram.

Grammar and Writing

✓ Recognize and use present tense verbs.

✓ Recognize and use past tense verbs.

✓ Recognize and use future tense verbs.

✓ Write a report.

✓ Write an autobiography.

✓ Write a myth.

Self-Evaluation Questions

- What do you now know about our neighbors in space?
- What questions do you still have about planets, the sun, the moon, and stars?
- How does what you've learned relate to the future?

UNIT 6

Arts Festivals

People have arts festivals to celebrate the fun of making and sharing art.

Readings

1

Arts Festival!

2

How to Make Puppets

3

The Music Goes On

The Big Question

What can be shown or take place at an arts festival?

Listening and Speaking

You will talk about art that you like to make.

Writing

You will write a newspaper article about your school.

Quick Write

Look at the picture of the puppets. Tell how you would make a puppet.

Bonus Reading

My Journal

What Do You Know about Arts Festivals?

Words to Know

1. Use these words to talk about arts festivals.

 **puppets**

 **mural**

 **mask**

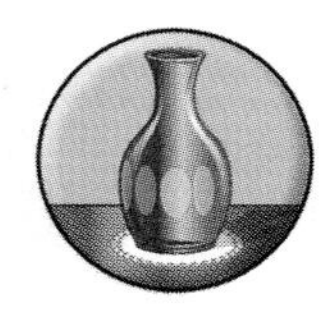 **vase**

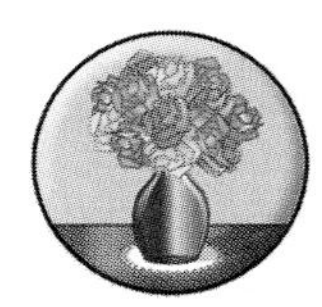 **paper flowers**

---

2. What can you do at an arts festival?

I can make ______________ .

 **puppets**

 **paper flowers**

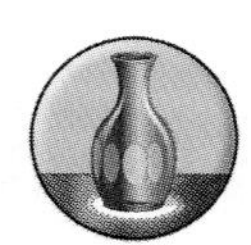 **a vase**

 **a mask**

 **a mural**

3. What material do you use?

To make ______________, I use ______________.

a sock

tissue paper

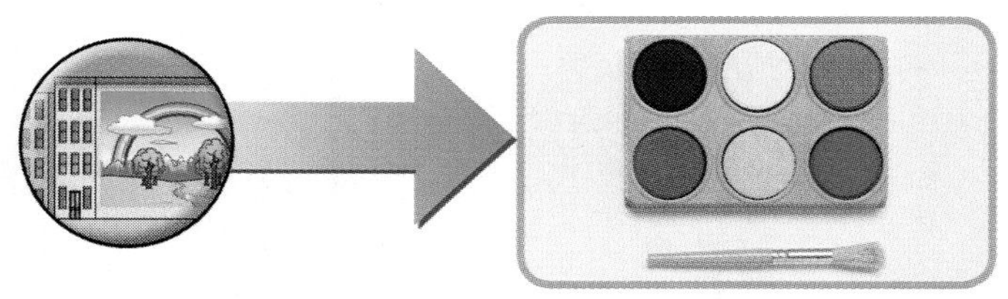

a paintbrush *and* **paints**

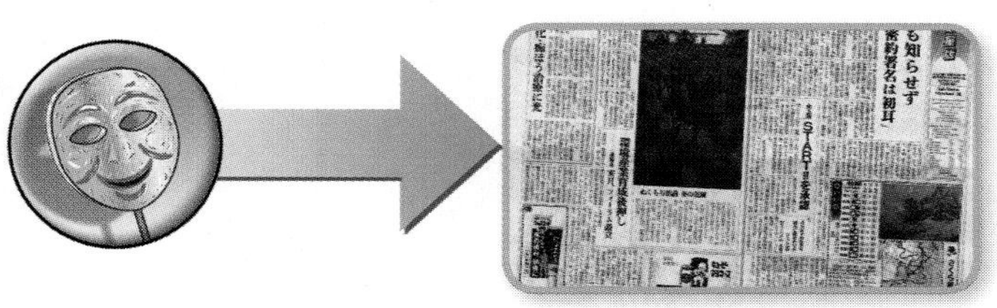

newspaper *and* **paste**

Your Stories about Arts Festivals

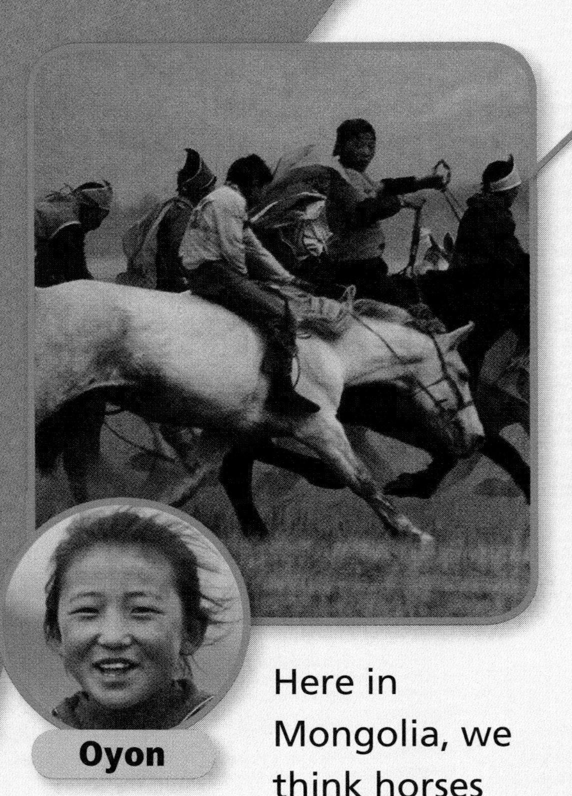

Here in Mongolia, we think horses are very important. We have horse races. We also celebrate horses in art. For the Rainbow Horse Festival, artists made 88 horse sculptures. Children painted the horse sculptures. It was a great festival.

Stacey

There is a big storytelling festival where I live in Tennessee. People come from all over to tell stories. The storytellers make us laugh. They tell tales about the past. Children can also tell stories at the festival.

Aidan

I live in Galway, Ireland. There is an arts festival for children. We go to see musicians, actors, and dancers. Then they teach us how to be artists, too! At the festival, my sister learned to play an Irish drum.

I live in Anguilla, in the Caribbean Sea. We have an arts festival. Artists from around the world show their paintings. There is a contest for the best one. The winner's picture is put on a postage stamp.

What about you?

1. What kind of art do you like to make or see?
2. How are these students' stories similar to yours?
3. Do you have other stories about arts festivals? Tell your story!

Reading 1

ARTS FESTIVAL!

Key Words

festival

annual

advertise

schedule

supplies

Vocabulary

Arts Festival! **tells about a big event in the town of Red Tree.**

Words in Context

1 My neighborhood has a Cinco de Mayo **festival**. It is like a big party. We celebrate our Mexican history. There is delicious food. The festival is an **annual** event. It happens once a year.

2 This is a poster to **advertise** a dance at a school. People will see the poster and come to the dance.

3 This **schedule** tells what Class 3-A does each morning.

4 Here are some of my school **supplies**. I have pencils, a pencil sharpener, an eraser, and a ruler.

3 **Class 3-A Morning Schedule**

8:30–8:45 Morning Greeting

8:45–9:30 Science

9:30–10:15 Art

10:15–11:00 Math

11:00–12:00 Reading

12:00–12:45 Lunch

4

Practice

Use each key word in a sentence.

Make Connections

What art do you like to make? Do you like to draw, dance, or sing? Tell what you would do at an arts festival.

Academic Words

illustrate
make something clear by giving examples

available
easy to get

pages 133–134

Reading 1

FUNCTIONAL WRITING

Poster • Schedule • Business Letter

The Big Question

Why is it important to advertise an arts festival?

Reading Strategy

Identify Author's Purpose

An author is a writer. Authors write for different reasons.

- An author may write to tell about something.
- An author may write to get readers to do something.
- An author may write something for readers to enjoy.
- As you read, look for the author's purpose.

ARTS FESTIVAL!

by Rouenna Albright

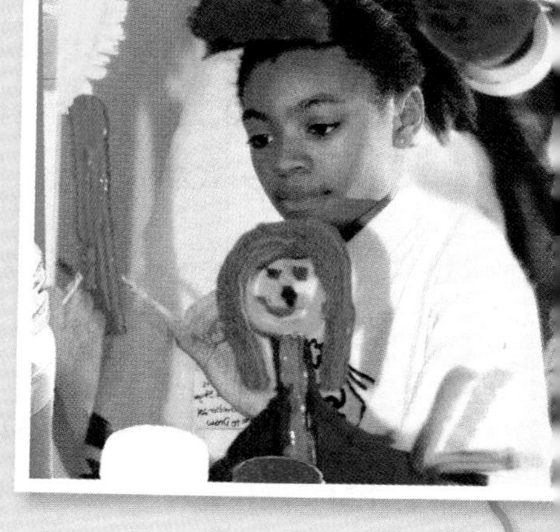

The town of Red Tree has an arts festival each year. It is called the Summer Arts Festival. All the people in the town come.

Children and adults can take art classes. They can go to a demonstration to learn how to make pottery or a collage.

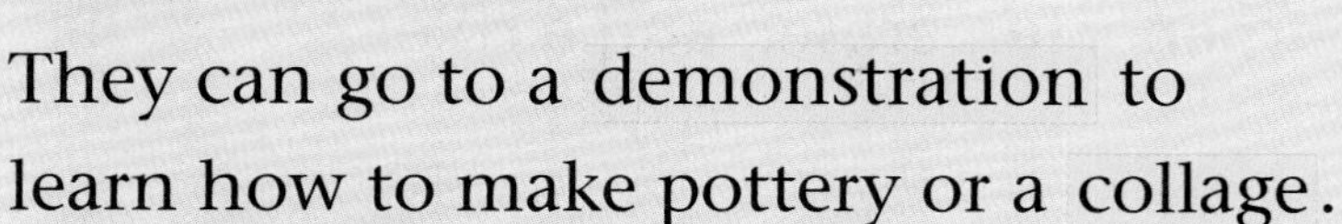

People work together to get ready for the arts festival. One person makes a poster. Another person makes a schedule. Ms. Tan, the art teacher, writes a letter.

adults fully grown people

demonstration showing how to do something

collage picture made by sticking different pictures onto a surface

Poster

This poster tells about the arts festival. It tells what day the festival is. It tells where the festival will be. The poster helps advertise the festival. People put up posters around Red Tree. Other people will see the posters. They will want to come to the festival.

Come to the
Summer Arts Festival!

When? Saturday, June 3, 10 AM
Where? The Middle School Field and Gym
What? Art Activities for All Ages

AND The Great Puppet-Making Contest
Make your own puppet. Win a prize.

Join your friends and neighbors
at the festival.

How will the poster help advertise the festival?

Business Letter

Ms. Tan writes a formal letter. In her letter, Ms. Tan asks for a donation to the festival.

---

donation something someone gives

Ms. Jun Tan
Red Tree Arts Center
233 Ferry Road
Red Tree, CA 92688

May 14, 2010

Ms. Kay Cork
Cork Arts and Crafts
531 South Drive
Red Tree, CA 92688

Dear Ms. Cork,

The Summer Arts Festival will take place in June. This year, there will be a puppet-making contest. Anyone can enter.

I am writing to ask for your help. We need art supplies for making puppets. We need colored paper, paste, crayons, and markers.

Many people in Red Tree come to the festival. Your donation would be a great way to advertise the store. It will also help the artists of Red Tree!

Thank you,

Jun Tan
Art Teacher

Schedule of Events

This schedule tells when events will take place.

Summer Arts Festival

10:00	Morning Classes Painting Drawing Crafts
11:00	Pottery Demonstration
12:00	Family Painting Class
1:00	Afternoon Classes Painting Drawing Pottery
2:00	Collage Demonstration
3:00	Puppet-Making Contest
4:00	Art Show Prizes for Best Puppets

pages 135–136

Reading Strategy

Identify Author's Purpose

- Think about the poster, schedule, and letter. What was each author's purpose?
- How did looking for the author's purpose help you to understand?

Think It Over

1. Where does the Summer Arts Festival take place?
2. What time is the pottery demonstration?
3. Why does Ms. Tan ask for art supplies in her letter?

Phonics & Fluency

Phonics

Diphthongs: *ou, ow*

Read the words. Listen for the vowel sounds.

ou	*ow*
out sound	how brown

Rule Box

The diphthongs *ou* and *ow* have the sound you hear in ***house***.

Practice

Read the sentences with a partner. Take turns.

- Our town is Red Tree.
- How do you make a puppet?
- I will use this brown yarn.
- She drew a mouth on the face.
- Find out what you can do!

1. List words with *ou*.
2. List words with *ow*.
3. Add three more words to each list.

page 137

Fluency

Look Ahead

Sometimes readers look for hard words before they read. Then they try to figure them out.

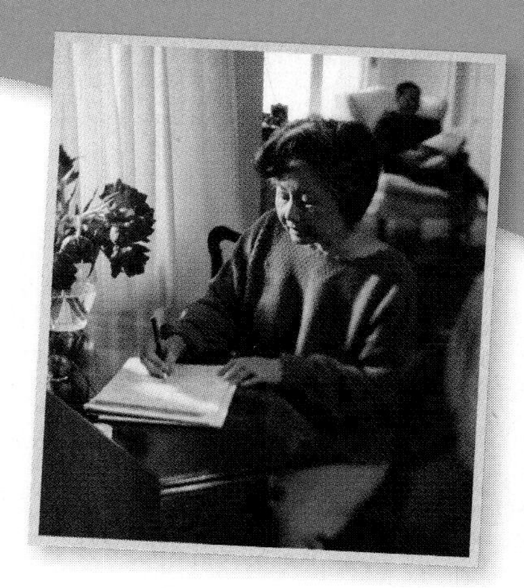

Practice

Pick one passage.	Find any hard words.	Practice saying those words.	Read the passage aloud.

1 Each year, the town of Red Tree has an arts festival. The people get ready for the festival in many ways.

2 People work together to get ready for the arts festival. One person makes a poster. Another person makes a schedule. Ms. Tan, the art teacher, writes a letter.

3 This poster tells about the arts festival. It tells what day the festival is. It tells where the festival will be. The poster helps advertise the festival. People put up posters around Red Tree. Other people will see the posters. They will want to come to the festival.

Reading 1

Comprehension

Author's Purpose

Authors have different reasons for writing. Here are ways to find the **author's purpose**.

If the selection . . .		the author's purpose is to
tells about something,	→	inform.
tries to get the reader to do something,	→	persuade.
is written for the reader to enjoy,	→	entertain.

Learning Strategy

Summarize

Summarize the selection for a partner.

Ask your partner to respond to the Big Question for this reading.

page 138

Practice

Think about the parts of *Arts Festival!* Tell if the author's purpose is to inform, persuade, or entertain.

1. The Summer Arts Festival poster
2. The Summer Arts Festival schedule
3. Jun Tan's formal letter

Use a T-Chart

You can use a T-Chart to show the author's purpose.

Practice

Copy the T-Chart. Fill in each author's purpose. Then fill in the author's purpose for passages 1, 2, and 3 below.

Selection	Author's Purpose
poster	inform
schedule	
formal letter	
1.	
2.	
3.	

1. Larry hopped into the room. It was his first day. The children looked at him. Some of them laughed. Larry did not care. He was happy to be the first rabbit to take art class.

2. We should have art every day. Then we would have more time to paint. We would also learn more about painting.

3. Painting is an old form of art. People have used paints for more than 20,000 years. The first paintings were in a cave.

Extension

Reread the passage about Larry (Number 1). Create a story that tells what Larry does in art class. Share it with a partner.

Reading 1

Grammar & Writing

Commas in a Series

You can list things in a sentence. Put commas after each item in the list.

Bring a ruler, an eraser, and a pencil to school.

Do not put a comma after the last thing in the list.

Practice

Write each sentence. Use commas after each item in the list.

1. I will work at the fair on Friday Saturday and Sunday.
2. This year we are selling shirts baseball caps and posters.
3. My brother sister and uncle will be there on Saturday.

page 139

Write a Formal Letter

You can write a formal letter to ask to do something. Jahaira wrote this letter.

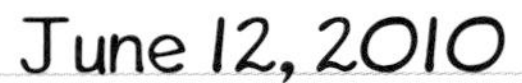
June 12, 2010

Ms. Jun Tan
233 Ferry Road
Red Tree, CA 92688

Dear Ms. Tan,
My grandmother is teaching me how to paint on bark cloth. May we give a class at the Arts Festival? We would bring the materials. Children would like to learn this.

Sincerely,
Jahaira Zepeda

SPELLING TIP

In some words, *sch* spells the sound /sk/.

school schedule

page 140

Practice

Write a formal letter asking to do something.

- Tell what you would like to do.
- Tell why you think it is a good idea.
- Use the correct parts of a letter.

Writing Checklist

- ✓ Did you tell what you would like to do?
- ✓ Did you tell why you think it is a good idea?
- ✓ Did you use the correct parts of a letter?
- ✓ Can a partner understand your letter?

Vocabulary

How to Make Puppets tells how to make a puppet.

Key Words

puppets
scissors
stapler
yarn
buttons

Words in Context

1. **Puppets** can be big or small. Some you move with strings. Some can fit on your fingers.

2. Some **scissors** cut paper. Other scissors cut cloth.

3 A **stapler** is a useful tool. This boy staples pieces of paper to make a paper chain.

4 They are knitting with **yarn**. The grandmother helps the girl.

5 **Buttons** come in many shapes and sizes. Would you like these buttons on a shirt?

Practice

Use each key word in a sentence.

Make Connections

Do you like to make crafts? What would you make with yarn, buttons, and cloth?

Academic Words

contribute
give money or help

design
drawing or plan

pages 141–142

FUNCTIONAL WRITING

Directions

Why is it important to read directions to make a craft?

Reading Strategy

Set a Purpose for Reading

As you read, think about your purpose for reading.

- You can read to have fun.
- You can read to learn new facts or ideas.
- You can read to learn how to do something.

How to Make Puppets

by Pravina Cole

People have been making puppets for thousands of years. Children like to play with puppets. People can use puppets to tell stories, too.

Do you know how to make a puppet? You can learn. Read the directions. First, you need to gather the supplies.

---

gather get things and put them together

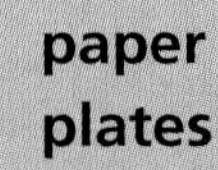

What You Will Need

white paper plates

scissors

stapler

glue

yarn

buttons

colored paper

crayons, markers, or paint

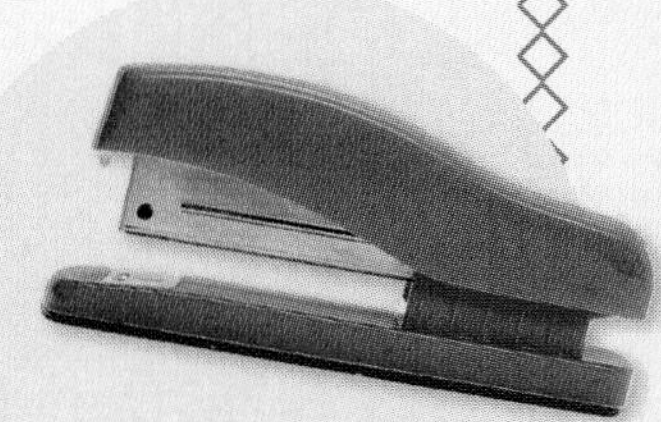

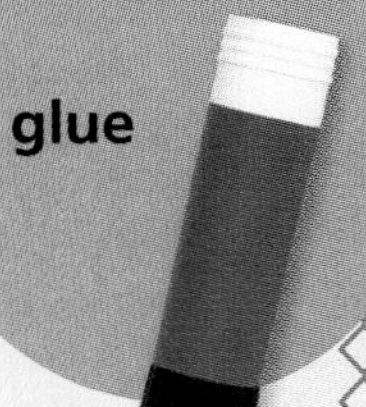

What things do you need to make a puppet?

1. Staple two paper plates together. The top of the plates should face inside. Do not staple all the way around. Leave a space at the bottom open.

2. With scissors, cut off the bottom part of the top paper plate. This will make a place for you to put your hand.

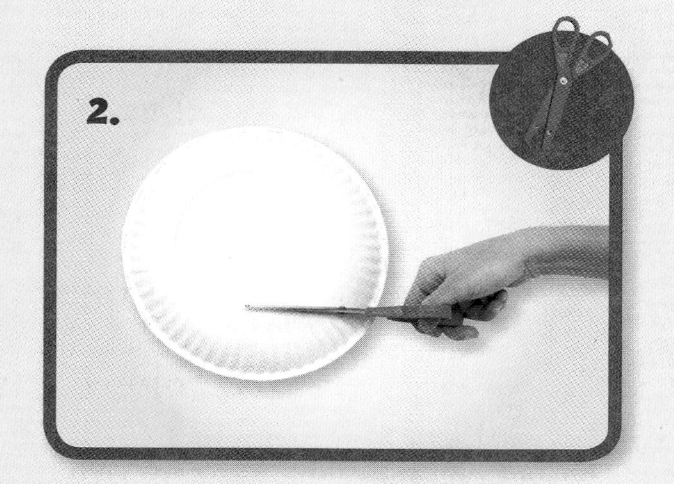

3. Use buttons and colored paper. Use crayons, paint, or markers. Make eyes, a nose, and a mouth for your puppet. Use yarn or paper to make hair or a hat.

4. Now you have made a puppet. Put your hand inside the space between the two paper plates. You can move the puppet by moving your hand.

Can you make your puppet talk? What will it say?

Use your puppet to put on a show or to tell a story.

pages 143–144

Reading Strategy

Set a Purpose for Reading

- What was your purpose for reading this selection?
- How did thinking about your purpose for reading help you understand the selection?

Think It Over

1. What can you use to make a face on a puppet?
2. What can you use to add hair to a puppet?
3. How can you make a puppet move?

A Closer Look at...

Puppets

▲ **Puppeteer**

The person who works a puppet is a puppeteer. This puppeteer and puppet are in India.

▲ **Sock puppet**

A sock puppet is easy to make. You just need a clean sock and some buttons.

▲ **Shadow puppets**

This is a shadow puppet show in Indonesia. Can you see the sticks? Puppeteers use the sticks to move the puppets.

▲ Behind the stage

These puppeteers watch their puppets on a video screen. They can see the stage during the show.

▲ Marionette

Marionettes are puppets that hang from strings. When the puppeteer moves the strings, the puppet moves.

▲ Puppets that teach

These puppets help teach children about people with physical challenges. One puppet is in a wheelchair. The other cannot see.

Activity to Do!

These two pages use pictures and words to tell about puppets.

- Choose another toy.
- Find pictures to show that toy.
- Post your pictures and captions in your classroom.

Word Analysis & Fluency

Word Analysis

Use a Dictionary

Read this dictionary entry.

gath • er (gath ər) verb **1** to bring or come together <gather your things>. **2** to gain little by little <gather speed>. **3** to come to a conclusion <gather that you're going>. **gathered**, **gathering**.

Practice

Work with a partner.

- The entry for **gather** has more than one meaning.
- Find the meaning that makes sense in each sentence.

1. Anna started to **gather** speed on her bike.
2. **Gather** your school supplies.
3. I **gather** that this selection is about making puppets.

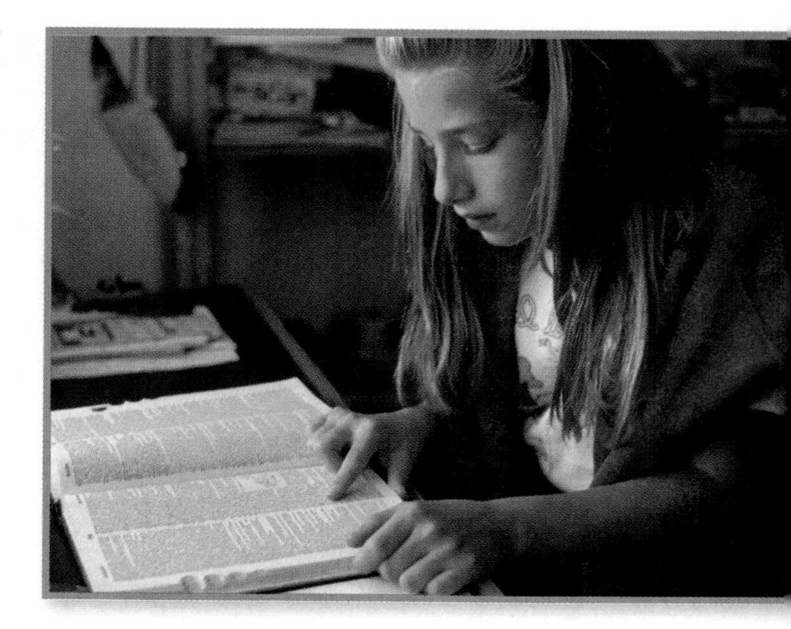

page 145

Fluency

Read for Speed and Accuracy

You should read quickly. But never read so quickly that you lose your understanding.

Read for one minute. → **Count the words you read.** → **Study any hard words.** → **Read and count again.**

Do you know how to make a puppet? You can learn. 11
Read the directions. First you need to gather the supplies. 21

1. Put two paper plates together. The top of the plates 31
   should face inside. Staple the paper plates together 39
   around the edges. Do not staple all the way around. 49
   Leave a space at the bottom open. 56
2. With scissors, cut off the bottom part of the top 66
   paper plate. This will make a place for you to put 77
   your hand. 79
3. Use buttons and colored paper. Use crayons, paint, 87
   or markers. Make eyes, a nose, and a mouth for 97
   your puppet. 99
4. Use yarn or paper to make hair or a hat. 109

Now you have made a puppet. Put your hand inside 119
the space between the two paper plates. You can move 129
the puppet by moving your hand. 135

Comprehension

Learning Strategy

Summarize

Summarize the selection for a partner.

Ask your partner to respond to the Big Question for this reading.

page 146

Purpose for Reading

You read different selections for different reasons.

Your **purpose for reading** may be
- to enjoy reading.
- to learn new facts or ideas.
- to learn how to do something.

Practice

Look back at the selection. Find clues that tell your purpose for reading.

1. Read the title. What does it tell you about the selection?
2. What do you learn in steps 1, 2, and 3?
3. What can you do when you put your hand between the two plates?
4. What is your purpose for reading?

Use a Sequence Chart

To make a puppet, you have to follow the steps in the right order.

Practice

Complete this Sequence Chart. List the steps given below in the right order.

- Cut off the bottom part of the top paper plate. This will make a place for you to put your hand.
- Place your hand inside the space between the two paper plates. You can move the puppet by moving your hand.
- Staple the paper plates together around the edges. Leave a space at the bottom open.
- Make eyes, a nose, and a mouth for your puppet. Add hair or a hat.

Gather supplies.
↓
↓
↓
↓
↓
Use your puppet to put on a show or to tell a story.

Grammar & Writing

Directive Sentences

Directive sentences tell the reader to do something.

Put two paper plates together.

Staple the paper plates together around the edges.

Practice

Read the paragraph below. Copy the directive sentences. There will be five directive sentences.

Making Animal Puppets

What is your favorite animal? Draw a small picture of the animal. Is it happy or sad? Show a smile or frown on its face. What color is your animal? Color it. Next, use scissors to cut out your picture. Tape the back of the animal picture to the pencil.

page 147

Write Directions

You write directions to explain how to do something. You have to tell the steps in order. Read Raul's directions.

Breaking the Piñata

1. Fill a piñata with candy. Hang it from a tree.
2. Put a blindfold on one child.
3. Give the child a stick. Spin the child around three times. Then the child tries to hit the piñata.
4. Give each child a turn.
5. When the piñata breaks, children can run to get the candy.

SPELLING TIP

The letter *g* has the /j/ sound when it is followed by an *e*, an *i*, or a *y*.

gentle	age
giant	gym

page 148

Practice

Tell how to play a game you know. Write a title. List the steps to play the game. Use directive sentences!

Writing Checklist

- ✓ Did you write a title?
- ✓ Did you write the steps in order?
- ✓ Did you use directive sentences?
- ✓ Can a partner understand how to play the game?

Vocabulary

***The Music Goes On* tells about a festival with music and dance.**

Key Words

microphone
guitar
trumpet
performer
soles
rhythm

Words in Context

1 The men sing into a **microphone**. It makes their voices louder.

2 These boys play **guitar** in a city in Mexico.

3 This boy plays **trumpet**. He is a **performer** in his high school band.

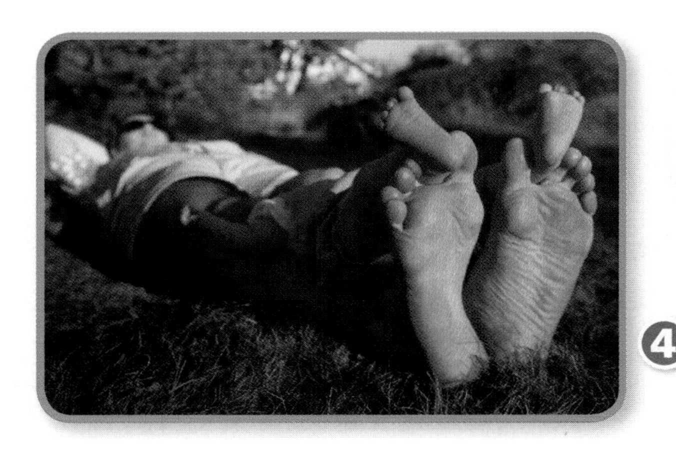

④ The bottoms of feet are called **soles**. The bottoms of shoes are called soles, too.

⑤ The drummer keeps the **rhythm** of a song. A rhythm is a pattern of beats.

Practice

Use each key word in a sentence.

Make Connections

Where does your family come from? What special music comes from there? What special dances? Ask a family member to tell you about these traditions.

Academic Words

source
where something comes from

select
choose by thinking carefully

pages 149–150

FUNCTIONAL WRITING

Newspaper Article

Can music and dance be part of an arts festival? Why?

Reading Strategy

Draw Conclusions

To draw a conclusion from what you read, put together details from the selection.

- Where do the performers live?
- What countries do the music and dance they perform come from?
- What can you conclude about the people who live in River City?

The Music Goes On

by Tony Paschall

Last week, people who love music went to River City Park. The River City Music Festival gave them special sounds and sights. People heard great music. They saw beautiful dancers.

This year, the festival had an international theme. The music and dance came from many different countries.

Larry Dodd played trumpet at the River City Music Festival.

---

international about more than one country

theme main idea

The Firehouse band played on Main Street.

The festival began on Saturday morning. Larry Dodd played a trumpet solo. The crowd loved it. Then, his jazz group joined him. They played many popular jazz songs.

Later, Larry said, "I was nervous but happy."

The Jalisco Mariachi Band played in the afternoon. Each member wore the clothing and sombrero of a Mexican cowboy. Gaspar Vargas was the leader. He sang and played guitar.

On Main Street, happy crowds listened to the Firehouse Brass Quartet. Firefighters started this band many years ago. They play at the festival every year.

The Jalisco Mariachi Band played a favorite song, "La Cucaracha."

solo piece of music that only one person plays

jazz a type of music with strong beats and solo parts

sombrero a Mexican hat with a wide, round edge

Check Up Where do you think the Jalisco Mariachi Band comes from? Why?

Shakira Gopal performed an Indian dance.

Step dancers moved to Irish music.

Young people are an important part of the festival. Many girls and boys sang, danced, and played music.

River City's Shakira Gopal performed a dance from India. Shakira said, "My family loves music. My mother taught me to dance. My father plays the *sitar* and a drum called the *tabla*."

The step dancers of the Irish Culture Center stamped the soles of their shoes to the beat of wild Irish music.

Young drummer Jorge Alameda excited the crowds with thrilling Latin rhythms.

---

performed showed to an audience

sitar stringed musical instrument from India

stamped put your foot down hard

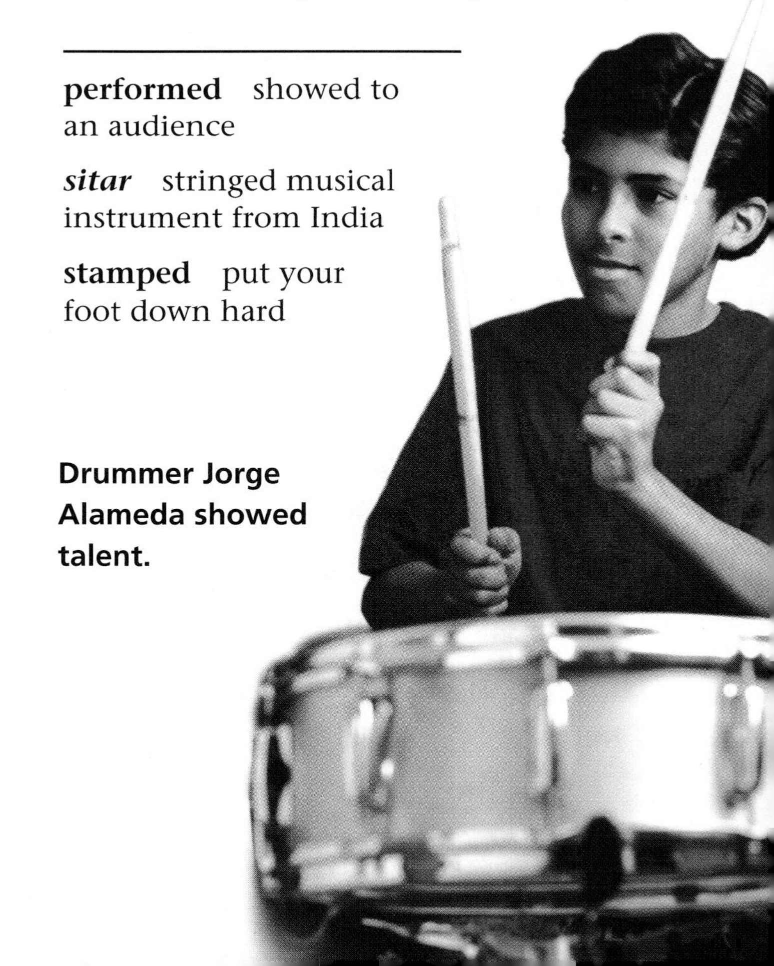

Drummer Jorge Alameda showed talent.

In his first time at the microphone, singer Mike Chen looked like a future star. He wrote the words and music for his songs.

In the evening, local rock-and-roll bands played for two hours. The River City Music Festival ended Sunday night with dancing and cheers. But as any music lover will tell you, the music goes on.

Mike Chen sang his own songs.

pages 151–152

Reading Strategy

Draw Conclusions

- What can you conclude about the people who live in River City?
- What led you to that conclusion?

Think It Over

1. What is a *tabla*?
2. What did the step dancers do?
3. How did dancers fit the theme of the festival?

Word Analysis & Fluency

Word Analysis

Multi-Syllable Words

Read the words in the chart.

1 Syllable	2 Syllables	3 Syllables
jazz	lead/er	af/ter/noon
my	head/ed	beau/ti/ful
theme	trum/pet	Sat/ur/day

Rule Box

Each syllable has one vowel sound. The vowel sound may be spelled with more than one vowel letter.

Practice

Work with a partner. Make a chart with three columns like the one above.

- Write each word below in the correct column.
- Add two new words to each column.

tradition	music	crowd	festival	great
microphone	drum	solo	dancers	

page 153

Fluency

Read with Expression

When you read aloud, use your voice to show feelings.

Practice

Read silently.	Read aloud.	Get comments.	Read aloud again.

Young people are an important part of the festival. Many girls and boys sang, danced, and played music.

River City's Shakira Gopal performed a traditional dance from India. Shakira said, "My family loves music. My mother taught me to dance. My father plays the *sitar* and a drum called the *tabla*."

The step dancers of the Irish Culture Center stamped the soles of their shoes to the beat of wild Irish music.

Young drummer Jorge Alameda excited the crowds with thrilling Latin rhythm.

Reading 3

Comprehension

Draw a Conclusion

To **draw a conclusion**, use details from the selection to make your own ideas. The 5 W questions can help you identify important details. The 5 W questions are *who, what, where, when,* and *why*.

Learning Strategy

Summarize

Summarize the selection to a partner.

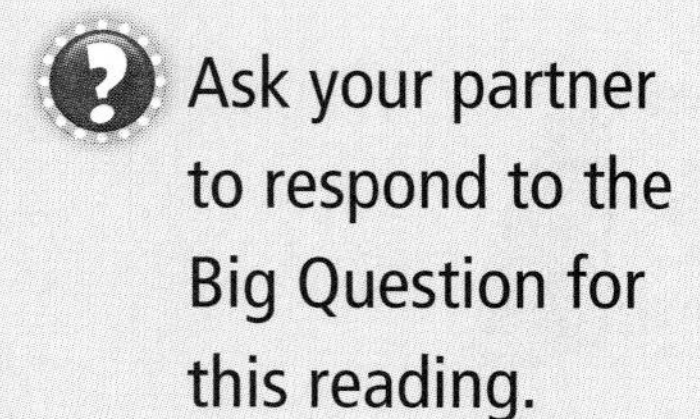

Ask your partner to respond to the Big Question for this reading.

Practice

Answer the questions. Try to draw a conclusion about the performers.

- Who are the performers in the Firehouse Brass Quartet?
- How many times had Mike Chen performed before?
- What can you conclude about the performers? Do you think they are paid, or do they make music just for fun?
- Explain how you reached that conclusion.

page 154

Use a 5 W Chart

Use a 5 W Chart to ask questions about the River City Music Festival.

Practice

Copy the chart. Use your answers to draw a conclusion about the music festival.

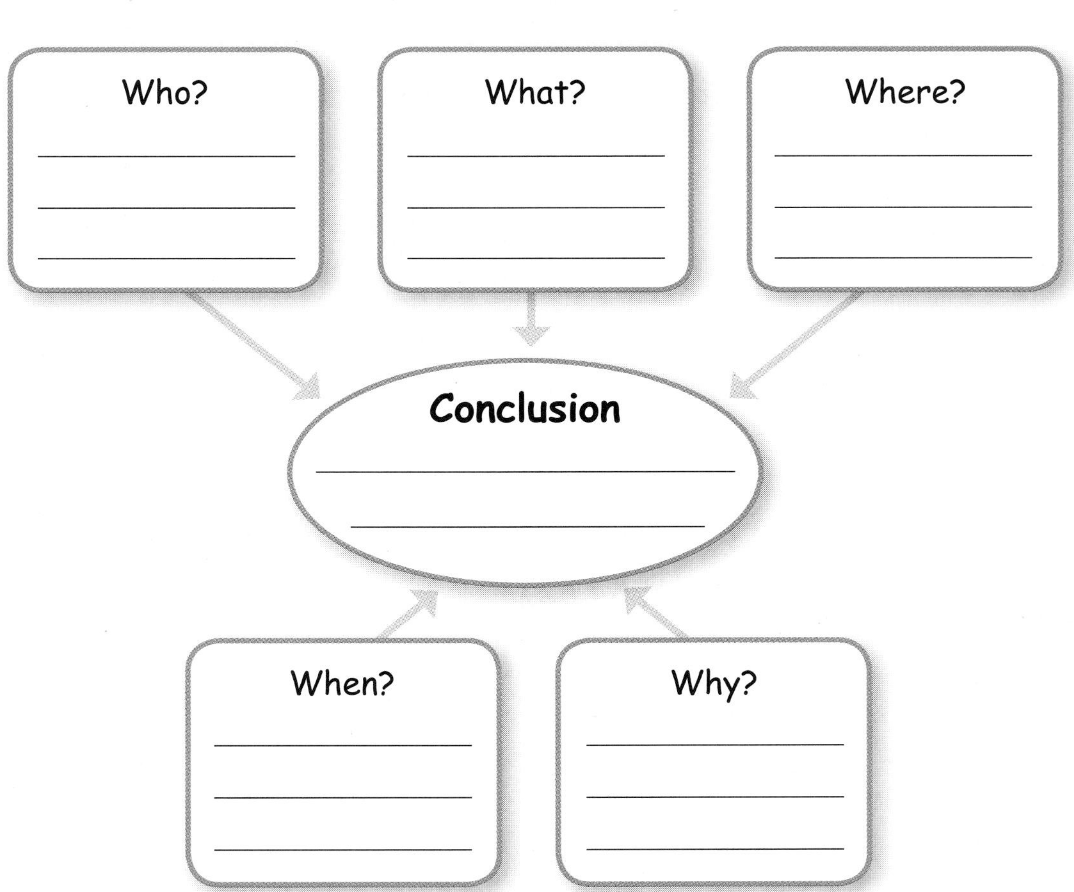

Extension

Create a dance that shows how you feel about your family. You may want to have music, too. Perform your dance for the class.

Reading 3

Grammar & Writing

Direct Quotation

A **direct quotation** tells the exact words a person said.

> **Larry said,** "I got my start at the festival."
>
> "My mother taught me to dance," **Shakira said.**

Rule Box

Each sentence has two parts. One part tells who is talking. The other part tells what the person said. The quotation marks show the words that are being said. A comma separates the two parts.

Practice

Copy the sentences. Add quotation marks to show the direct quotations.

1. Julia said, I want to be a drummer someday.
2. I can teach you how to play, said Jorge.
3. How long do you think it will take to learn? she asked.
4. Jorge said, Many years.

page 155

Write a Newspaper Article

Angie wrote this newspaper article. She answered the 5 W questions. She used direct quotations.

LAKE PARK, MN May 20—
Mrs. Brown's class has a snail garden! The class keeps the snails in an empty fish bowl. They are learning what snails like to eat.

"I thought it would be yucky," said Lisa. "But it's fun."

Bruce said, "Having a snail on my hand felt strange."

Mrs. Brown said that the class has had the snails for three weeks. "They are easy to keep," she said. "And the children think of new things to find out about snails."

SPELLING TIP

You can type your article on a computer. Use the spell check to check your spelling. But be careful. The spell check does not find everything.

page 156

Practice

Write a newspaper article.

- Tell about something that happened at your school.
- Answer the 5 W questions.
- Include a direct quotation in your story.
- Indent each paragraph.

Writing Checklist

- ✓ Does your article tell what happened?
- ✓ Did you tell *who, what, where, when*, and *why*?
- ✓ Did you use a direct quotation?
- ✓ Can a partner understand your newspaper article?

My Journal

by Neva Crespo

The art fair was great!

We got to make masks of our faces. Mr. Okawa showed us how.

At first, I was scared. I was afraid making a mask would be too messy. But I tried it. It was fun!

Then we painted the masks. I painted my mask blue, green, red, and yellow.

It's a cool mask. I will hang it on my wall.

We made painted animals using boxes and things. We used clay to make pots. The most fun was making a big painting. Ms. Burns drew a plan for the picture on a piece of paper. Then we helped her paint it. We all got to add our own ideas. The painting will hang in our school all year. Next year, we will make another.

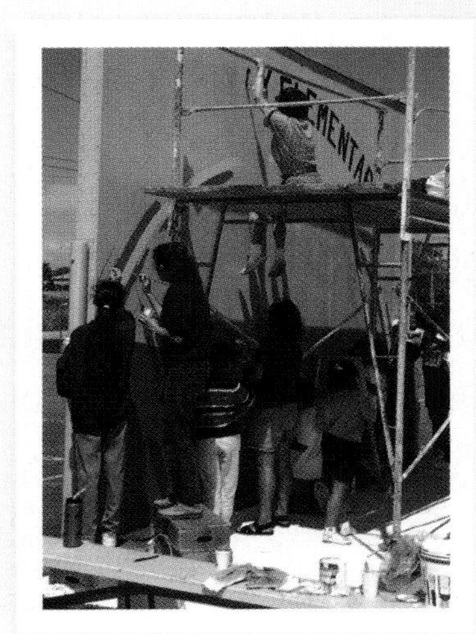

I like to make any kind of art. But I think I like painting the most.

UNIT 6 Wrap Up

The Big Question

What can be shown or take place at an arts festival?

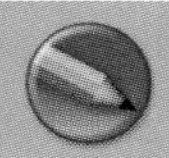

Written

Invitation

Write a letter to a neighbor. Invite your neighbor to a school arts festival. Tell why it will be fun to come to the festival.

Festival Story

Write a story about a girl or boy who goes to an arts festival. Describe what your character sees and does at the festival.

Oral

Group Plan

Work with a group. Plan an arts festival at your school. Plan what art you want to have and how to display it. Plan what will go on. Present your plan to your class.

Artist Interview

Interview an artist in your community. Ask about what the artist has made and shown. Make a list of questions. Then tell the class about the artist's work.

Visual/Active

Advertising Poster

Make a poster to advertise an arts festival. Answer the 5 W questions in your poster.

Festival Collage

Find photos of artwork on the Internet or in magazines. Make a collage of all different kinds of art that might be displayed at an arts festival.

✓ Learning Checklist

Word Analysis and Phonics

- ✓ Read words with the diphthongs *ou, ow.*
- ✓ Use a dictionary.
- ✓ Read multi-syllable words.

Comprehension

- ✓ Identify author's purpose.
- ✓ Use a T-Chart.
- ✓ Set a purpose for reading.
- ✓ Use a Sequence Chart.
- ✓ Draw a conclusion.
- ✓ Use the 5 W Chart.

Grammar and Writing

- ✓ Recognize and use commas in a series.
- ✓ Recognize directive sentences.
- ✓ Recognize and write a direct quotation.
- ✓ Write a formal letter.
- ✓ Write directions.
- ✓ Write a newspaper article.

Self-Evaluation Questions

- What have you learned about arts festivals?
- What questions do you still have about arts festivals?
- What work are you most proud of doing in this unit?

Handbook

How to Learn Language

Learning a language involves listening, speaking, reading, and writing. You can use these tips to make the most of your language learning.

LISTENING

1. Listen with a purpose.
2. Listen actively.
3. Take notes.
4. Listen to speakers on the radio, television, and Internet.

SPEAKING

1. Think before you speak.
2. Speak appropriately for your audience.
3. Practice reading aloud to a partner.
4. Practice speaking with friends and family members.
5. Remember, it is okay to make mistakes.

READING

1. Read every day.
2. Use the visuals to help you figure out what words mean.
3. Reread parts that you do not understand.
4. Read many kinds of literature.
5. Ask for help.

WRITING

1. Write something every day.
2. Plan your writing before you begin.
3. Read what you write aloud. Ask yourself whether it makes sense.
4. Check for spelling and grammar mistakes.

How to Study

Here are some tips for developing good study habits.

- **Schedule a time for studying.** It is easier to develop good study habits if you set aside the same time every day to study. Once you have a study routine, it will be easier for you to find time to prepare for larger projects or tests.
- **Create a special place for studying.** Find a study area where you are comfortable and where you have everything you need for studying. If possible, choose an area that is away from telephones or television. You can play music if it helps you to concentrate.
- **Read the directions first.** Make sure you understand what you are supposed to do. Ask a partner or your teacher about anything you do not understand.
- **Preview the reading.** Look at the pictures, illustrations, and captions in the reading. They will help you understand the text.
- **Learn unfamiliar words.** Try to figure out what unfamiliar words mean by finding context clues in the reading. If you still can't figure out the meaning, use a dictionary.
- **Take notes.** Keep notes in a notebook or journal of important things you want to remember from the reading.
- **Ask questions.** Write any questions you have from the reading. Discuss them with a partner or your teacher.

How to Build Vocabulary

Use these ideas to help you remember the meanings of new words.

Keep a Vocabulary Notebook Keep a notebook of vocabulary words and their definitions. Test yourself by covering either the word or the definition.

Make Flashcards On the front of an index card, write a word you want to remember. On the back, write the meaning. Use the cards to review the words with a partner or family member.

Say the Words Aloud Use your new words in sentences. Say the sentences to a partner or a family member.

How to Use a Book

The Title Page The title page states the title, the author, and the publisher.

The Table of Contents The table of contents is at the front of a book. The page on which a chapter begins is next to its name.

The Glossary The glossary is a small dictionary at the back of a book. It will tell you the meaning of a word, and sometimes how to pronounce it. Use the glossary the same way you would use a dictionary.

The Index The index is at the back of a book. It lists subjects and names that are in the book, along with page numbers where you can find information.

The Bibliography The bibliography at the back of a book or chapter lets you know the books or sources where an author got information.

How to Use a Dictionary and Thesaurus

The Dictionary

You can find the **spelling**, **pronunciation**, **part of speech**, and **definitions** of words in the dictionary.

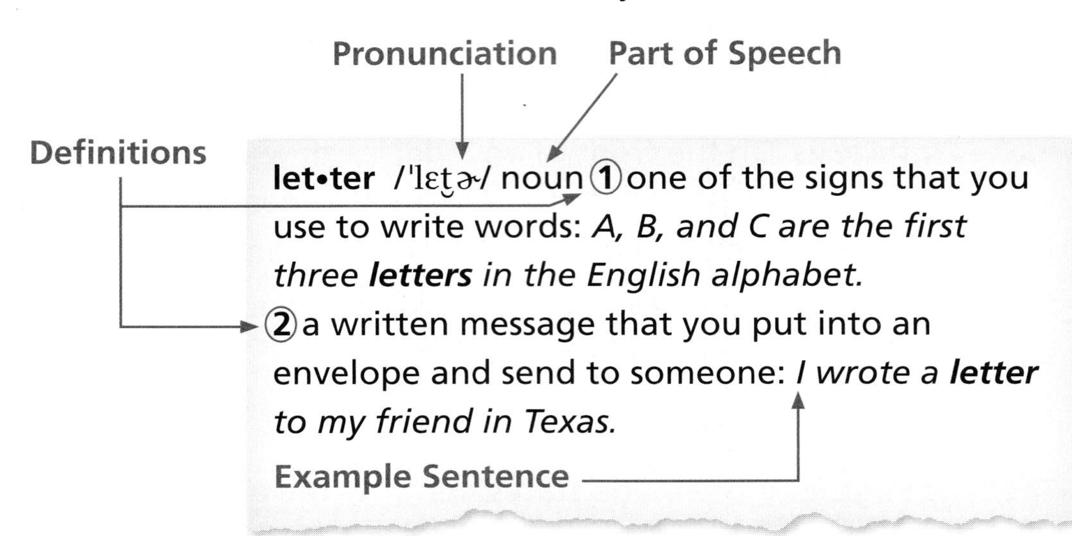

let•ter /ˈlɛt̬ɚ/ noun ① one of the signs that you use to write words: *A, B, and C are the first three **letters** in the English alphabet.*
② a written message that you put into an envelope and send to someone: *I wrote a **letter** to my friend in Texas.*

The Thesaurus

A thesaurus is a specialized dictionary that lists **synonyms**, or words with similar meanings, and **antonyms**, or words with opposite meanings. Words in a thesaurus are arranged alphabetically. You can look up the word just as you would look it up in a dictionary.

Main entry: sad
Part of speech: adjective[1]
Definition: unhappy
Synonyms: bitter, depressed, despairing, down, downcast, gloomy, glum, heartbroken, low, melancholy, morose, pessimistic, sorry, troubled, weeping
Antonyms: cheerful, happy

How to Take Tests

Taking tests is part of going to school. Use these tips to help you answer the kinds of questions you often see on tests.

True-False Questions

- If a statement seems true, make sure it is *all* true.
- The word *not* can change the meaning of a statement.
- Pay attention to words such as *all*, *always*, *never*, *no*, *none*, and *only*. They often make a statement false.
- Words such as *generally*, *much*, *many*, *sometimes*, and *usually* often make a statement true.

Multiple Choice Questions

- Try to answer the question before reading the choices. If your answer is one of the choices, choose it.
- Eliminate answers you know are wrong.
- Don't change your answer unless you know it is wrong.

Matching Questions

- Count each group to see whether any items will be left over.
- Read all the items before you start matching.
- Match the items you know first.

Fill-In-the-Blank Questions or Completions

- Read the question or incomplete sentence carefully.
- Look for clues in the question or sentence that might help you figure out the answer.
- If you are given possible answers, cross each out as you use it.

Short Answers and Essays

- Take a few minutes to organize your thoughts.
- Give only the information that is asked for.
- Answer as clearly as possible.
- Leave time to proofread your response or essay.

How to Read Maps and Diagrams

Informational texts often use maps, diagrams, graphs, and charts. These tools help illustrate and explain the topic.

Maps

Maps show the location of places such as countries, states, and cities. They can also show where mountains, rivers, lakes, and streets are located. A compass rose on the map shows which way is north. A scale shows how miles or kilometers are represented on the map.

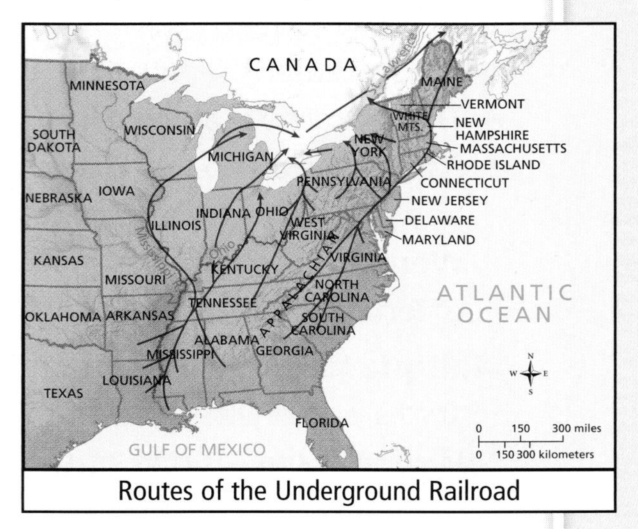

Routes of the Underground Railroad

Diagrams

Diagrams are drawings that explain things or show how things work. Some diagrams show pictures of how objects look on the outside or on the inside. Others show the different steps in a process.

This diagram shows the steps of the Scientific Method. It helps you understand the order and importance of each step.

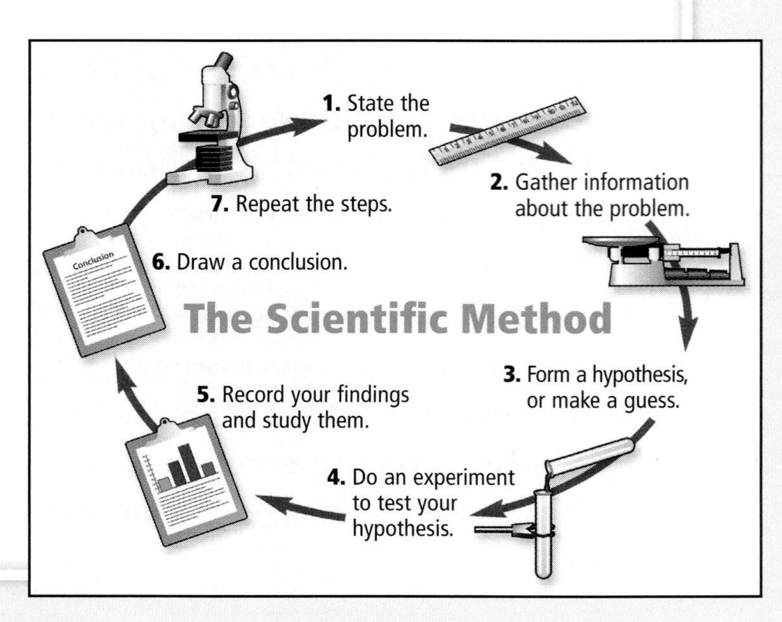

How to Read Graphs

Graphs show how two or more kinds of information are related or alike. Three common kinds of graphs are **line graphs, bar graphs,** and **circle graphs**.

Line Graph

A **line graph** shows how information changes over a period of time. This line graph explains how the Native American population in Central Mexico changed over 100 years.

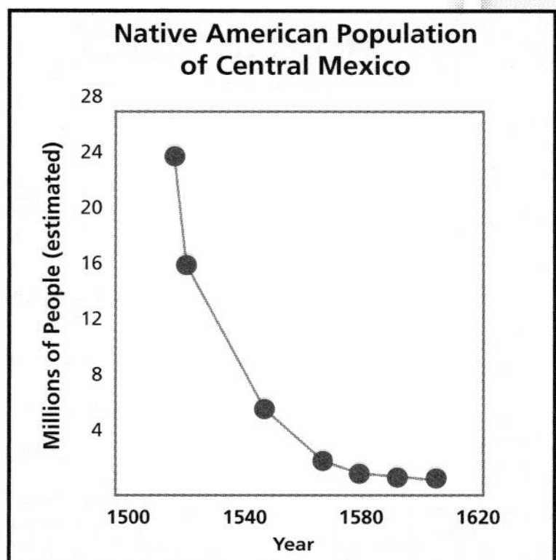

Bar Graphs

We use **bar graphs** to compare information. For example, this bar graph compares the populations of the 13 United States in 1790.

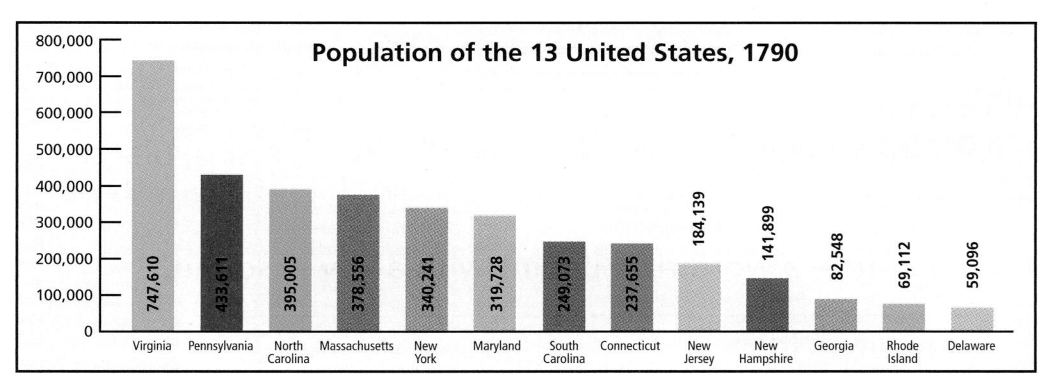

Circle Graphs

A **circle graph** is sometimes called a pie chart because it looks like a pie cut into slices. Circle graphs are used to show how different parts of a whole compare to each other.

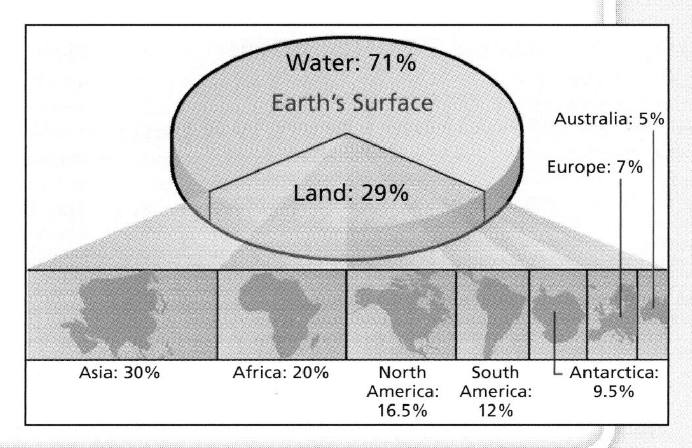

Parts of Speech

In English there are eight **parts of speech**: nouns, pronouns, adjectives, verbs, adverbs, prepositions, conjunctions, and interjections.

Nouns

Nouns name people, places, or things.

A **common noun** is a general person, place, or thing.

> person — thing — place
> The **student** brings a **notebook** to **class**.

A **proper noun** is a specific person, place, or thing.

> person — place — thing
> **Joe** went to **Paris** and saw the **Eiffel Tower**.

Articles

Indefinite articles are *a* or *an*. They refer to a person, place, or thing.

Use *an* before a word that begins with a vowel sound.

> I have **an** idea.

Use *a* before a noun that begins with a consonant sound.

> May I borrow **a** pen?

The is called a **definite article**. Use *the* to talk about specific people, places, or things.

> Please bring me **the** box from your room.

Pronouns

Pronouns are words that take the place of nouns or proper nouns.

proper noun — pronoun
Ana is not home. **She** is babysitting.

	Subject Pronouns	Object Pronouns
Singular	I, you, he, she, it	me, you, him, her, it
Plural	we, you, they	us, you, them

A **subject pronoun** replaces the subject of a sentence. A **subject** is who or what a sentence is about.

subject — subject pronoun (singular)
Dan is a student. **He** goes to school every day.

Object pronouns replace a noun or proper noun that is the object of a verb. An **object** receives the action of a verb.

object — object pronoun (singular)
Lauren gave **Ed** the notes. Lauren gave **him** the notes.

Possessive pronouns replace nouns or proper nouns. They show who owns something.

	Possessive Pronouns
Singular	mine, yours, hers, his
Plural	ours, yours, theirs

Verbs

Verbs express an action or a state of being.

An **action verb** tells what someone or something does or did.

Verbs That Tell Actions You Can See		Verbs That Tell Actions You Cannot See	
dance	swim	know	sense

A **linking verb** shows no action. It links the subject with another word that describes the subject.

Examples of Linking Verbs		
look	smell	is
are	appear	seem

A helping verb comes before the main verb. They add to a verb's meaning.

	Helping Verbs
Forms of the verb *be*	am, was, is, were, are
Forms of the verb *do*	do, did, does
Forms of the verb *have*	have, had, has
Other helping verbs	can, must, could, have (to), should, may, will, would

Adjectives

Adjectives describe nouns. An adjective usually comes before the noun it describes.

tall grass	big truck

An adjective can come *after* the noun it describes. This happens in these kinds of sentences.

> The bag is **heavy**. The books are **new**.

Adverbs

Adverbs describe the action of verbs. They tell *how* an action happens. Adverbs answer the question *Where?, When?, How?, How much?,* or *How often?*

Many adverbs end in *-ly*.

easily	slowly

Some adverbs do not end in *-ly*.

seldom	fast	very

In this sentence, the adverb *everywhere* modifies the verb *looked*. It answers the question *Where?*

> verb adverb
> Nicole looked **everywhere** for her book.

Prepositions

Prepositions show time, place, and direction.

Time	Place	Direction
after before	above below	across down

In this sentence, the preposition *above* shows where the bird flew. It shows place.

preposition
A bird flew **above** my head.

In this sentence, the preposition *across* shows direction.

preposition
The children walked **across** the street.

A **prepositional phrase** starts with a preposition and ends with a noun or pronoun. In this sentence, the preposition is *near* and the noun is *school*.

prepositional phrase
The library is **near the new school**.

Conjunctions

A **conjunction** joins words, groups of words, and whole sentences. Common conjunctions include *and*, *but*, and *or.*

The conjunction *and* joins two proper nouns: *Allison* and *Teresa*.

proper noun — proper noun
Allison **and** Teresa are in school.

The conjunction *or* joins two prepositional phrases: *to the movies* and *to the mall*.

prepositional phrase — prepositional phrase
They want to go to the movies **or** to the mall.

The conjunction *but* joins two independent clauses.

independent clause — independent clause
Alana baked the cookies, **but** Eric made the lemonade.

Interjections

Interjections are words or phrases that express emotion.

Interjections that express strong emotion are followed by an exclamation point.

Wow! Did you see that catch?

A comma follows interjections that express mild emotion.

Gee, I'm sorry that your team lost.

Sentences

Clauses

Clauses are groups of words with a subject and a verb.

- An **independent clause** can stand on its own as a complete sentence.
- A **dependent clause** cannot stand alone as a complete sentence.

Sentences

A simple sentence is an independent clause. It has a subject and a verb.

subject verb
The dog barked.

A **compound sentence** is made up of two or more simple sentences, or independent clauses.

independent clause — independent clause
The band has a lead singer, **but** it needs a drummer.

Sentence Types

Declarative sentences are statements. They end with a period.

We are going to the beach on Saturday.

Interrogative sentences are questions. They end with a question mark.

Will you come with us?

Imperative sentences are commands. They end with a period or an exclamation point.

Put on your life jacket. Now jump in the water!

Exclamatory sentences express strong feeling. They end with an exclamation point.

I swam all the way from the boat to the shore!

Punctuation

End Marks

End marks come at the end of sentences. There are three kinds of end marks: periods, question marks, and exclamation points.

Periods

- Use a period to end a statement (declarative sentence).
- Use a period to end a command or request (imperative sentence).
- Use a period after a person's initial or abbreviated title.
- Use a period after abbreviations.

Question Marks and Exclamation Points

- Use an exclamation point to express strong feelings.
- Use a question mark at the end of a question.

Commas

Commas separate parts of a sentence or phrase.

- Use a comma to separate two independent clauses linked by a conjunction.
- Use commas to separate the parts in a series. A series is a group of three or more words, phrases, or clauses.
- Use a comma to set off introductory words or phrases.
- Use commas to set off an interrupting word or phrase.
- Use a comma to set off a speaker's quoted words.
- Use commas to set off the name of the person being addressed in a letter or speech.

Semicolons and Colons

Semicolons can connect two independent clauses. Use them when the clauses are closely related in meaning or structure.

Colons introduce a list of items or important information. Also use a colon to separate hours and minutes when writing the time.

Quotation Marks

Quotation marks set off direct quotations, dialogue, and some titles.

- Commas and periods always go inside quotation marks.
- If a question mark or exclamation point is not part of the quotation, it goes outside the quotation marks.
- Use quotation marks to set off what people say in a dialogue.
- Use quotation marks around the titles of short works of writing.

Apostrophes

Apostrophes can be used with singular and plural nouns to show ownership or possession. To form the possessive, follow these rules:

- For singular nouns, add an apostrophe and an *s*.
- For singular nouns that end in *s*, add an apostrophe and an *s*.
- For plural nouns that do not end in *s*, add an apostrophe and an *s*.
- For plural nouns that end in *s*, add an apostrophe.
- Apostrophes are also used in contractions, to show where a letter or letters have been taken away.

Capitalization

There are five main reasons to use capital letters:

- to begin a sentence
- to write the pronoun ***I***
- to write the names of proper nouns
- to write a person's title
- to write the title of a work (artwork, written work)

Modes of Writing

Narration is used to tell a story. Here are some types of narration.

- Autobiography is the story of a person's life, told by the writer.
- Biography is the story of a person's life told by another person.
- A short story is a short, fictional narrative.

Exposition gives information or explains something. Here are some types of exposition.

- Compare and Contrast writing analyzes the similarities and differences between two or more things.
- Cause and Effect writing explains why something happened and what happens as a result.
- Problem and Solution writing describes a problem and offers one or more solutions to it.
- How-To writing explains how to do or make something.
- Description paints a picture of a person, place, thing, or event.

Persuasion is writing that tries to convince people to think or act in a certain way.

Functional writing is writing for real-world uses. Here are some types of functional writing.

- You might fill out a form to sign up for lessons, take a field trip, or apply for a library card.
- You might create an invitation to a holiday party.

The Writing Process

The writing process is a series of steps that helps you write clearly.

Step 1: Pre-write

When you pre-write, you explore ideas and choose a topic. You identify your audience, and you choose your purpose for writing.

To choose a topic, try one or more of these strategies.

- **List** many ideas that you might want to write about.
- **Freewrite** about some ideas for five minutes.
- **Brainstorm** a list of ideas with a partner.

To identify your audience, think about who will read your writing. What do they already know? What do you need to explain?

To identify your purpose for writing, ask:

- Do I want to entertain my audience?
- Do I want to inform my audience?
- Do I want to persuade my audience?

Now, decide on the best form for your writing. Gather and organize the details that will support your topic.

Step 2: Draft

You start writing in this step. Put your ideas into sentences. Put your sentences into paragraphs. Begin to put your paragraphs in order. Don't worry too much about grammar and spelling. You will have a chance to correct any errors later.

Step 3: Revise

This is the time to look at your ideas and the organization of your writing. Read your first draft. Ask yourself:

- Are the ideas presented in the best order?
- Is there a clear beginning, middle, and end?
- Does each paragraph have a main idea and supporting details?

Ask a partner to read your writing and make comments about it. This is called a peer review. Decide what changes you want to make. Then rewrite your draft.

Step 4: Edit/Proofread

This is the time to look at word choice, sentence fluency, and writing conventions. Reread your paper. Proofread for mistakes in spelling, grammar, and punctuation. Correct any mistakes you find.

When you edit and proofread your draft, use these proofreading marks to mark the changes.

Editing/Proofreading Marks		
To:	**Use This Mark:**	**Example:**
add something	∧	We ate rice, bean∧ and corn. (s)
delete something	(delete mark)	We ate rice, beans, and corns.
start a new paragraph	¶	¶ We ate rice, beans, and corn.
add a comma	(comma mark)	We ate rice, beans and corn.
add a period	⊙	We ate rice, beans, and corn⊙
switch letters or words	(switch mark)	We ate rice, baens, and corn.
change to a capital letter	a (triple underline)	we ate rice, beans, and corn.
change to a lowercase letter	A (slash)	WE ate rice, beans, and corn.

Proofreading Checklist

- Check your spelling. Look up words you aren't sure of in the dictionary.
- Check your grammar and usage. Use the Grammar Handbook to help you correct sentences.
- Review capitalization and punctuation. Make sure each sentence begins with a capital letter and uses proper end punctuation.

Step 5: Publish

Once you have revised and proofread your paper, share it with others. Look at these publishing ideas.

- Post your paper on the bulletin board.
- Photocopy your paper. Hand it out to your classmates and family members.
- Attach it to an email and send it to friends.
- Send it to a school newspaper or magazine for possible publication.

Once you have shared your work with others, you may want to put it in your portfolio. A portfolio is a folder or envelope in which you keep your writing. If you keep your work in a portfolio, you can look at what you have written over a period of time. This will let you see if your writing is improving. It will help you become a better writer.

Build Your Portfolio

You may want to keep your completed writing in your portfolio. It is a good idea to keep your drafts, too. Keep comments you receive from your teacher or writing partner, as well.

Reflect on Your Writing

Make notes on your writing in a journal. Write how you felt about what you wrote. Use these questions to help you get started.

- What new things did you learn about your topic?
- What helped you organize the details in your writing?
- What helped you revise your writing?
- What did you learn about yourself as you wrote?

Rubric for Writing

A rubric is a tool that helps you assess, or evaluate, your work. This rubric shows specific details for you to think about when you write. The scale ranges from 4 to 1, with 4 being the highest score and 1 being the lowest.

Score	Description
4	Writing is clearly focused on the task. Writing is well organized. Ideas follow a logical order. Main idea is fully developed and supported with details. Sentence structure is varied. Writing is free of fragments. There are no errors in writing conventions.
3	Writing is focused, with some unnecessary information. There is clear organization, with some ideas out of order. The main idea is supported, but development is uneven. Sentence structure is mostly varied, with some fragments. Writing conventions are generally followed.
2	Writing is related to the task but lacks focus. Organization is not clear. Ideas do not fit well together. There is little or no support for the main idea. No variation in sentence structure. Fragments occur often. Frequent errors in writing conventions.
1	The writing is generally unfocused. There is little organization or development. There is no clear main idea. Sentence structure is unvaried. There are many fragments. Many errors in writing conventions and spelling.

Writing and Research

Sometimes when you write, you need to do research to learn more information about your topic. You can do research in the library, on the Internet, and by viewing or listening to information media.

Library Reference

Encyclopedias contain basic facts, background information, and suggestions for additional research.

Biographical references provide brief life histories of famous people in many different fields.

Almanacs contain facts and statistics about many subjects, including government, world history, geography, entertainment, business, and sports.

Periodicals are past editions of magazines. Use a periodical index to find articles on your topic.

Vertical files contain pamphlets on a wide variety of topics.

Electronic databases provide quick access to information on many topics.

Citing Sources

When you do research, you read what other people wrote. The material you research is called the source or reference. When you tell who wrote the material, this is called citing the source. It is important to cite each source you use when you write.

In your paper, note each place in which you use a source. At the end of the paper, provide a list that gives details about all your sources. A bibliography and a works cited list are two types of source lists.

- A **bibliography** provides a listing of all the material you used during your research.
- A **works cited list** shows the sources you have quoted in your paper.

Plagiarism

Plagiarism is presenting someone else's words, ideas, or work as your own. If the idea or words are not yours, be sure to give credit by citing the source in your work. It is a serious offense to plagiarize.

Look at the chart of the Modern Language Association (MLA). Use this format for citing sources. This is the most common format for papers written by middle and high school students, as well as college students.

MLA Style for Listing Sources

Book	Pyles, Thomas. *The Origins and Development of the English Language*. 2nd ed. New York: Harcourt Brace Jovanovich, Inc., 1971.
Signed article in a magazine	Gustaitis, Joseph. "The Sticky History of Chewing Gum." *American History* Oct. 1998: 30–38.
Filmstrips, slide programs, videocassettes, DVDs	*The Diary of Anne Frank*. Dir. George Stevens. Perf. Millie Perkins, Shelly Winters, Joseph Schildkraut, Lou Jacobi, and Richard Beymer. Twentieth Century Fox, 1959.
Internet	*National Association of Chewing Gum Manufacturers*. 19 Dec. 1999. <http://www.longmancornerstone.com> [Indicate the date you found the information.]
Newspaper	Thurow, Roger. "South Africans Who Fought for Sanctions Now Scrap for Investors." *Wall Street Journal* 11 Feb. 2000.
Personal interview	Smith, Jane. Personal interview. 10 Feb. 2000.

Internet Research

The Internet is an international network of computers. The World Wide Web is a part of the Internet that lets you find and read information.

To do research on the Internet, you need to open a search engine. Type in a keyword on the search engine page. **Keywords** are words or phrases on the topic you want to learn about. For example, if you are looking for information about your favorite musical group, you might use the band's name as a keyword.

To choose a keyword, write a list of all the words you are considering. Then choose a few of the most important words.

Tips

- Spell the keywords correctly.
- Use the most important keyword first, followed by the less important ones.
- Open the pages at the top of the list first. These will usually be the most useful sources.

How to Evaluate Information from the Internet

When you do research on the Internet, you need to be sure the information is correct. Use the checklist to decide if you can trust the information on a Web site.

- ✓ Look at the address bar. A URL that ends in "edu" is connected to a school or university. A URL that ends in "gov" means it is a site posted by a state or federal government. These sites should have correct information.
- ✓ Check that the people who write or are quoted on the site are experts, not just people telling their ideas or opinions.
- ✓ Check that the site is free of grammatical and spelling errors. This is often a hint that the site was carefully designed and researched.
- ✓ Check that the site is not trying to sell a product or persuade people.
- ✓ If you are not sure about using a site as a source, ask an adult.

Information Media

Media is all the organizations that provide news and information for the public. Media includes television, radio, and newspapers. This chart describes several forms of information media.

Types of Information Media	
Television News Program	• Covers current news events • Gives information objectively
Documentary	• Focuses on one topic of social interest • Sometimes expresses controversial opinions
Television Newsmagazine	• Covers a variety of topics • Entertains and informs
Radio Talk Show	• Covers some current events • Offers a place for people to express opinions
Newspaper Article	• Covers one current event • Gives details and background about the event
Commercial	• Presents products, people, or ideas • Persuades people to buy or take action

How to Evaluate Information from Various Media

Because the media presents large amounts of information, it is important to learn how to analyze this information. Some media sources try to make you think a certain way instead of giving you all the facts. Use these techniques to figure out whether you can trust information from the media.

- ✓ Sort facts from opinions. A fact is a statement that can be proven true. An opinion is how someone feels or thinks about something. Make sure any opinions are supported by facts.
- ✓ Be aware of the kind of media you are watching, reading, or listening to. Is it news or a documentary? Is it a commercial? What is its purpose?
- ✓ Watch out for bias. **Bias** is when the source gives information from only one point of view. Try to gather information from several points of view.
- ✓ Discuss what you learn from different media with your classmates or teachers. This will help you determine if you can trust the information.
- ✓ Read the entire article or watch the whole program before reaching a conclusion. Then, develop your own views on the issues, people, and information presented.

How To Use Technology in Writing

Writing on a Computer

You can write using a word processing program. This will help you when you follow the steps in the Writing Process.

- When you write your first draft, save it as a document.
- As you type or revise, you can move words and sentences using the cut, copy, and paste commands.
- When you proofread, you can use the grammar and spell check functions to help you check your work.

Keeping a Portfolio

Create folders to save your writing in. For example, a folder labeled "Writing Projects—September" can contain all of the writing you do during that month.

Save all the drafts of each paper you write.

Computer Tips

- Rename each of your revised drafts using the SAVE AS function. For example, if your first draft is "Cats," name the second draft "Cats2."
- If you share your computer, create a folder for only your work.
- Always back up your portfolio on a server or a CD.

Glossary

achieve succeed in doing something (p. 225)

advertise use notices, photographs, movies, etc. to try to persuade people to buy, do, or use something (p. 262)

amazing very surprising and exciting (p. 124)

annual happening every year (p. 262)

area part of a place (p. 35)

available easy to get (p. 263)

bark hard skin that covers the outside of a tree (p. 240)

benefit help (p. 159)

bicycles vehicles with two wheels that you sit on and ride by moving your legs (p. 158)

billions at least twice more than the number 1,000,000,000 (p. 210)

brighter more sunny; having more light (p. 86)

butterfly insect that has large wings with bright colors on them (p. 112)

buttons small round objects that you push through a hole to fasten clothes (p. 274)

camels animals with long necks and one or two humps on their backs that live in the desert (p. 124)

camouflage act of hiding something by making it look the same as the things around it (p. 136)

canoe narrow, light boat which you move using a paddle (p. 240)

caterpillar young form of some insects, that looks like a worm with many legs (p. 112)

caves hollow places under the ground or in the side of a mountain (p. 124)

celebrate have a special meal or party because of a particular event (p. 34)

challenge something hard to do (p. 225)

chrysalis moth or butterfly when it has a hard outer shell, before it becomes a larva and then an adult (p. 112)

city very large town (p. 8)

clouds masses of very small drops of water floating in the sky (p. 86)

community place where people live (p. 9)

conclude decide something is true based on what you know (p. 175)

consequence result of an action (p. 61)

context things around something that help to explain it (p. 87)

continents one of the large areas of land on Earth, such as Africa, Europe, and Australia (p. 210)

contribute give money or help (p. 275)

costume clothes worn for a special reason, or that represent a country or time in history (p. 188)

craters round holes in the ground made by something that has fallen or exploded on them (p. 210)

create make something (p. 21)

crowd large group of people (p. 34)

culture the way a group of people does things (p. 21)

D

design drawing or plan (p. 275)

dessert sweet food that you eat at the end of a meal (p. 20)

dinner main meal of the day, usually eaten in the evening (p. 75)

donate give something to a person or organization that needs help (p. 158)

E

elements important parts that make up something (p. 75)

F

feature important part of something (p. 125)

festival set of special events of a particular type (p. 262)

final coming at the end; last (p. 87)

flight trip in an airplane or space shuttle (p. 224)

flower part of the plant which has the seeds and is brightly colored (p. 8)

fold bend a piece of paper or cloth so that one part covers the other (p. 20)

friend person you like and trust very much (p. 140)

function purpose (p. 137)

garden piece of land where flowers or vegetables are grown around a house or in a public place (p. 60)

gathers comes together in a group (p. 34)

guitar musical instrument with six strings, a long neck, and a wooden or plastic body (p. 288)

habitats natural places where plants or animals live (p. 136)

habits things that you always do, often without thinking about it (p. 124)

handprints marks on a surface that are made by a hand or hands (p. 240)

hatch come out of an egg (p. 112)

helmets hard hats that cover and protect your head (p. 158)

identify tell what something is (p. 75)

illustrate make something clear by giving examples (p. 263)

initial first; at the beginning (p. 113)

insect very small creature such as a fly, that has six legs (p. 136)

instinct natural ability to behave in a particular way without having to think about it or learn it (p. 174)

lab room or building in which a scientist works (p. 174)

label word or phrase that describes something (p. 211)

leaf one of the flat green parts of a plant or tree that grow out of branches or a stem (p. 112)

link join things or pieces together (p. 241)

location particular place or position (p. 211)

luck good and bad things that happen to you by chance (p. 8)

mail letters and packages that you send or receive (p. 8)

mask something that covers all or part of your face (p. 188)

method plan for doing something (p. 125)

microphone piece of equipment that makes your voice sound louder (p. 288)

mix put different things together to make something new; join together (p. 20)

moth insect like a butterfly that flies at night (p. 136)

neat very good or pleasant (p. 8)

neighborhood small area of a town and the people who live there (p. 60)

observe watch someone or something carefully (p. 224)

occur happen; take place (p. 61)

painting painted picture (p. 188)

patterns arrangements of shapes, lines, or colors (p. 136)

plains large areas of flat land (p. 124)

planets large objects in space like Earth that move around a star such as the sun (p. 210)

plants living things that have leaves and roots (p. 60)

prey animal that is hunted and eaten by another animal (p. 136)

process set of steps that makes something happen (p. 113)

proof facts that prove something is true (p. 174)

puppets small figures of people or animals that you can move by pulling the strings, or by putting your hand inside them (p. 274)

Q

quilt soft thick cover for a bed (p. 188)

R

rainbow large curve of different colors that appears in the sky after it rains (p. 240)

reaction response (p. 137)

reflection what you see in a mirror or water (p. 74)

respond answer (p. 189)

rhythm regular sound like a drum in music (p. 288)

roars makes a deep loud noise (p. 74)

robe long loose piece of clothing that covers most of your body (p. 188)

role part that someone or something plays (p. 9)

rotates goes around like a wheel (p. 219)

S

satellite object sent into space to receive signals from one part of the world and send them to another (p. 224)

schedule plan of what you will do and when you will do it (p. 262)

scientists people who study or work in science (p. 174)

scissors instrument with two sharp blades joined together used for cutting paper, cloth, etc. (p. 274)

seeds small grains from which new plants grow (p. 60)

select choose by thinking carefully (p. 289)

significant important (p. 159)

similar almost the same (p. 35)

soles bottoms of your feet or shoes (p. 288)

source where something comes from (p. 289)

space shuttle type of vehicle that can carry people into space and then return to Earth to be used again (p. 224)

spacewalks moving around outside a space shuttle while in space (p. 224)

sphere solid round shape like a ball (p. 210)

spiders small creatures with eight legs that use threads from their bodies to makes webs (p. 86)

stapler tool used for putting in staples to hold pieces of paper together (p. 274)

stronger having more power or force (p. 286)

summary short statement that tells the main points (p. 241)

supplies things that you need for your daily life (p. 286)

tadpole small creature that lives in the water and becomes a frog or toad (p. 112)

teepee round tent used by some Native Americans (p. 188)

theory idea that explains something (p. 175)

tools things that help you build or repair other things (p. 174)

tradition custom of a group (p. 189)

trumpet musical instrument that you blow into, shaped like a bent metal tube that is wide at one end (p. 288)

volunteers people who offer to do things without expecting to be paid (p. 158)

webs nets of sticky thin threads made by a spider or spiders (p. 86)

weekend Saturday and Sunday (p. 34)

well a deep hole in the ground from which water is taken (p. 74)

yarn thick thread used by someone to knit something (p. 274)

Index

Credits

TEXT CREDITS: Vivian Binnamin. "Cool Hector" by Vivian Binnamin. **Mary Ann Hoberman.** "A Year Later" by Mary Ann Hoberman. Printed by Permission.

ILLUSTRATORS: Ellen Joy Sasaki 10–18, **Laurie Keller** 22–27, 29–32 **Kathryn Mitter** 37–40, 44–46 **Aleksey and Olga Ivanov** 62–71 **Tim Haggerty** 76–79, 81–84 **Stephen Alcorn** 88–97, 99–100 **Felipe Ugalde** 148–159 **Laura Jacobsen** 176–179, 183–184, 186 **Johnnee Bee** 212–217 **Nathan Hale** 227–229, 234–235, 237 **Joel Nakamura** 242–248.

COVER: Will Terry

UNIT 1: 2–3 Digital Vision/Getty Images; 3 bottom, ©Shehzad Noorani/WoodfinCamp/IPN; 5 top, Getty Images-Stockbyte; 5 top middle, Dwayne Newton/PhotoEdit Inc.; 5 bottom middle, David Young-Wolff/PhotoEdit Inc.; 5 bottom, Robert Fried Photography; 6 top left, Richard Hutchings/Silver Burdett Ginn; 6 bottom left, Robert W Ginn/PhotoEdit Inc.; 6 top right, © Tony Arruza/CORBIS; 6 bottom right, © Ric Ergenbright/CORBIS; 7 top left, Alan Evrard/Robert Harding World Imagery; 7 bottom left, © David Turnley/CORBIS; 7 top right, © Jon Hicks/CORBIS; 7 bottom right, ©Ellen Senisi; 8 top, Michael Newman/PhotoEdit Inc.; 8 bottom, David Young-Wolff/PhotoEdit Inc.; 9 top, © Jim Cummins/Corbis; 9 middle, Canstock Images/Alamy Images; 9 bottom, Mary Kate Denny/PhotoEdit Inc.; 19, Lea/Omni-Photo Communications, Inc.; 20 top, Ian O'Leary/Dorling Kindersley Media Library; 20 bottom, Novastock/The Stock Connection; 21 top, Walter Hodges/Getty Images Inc.-Stone Allstock; 21 bottom, Myrleen Ferguson Cate/PhotoEdit Inc.; 28, Pearson Scott Foresman; 32, ©Ellen Senisi; 34 top, Myrleen Ferguson Cate/PhotoEdit Inc.; 34 middle, PeterReid/The Stock Connection; 34 bottom, Chad Ehlers/The Stock Connection; 35 top, Deborah Davis/PhotoEdit Inc.; 35 bottom, Tony Freeman/PhotoEdit Inc.; 42 top left, Rob Lewine/Corbis/Bettman; 42 top right, Cleve Bryant/PhotoEdit, Inc. ; 42 middle left, Michael Newman/PhotoEdit, Inc.; 42 middle, Michael Newman/PhotoEdit, Inc.; 42 middle right, Tony Freeman/ PhotoEdit, Inc.; 42 bottom left, Tony Freeman/ PhotoEdit, Inc.; 42 bottom right, David Mager/Pearson Learning Photo Studio; 43 top left, Rob Lewine/Corbis/Bettman; 43 top right, Rob Lewine/Corbis/Bettman; 43 middle, Tony Freeman/ PhotoEdit, Inc.; 43 bottom left, Michael Newman/PhotoEdit, Inc.; 43 bottom right, Rob Lewine/Corbis/Bettman; 48, Dorling Kindersley Media Library; 49, Barbara Penoyar/ Getty Images, Inc.- Photodisc.; 50, © Richard Powers/Corbis; 51 top, ©Shehzad Noorani/WoodfinCamp/IPN; 51 bottom, ©Yann Layma/Getty Images

UNIT 2: 54–55 Jonathan Nourok/PhotoEdit Inc.; 55 bottom, Joe McBride/Getty Images Inc. - Stone Allstock; 57 top, Scott Montgomery/Getty Images Inc. - Stone Allstock; 57 top middle, David Mager/Pearson Learning Photo Studio; 57 middle bottom, Silver Burdett Ginn; 57 bottom, Lawrence Migdale/Pix; 58 top left, Getty Images Inc. - Hulton Archive Photos; 58 bottom left, Ron Giling/Lineair/Peter Arnold Inc.; 58 top right, Philip Gatward/ Dorling Kindersley Media Library; 58 bottom right, ADAM BUCHANAN/ Danita Delimont Photography; 59 top left, Michael Newman/PhotoEdit, Inc.; 59 bottom left, © Wolfgang Kaehler/CORBIS; 59 top right, © Martin Rogers/CORBIS; 59 bottom right, Gary Braasch Photography; 60, © Ralf-Finn Hestoft/CORBIS; 72, Tony Freeman/ PhotoEdit, Inc.; SGM/ AGE Fotostock America, Inc.; 74 top right, Dorling Kindersley Media Library; 74 top left, JONELLE WEAVER/ Getty Images, Inc. – Taxi; 74 top middle, Ian O'Leary/Dorling Kindersley Media Library; 74 top middle right, © Owen Franken/CORBIS; 74 middle right, © Joe Sachs/Corbis/PunchStock; 74 bottom , Robert Fried Photography; 75 top left, Dorling Kindersley Media Library; 75 top middle, Porterfield/Chickering/ Photo Researchers, Inc.; 75 top right, Dorling Kindersley Media Library; 75 middle, Jerry Young/ Dorling Kindersley Media Library; 75 bottom, Dorling Kindersley Media Library; 80, Richard Embery/ Pearson Education/PH College; 85, Susanna Price/

Dorling Kindersley Media Library; 86 top right, Brian Cosgrove/ Dorling Kindersley Media Library; 86 top middle right, Brian Cosgrove/ Dorling Kindersley Media Library; 86 middle, Linda Whitwam/Alamy, Newscom, Rex Active/ Dorling Kindersley Media Library; 86 bottom, Paul Harris/Getty Active/ Dorling Kindersley Media Library; 87 top left, Gerard Fuehrer/ DRK Photo; 87 top right, Scott Camazine/Photo Researchers, Inc.; 87 middle, Nuridsany et Perennou/ Photo Researchers, Inc.; 87 bottom left, Spencer Grant/PhotoEdit, Inc.; 87 bottom right, © Michel Arnaud/Beateworks/Corbis; 98, SBG Stock/ Pearson Education Corporate Digital Archive; 52, Hart, G. K. & Vikki/ Getty Images Inc. - Image Bank; 102-103, Joe McBride/Getty Images Inc. - Stone Allstock

UNIT 3: 106–107 Peter Bassett/Nature Picture Library; 106 bottom right, Oxford Scientific Films/ Animals, Animals; 106 bottom middle, Tony Heald/Nature Picture Library; 107 bottom right, John D. Cunningham/Visuals Unlimited; 109 top, Gary W. Carter/ Corbis/Bettmann; 109 top middle, Mickey Gibson/ Animals Animals/Earth Scenes; 109 middle bottom left, Dorling Kindersley Media Library; 109 bottom middle right, Frank Greenaway/ Dorling Kindersley Media Library; 109 bottom left, Andy Crawford and Kit Houghton/ Dorling Kindersley Media Library; 109 bottom right, John Giustina/ Getty Images – Photodisc; 110 top left, Castaneda, Inc., Luis/ Getty Images Inc. - Image Bank; 110 bottom left, David Mager/Pearson Learning Photo Studio; 110 top right, Leszczynski, Zig/ Animals Animals/ Earth Scenes; 110 bottom right, Angus Beare/ Dorling Kindersley Media Library; 111 top left, E.A. KUTTAPAN/ Nature Picture Library ; 111 bottom left, Nicholas DeVore/ Getty Images Inc. - Stone Allstock; 110 top right, Schafer & Hill/ Getty Images Inc. - Stone Allstock ; 111 bottom right, © CIXOUS LIONEL/CORBIS SYGMA; 112 top, John Cancalosi/ Nature Picture Library; 112 [1], Kim Taylor/ Dorling Kindersley Media Library; 112 [2], Kim Taylor/ Dorling Kindersley Media Library; 112 [3], Kim Taylor/ Dorling Kindersley Media Library; 112 [4]. Dave King/Dorling Kindersley Media Library; 112 [5], Dave King/Dorling Kindersley Media Library; 112 [6] Geoff Dann/ Dorling Kindersley Media Library; 113 top, G.I. Bernard/ Animals, Animals; 113 bottom, Suzanne & Joseph Collins/Photo Researchers; 114 top, J.H. Robinson/Photo Researchers; 114 bottom, Tim Davis/Photo Researchers; 115 top tab, J.H. Robinson/Photo Researchers; 115 top, Breck P. Kent/Animals, Animals; 115 top middle, Rod Planck/Tom Stack & Assoc.; 115 middle bottom, Patti Murray/ Animals, Animals; 115 bottom, Rod Planck/Photo Researchers; 116 top tab, Tim Davis/Photo Researchers; 116 top, Oxford Scientific Films/ Animals, Animals; 116 middle, G.I. Bernard/Animals, Animals; 116 bottom, Oxford Scientific Films/ Animals, Animals; 117, Suzanne & Joseph Collins/Photo Researchers, Inc.; 118, Kim Taylor/Dorling Kindersley Media Library; 119, Patti Murray/ Animals, Animals; 120, Dorling Kindersley Media Library; 121, Rod Planck/Photo Researchers; 122, Oxford Scientific Films/ Animals, Animals; 123, Myrleen Ferguson Cate/PhotoEdit Inc.; 124 top, Art Wolfe/ Danita Delimont Photography; 124 bottom, Nick Bergkessel/ Photo Researchers, Inc.; 125 top, ©Ellen B. Senisi; 125 middle, William Ervin/ Photo Researchers, Inc.; 125 bottom, Jodi Cobb/ National Geographic Image Collection; 126, Tony Heald/Nature Picture Library; 127 top, Tony Heald/Nature Picture Library; 127 bottom, Anup Shah/ Nature Picture Library; 128 top left, Barry Mansell/Nature Picture Library; 128 top right, Chris Johns/ National Geographic Image Collection; 128 bottom left, John Eastcott and Yva Momatiuk/ National Geographic Image Collection; 128 bottom right, David Kjaer/Nature Picture Library; 129 top left, Ralph Wetmore/ Creative Eye/MIRA.com; 128 top right, Ted Levin/ Animals Animals/Earth Scenes; 129 bottom, Jim Stamates/ Getty Images Inc. - Stone Allstock; 130, Anup Shah/ Nature Picture Library; 131, Tony Heald/Nature Picture Library; 132, Tony Heald/Nature Picture Library; 133, Chris Johns/ National Geographic Image Collection; 134, David Kjaer/Nature Picture Library; 135, Geoff Dann/ Dorling

Kindersley Media Library; 137 top, ©William Manning/CORBIS; 137 bottom, Harry Taylor/ Dorling Kindersley Media Library; 138 top, Lynn Stone/Animals Animals/Earth Scenes; 138 bottom left, Norbert Rosing/Getty Images; 138 bottom right, Paul Nicklen/Getty Images; 139 top, Andrew Darrington/Alamy Images; 139 bottom, Andrew Darrington/Alamy Images; 140 top, Joel Sartore/National Geographic Image Collection; 140 middle, Jason Edwards/ National Geographic Image Collection; 140 right, Novastock/ The Stock Connection; 141 top, Roy Toft/National Geographic Image Collection; 141 bottom, John D. Cunningham/ Visuals Unlimited; 142, Andrew Darrington/ Alamy Images; 143, Norbert Rosing/Getty Images; 144, Jason Edwards/National Geographic Image Collection; 145, Paul Nicklen/Getty Images; 146, Novastock/ The Stock Connection; 147, Lynn Stone/Animals Animals/Earth Scenes

UNIT 4: 152–153 Image100/PunchStock; 152 bottom left, Steve Gorton and Gary Ombler/ Dorling Kindersley Media Library; 152 bottom right Jacka Photography; 155 top, Rob Michelson/GTRI/ Photo Researchers, Inc.; 155 top middle, Morrocco, Alberto, The Bridgeman Art Library International; 155 bottom middle, Ambient Images/Mira. com; 155 bottom, Dorling Kindersley Media Library; 156 top left, Angela Wyant/ Getty Images Inc. - Stone Allstock; 156 bottom left, Scott Cunningham/Merrill Education; 156 top right, © Gideon Mendel/Corbis; 156 bottom right, Dave Nagel/ Getty Images Inc. - Stone Allstock; 157 top left, Jonathan Nourok/ PhotoEdit Inc.; 157 bottom left, Dorling Kindersley Media Library; 157 top right, Pablo Eder/istockphoto; 157 bottom right, © David Turnley/CORBIS; 158, Mark Richards/ PhotoEdit, Inc.; 159 top, © Michael Jenner/ Corbis; 159 bottom, B. Daemmrich/ The Image Works; 160, © Jon Feingersh/CORBIS; 161 top, Skjold Photographs; 161 bottom, © Nik Wheeler/CORBIS; 162 top, Lawrence Migdale/ Pix; 162 bottom, © Mika/zefa/Corbis; 163 top, © Heide Benser/zefa/Corbis; 163 bottom, © Corbis; 164 top, argus / Hartmut Schwarzbach/ Peter Arnold, Inc.; 164 bottom, Jorgen Schytte/Peter Arnold, Inc.; 166 top, National Geographic Image Collection; 166 bottom left, Peter Downs/ Dorling Kindersley Media Library; 166 bottom right, Steve Gorton and Gary Ombler/ Dorling Kindersley Media Library; 167 top left, Norm Dettlaff/AP Wide World Photo 167 top right, Getty Images – Stockbyte; 167 middle, Philip Gatward/ Dorling Kindersley Media Library; 167 bottom, © Glyn Jones/Corbis; 168, Skjold Photographs; 169, © Corbis; 170, © Nik Wheeler/CORBIS; 171, argus / Hartmut Schwarzbach/ Peter Arnold, Inc.; 172, Jorgen Schytte/Peter Arnold, Inc.; 173, David Young-Wolff/ PhotoEdit Inc.; 174 top, Steve Shott/Dorling Kindersley Media Library; 174 middle, Jane Burton / Dorling Kindersley Media Library; 174 bottom, Peter Anderson/ Dorling Kindersley Media Library; 175 top, Art Resource/ Schomburg Center for Research in Black Culture 175 bottom, Michael K. Nichols/National Geographic Image Collection; 180 top, Alexander Weir; 181, Gavin Hunt; 182, Cal Vornberger/ Peter Arnold, Inc.; 185, Alexander Weir; 187, Peter Scoones/ Photo Researchers, Inc.; 188 top, Dave King/ Dorling Kindersley Media Library; 188 middle top, (c) Fine Art Photographic Library/ CORBIS; 188 middle bottom, Rafael Macia/ Photo Researchers, Inc.; 188 bottom, Michael A. Dulisse/The Stock connection; 189 top, The Bridgeman Art Library International; 189 bottom, Gary Ombler/ Dorling Kindersley Media Library; 190, Robert Fried Photography; 191 top right, Denver Art Museum; 191 left, Silver Burdett Ginn; 191 bottom right, Viesti Associates, Inc.; 192 top left, Robert Fried Photography; 192 top right, Viesti Associates, Inc.; 192 middle, Jacka Photography; 192 bottom, Betty Sederquist/ Ambient Images; 193 top, Doug Elbing/ Michigan State University Museum; 193 bottom, Robert Fried Photography; 194, Viesti Associates, Inc.; 195, Robert Fried Photography; 196, Doug Elbing/ Michigan State University Museum; 197, Denver Art Museum; 198, Betty Sederquist/

Ambient Images; 199, Wolfgang Kaehler Photography; 200, ©Stefano Bianchetti/ Corbis; 201, Digital Archive Japan/Alamy

UNIT 5: 204–205 Robert Karpa/Masterfile; 207 top, John Chumack / Photo Researchers, Inc.; 207 middle top, Warren Bolster/ Getty Images Inc. - Stone Allstock; 207 middle bottom, Dorling Kindersley Media Library; 207 bottom, Bobbé Christopherson; 208 top left, John R. Foster/ Photo Researchers, Inc.; 208 bottom left, Tony Freeman / PhotoEdit Inc.; 208 top right, Michael J. Doolittle/ The Image Works; 208 bottom right, Richard T. Nowitz/ Photo Researchers, Inc.; 209 top left, David Nunuk/ Photo Researchers, Inc.; 209 bottom left, Bruna Stude/ Omni-Photo Communications, Inc.; 209 top right, Stephen Dorey/ Alamy Images Royalty Free; 209 bottom right, Chris Stowers/ Dorling Kindersley Media Library; 210 top, Peter Cade/Stone/ Getty Images; 210 middle, NASA/ Corbis Los Angeles; 210 bottom, Lucio Rossi/Dorling Kindersley Media Library; 211 bottom left, MIKE BERCEANU / Photolibrary.com; 211 bottom middle, European Space Agency/Science Photo Library/ Photo Researchers, Inc.; 211 bottom right, NASA/ GSFC/ NOAA / USGS / Reuters/ Corbis/Reuters America LLC; 220, David Young-Wolff/ PhotoEdit Inc.; 221, Neil Armstrong/ The Granger Collection; 222, NASA/ Corbis Los Angeles; 223, ©Ellen Senisi; 224 top, NASA/ Finley Holiday Films/Dorling Kindersley Media Library; 224 bottom, Dorling Kindersley Media Library; 225 top, Tony Freeman/PhotoEdit Inc.; 225 bottom, Getty Images Inc. - Stone Allstock; 232 top left, NASA / Photo Researchers, Inc.; 232 top right, NASA/Science Source/ Photo Researchers, Inc.; 232 bottom left, NASA/John F. Kennedy Space Center; 232 bottom right, NASA Goddard Laboratory for Atmospheres; 233 top left, NASA / Photo Researchers, Inc.; 233 top right, JPL/ NASA Headquarters; 233 bottom, Corbis/Bettmann; 236, NASA/Johnson Space Center; 238, NASA/Johnson Space Center; 239, Corbis Royalty Free; 240 top left, Dorling Kindersley Media Library; 240 top middle, Pearson Education/ EMG Education Management Group; 240 top right, Michael S. Lewis/National Geographic Image Collection; 240 middle, Rod Planck/ Photo Researchers, Inc.; 240 bottom left, Donna Coleman/ istockphoto; 241 top, Mark E. Gibson/Ambient Images; 241 bottom, Ira Block/National Geographic Image Collection; 249, Tom Powers; 251, Bill Bachmann/Creative Eye/MIRA.com; 252, Getty Images

UNIT 6: 256–257 Angelo Cavalli/Robert Harding World Imagery/Getty Images; 256 right, ©Bill Bachmann/Index Stock Imagery; 257 bottom, Elizabeth Crews Photography; 259 top, Dorling Kindersley Media Library; 259 middle top, Steve Gorton/Dorling Kindersley Media Library; 259 middle bottom, Tim Ridley/Dorling Kindersley Media Library; 259 bottom left, Dorling Kindersley Media Library; 259 bottom right, Pearson Learning Photo Studio; 260 top left, Gordon Wiltsie/National Geographic Image Collection; 260 bottom left, Keren Su/ Danita Delimont Photography; 260 top right, Spencer Grant/ PhotoEdit Inc.; 260 bottom right, Pearson Learning Photo Studio; 261 top left, AP Wide World Photos; 261 bottom left, Angelo Cavalli/ Getty Images Inc. - Image Bank; 261 top right, Odile Noel/ Lebrecht Music & Arts Photo Library; 261 bottom right, © Peter TurnleyCorbis; 262, David Young-Wolff/PhotoEdit Inc.; 263 top, Peter Buckley/Pearson Education/PH College; 263 bottom, Dorling Kindersley Media Library; 264, ©Jay Paul for ART 180; 265 bottom, Getty Images; 268, David Mager/ Pearson Learning Photo Studio; 269, David Hanover/ Getty Images Inc. - Stone Allstock; 270, Jeff Greenberg/ PhotoEdit Inc.; 271, Jeff Greenberg/PhotoEdit Inc.; 272, Richard Hutchings/ PhotoEdit Inc.; 273, © Ellen Senisi; 274 top, Dorling Kindersley Media Library; 274 middle, Dave King/Dorling Kindersley Media Library; 274 bottom left, David Young-Wolff/PhotoEdit Inc.; 274 bottom right, Dave King/Dorling Kindersley Media Library; 275 top left, Barrie Watts/Dorling Kindersley Media Library; 275 top right, Andy Crawford/ Dorling Kindersley Media Library; 275 middle,

Bill Bachmann/Photo Researchers, Inc.; 275 bottom, Dave King/Dorling Kindersley Media Library; 277, bottom right, Getty Images; 277 bottom, PEARSON SCOTT FORESMAN; 280 top left, Dallas and John Heaton/The Stock Connection; 280 top right, Steve Gorton/Dorling Kindersley Media Library; 280 bottom, Vision Photo Agency / Pacific Stock; 281 top left, Lynn Johnson/ Aurora & Quanta Productions Inc; 281 top right, Andy Crawford and Gary Ombler/Dorling Kindersley Media Library; 281 bottom, Scott Cunningham/PH Merrill Publishing; 282, Renate Hiller; 287, Gary Conner/PhotoEdit Inc.; 288 top, Cleve Bryant/PhotoEdit Inc.; 288 middle, Robert Fried/ Stock Boston; 288 bottom, David Young-Wolff/ PhotoEdit Inc.; 289 top left, Chad Ehlers/The Stock Connection; 289 top right, Dorling Kindersley Media Library; 289 bottom, © Somos Images/Corbis/PunchStock; 290, Getty Images; 291 top, ©Jeff Greenberg/AGE Fotostock; 291 bottom, ©Bill Bachmann/Index Stock Imagery; 292 top left, ©Goncalo Diniz /AlamyImages; 292 top right, ©Scenicireland/ Christopher Hill Photographic /Alamy; 293, ©Scott Montgomery /Getty Images; 294, © Ellen B. Senisi; 295, ©Scenicireland /Christopher Hill Photographic /Alamy; 296, ©Bill Bachmann /Index Stock Imagery; 297, David Young-Wolff/ PhotoEdit Inc; 299, Will Hart/ PhotoEdit Inc; 300 top, ©Elizabeth Crews Photography; 300 bottom, ©Elizabeth Crews Photography; 301 top, David Mager/Pearson Learning Photo Studio; 301 bottom, David Young-Wolff/ PhotoEdit Inc.